The world is wired for love, made in the image of a loving God, and Dr. Tim Jennings's new book . . . shows us what this love should look like. It is an excellent handbook for loving God, ourselves, and our neighbors!

> Dr. Caroline Leaf, cognitive neuroscientist,
> author, speaker, and TV host of *The Dr. Leaf Show*

God designed us to navigate life's decisions at the highest level, operating from his law of love. Yet we so often default to simply trying harder, and it never works. Dr. Jennings's careful scholarship and moving stories will inspire you to live, heal, and succeed via a transformed heart, loving both God and others well. Highly recommended.

> John Townsend, PhD,
> *New York Times* bestselling author of *Boundaries*,
> founder of the Townsend Institute
> for Leadership and Counseling

Those who have discovered Tim Jennings's work to be transformational will find in *The God-Shaped Heart* yet another thirst-quenching spring for parched souls. Jennings offers a needed contribution to the community of faith that is erudite, accessible, and above all, useful in the renewal of the mind. Incisive and kind, practical and generous, our guide awakens us to God's design—and desire—for us as humans. For those who long for God's world of goodness and beauty, this is a book where that longing is waiting to be discovered.

> Curt Thompson, MD, author of *Anatomy of the Soul*
> and *The Soul of Shame*

The God-Shaped Heart is a book for anyone whose heart has been damaged by a Christianity focused on fear and punishment. It's a call for people to move beyond law, beyond reactivity, and most importantly beyond a low-level moral development and to grow into a complex, mature, responsible, and compassionate faith. The book is theologically and biblically solid and draws from many deep insights of neuroscience and human development. But beyond all this, what makes Jennings uniquely qualified to lead us into this rich and mature faith is that he speaks from experience—the experience of a lifetime working with people in his psychiatry practice and helping them move toward healing. Tim Jennings does not simply want to change your mind, he also wants to change your heart.

Derek Flood, author of *Disarming Scripture*

Dr. Jennings beautifully illustrates how the love of God through Jesus has the power to transform hearts and minds. As always, Dr. Jennings takes complex ideas and makes them remarkably accessible and practical. This book is hopeful and will clarify the most important concepts about God and his work to heal and restore our broken world.

Brad Cole, MD, associate professor of neurology
at Loma Linda University

THE
GOD-SHAPED
HEART

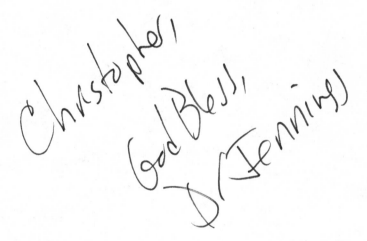

THE
GOD-SHAPED
HEART

HOW CORRECTLY UNDERSTANDING
GOD'S LOVE TRANSFORMS US

TIMOTHY R. JENNINGS, MD

BakerBooks

a division of Baker Publishing Group
Grand Rapids, Michigan

Published by Baker Books
a division of Baker Publishing Group
P.O. Box 6287, Grand Rapids, MI 49516-6287
www.bakerbooks.com

Printed in the United States of America

Library of Congress Cataloging-in-Publication Data is on file at the Library of Congress, Washington, DC.

ISBN 978-0-8010-7521-6

Unless otherwise indicated, Scripture quotations are from the Holy Bible, New International Version®. NIV®. Copyright © 1973, 1978, 1984, 2011 by Biblica, Inc.™ Used by permission of Zondervan. All rights reserved worldwide. www.zondervan.com

Scripture quotations labeled GNT are from the Good News Translation—Second Edition. Copyright © 1992 by American Bible Society. Used by permission.

Scripture quotations labeled KJV are from the King James Version of the Bible.

Scripture quotations labeled Message are from THE MESSAGE. Copyright © by Eugene H. Peterson 1993, 1994, 1995, 1996, 2000, 2001, 2002. Used by permission of NavPress. All rights reserved. Represented by Tyndale House Publishers, Inc.

Scripture quotations labeled NASB are from the New American Standard Bible®, copyright © 1960, 1962, 1963, 1968, 1971, 1972, 1973, 1975, 1977, 1995 by The Lockman Foundation. Used by permission. (www.Lockman.org)

Scripture quotations labeled NKJV are from the New King James Version®. Copyright © 1982 by Thomas Nelson, Inc. Used by permission. All rights reserved.

Scripture quotations labeled NLT are from the *Holy Bible*, New Living Translation, copyright © 1996, 2004, 2015 by Tyndale House Foundation. Used by permission of Tyndale House Publishers, Inc., Carol Stream, Illinois 60188. All rights reserved.

Scripture quotations labeled NRSV are from the New Revised Standard Version of the Bible, copyright © 1989, by the Division of Christian Education of the National Council of the Churches of Christ in the United States of America. Used by permission. All rights reserved.

All italics in Scripture quotations are the author's emphasis.

Some names and details of the people and situations described in this book have been changed or presented in composite form in order to ensure the privacy of those with whom the author has worked.

17   18   19   20   21   22   23   7   6   5   4   3   2   1

To the advancement
of God's kingdom
of love!

CONTENTS

Acknowledgments   11

1. Heart Disease in Christianity: *There Is Something Wrong*   13
2. The Infection   23
3. Growing Past the Rules   47
4. Spiritual Failure to Thrive   67
5. Law, Love, and Healing   89
6. The Evidence   101
7. Love and Worship   123
8. Love and the Institution   137
9. Rituals, Metaphors, and Symbols   157
10. The Little Theater   177
11. The Power of Love and Truth   203
12. Law or Love in the Real World   221
13. God's Action in the Old Testament: *Love or Law?*   237
14. Love and Eternal Judgment   259

Appendix A: Summary of God's Design Laws   281
Appendix B: Another Resource—*The Remedy*   287
Notes   291

ACKNOWLEDGMENTS

To my wife, Christie, who is a constant beacon of God's love and who patiently supported me throughout the writing of this book.

To my many friends and supporters, who have kept me in prayer and shared their love and encouragement with me—and many requests for this book. Thanks for your patience!

1

Heart Disease in Christianity

There Is Something Wrong

People look at the outward appearance, but the
LORD looks at the heart.

1 Samuel 16:7

She was terrified. Dust caked her mouth, and the tears that made
trails through the dirt on her face couldn't flow fast enough to
keep the painful grit out of her eyes. Her knees bled from being
dragged through the rough streets as she desperately clung to
the torn sheet barely covering her body. She frantically looked
for escape, but in every direction there was only the impenetrable wall of hate. She could feel their malice building, their
hunger for her blood, the dam holding back their pent-up sav-
agery about to break upon her.

She knew she deserved to die. She was taught from childhood
that what she had just been caught doing was punishable by

death, and she loathed who she had become. She remembered how her uncle had taken her innocence when she was only a child and then had told her how wicked and filthy she was. He called her vile names, and those insults replayed in her mind in a nonstop cacophony of self-loathing. Some part of her longed for escape; perhaps death would finally free her from the years of guilt, shame, insecurity, fear of rejection, and chronic loneliness—yes, loneliness. Though she had been with more men than anyone she knew, she always felt alone, unloved, worthless. Life was hard; perhaps it was better this way. Perhaps this was God's will for someone like her, someone who wasn't pure. Perhaps death was all she deserved. Let it come. Why fight it? She sank down in the dirt waiting for the stones to find her.

But the stones never came. One moment the vulgar taunts of the murderous mob were all she could hear, and the next—silence. Daring to open her eyes, she saw a pair of sandaled feet. Fearfully looking up, she thought she must be dreaming as she saw the kindest face she had ever seen, and he smiled at her.

How could he smile? But he was smiling, and in his smile she saw peace, compassion, and real concern for her. And then she noticed his eyes. They were intense, and she knew instantly that he saw her—not the nearly naked body the mob looked upon nor the frightened girl groveling in guilt and shame. No! He saw her! He saw the little girl, the bruised, battered, betrayed, exploited, misunderstood, and vilified little girl hiding behind years of bad choices, broken promises, and self-hatred. He saw the little girl inside longing to be loved, desperate to be whole—he saw *her*!

She held her breath as he asked her where her accusers were. With a voice barely above a whisper, not wanting to shatter this fragile moment, she told him they had gone. And then, the unbelievable happened and her world shook, her distorted self-image shattered, her understanding of reality changed. His voice was so compassionate, so tender, like the gentlest music, and she heard him say, "Neither do I condemn you." How? How could he not? He knew what she was, and what she had done. She knew what the law said, what the teachers said, and what the priests said. Everyone agreed she deserved to be condemned. But not this man! He said no, I don't condemn you! I love you and want you to be whole—go now and live a better life, live in harmony with God's design for life and relationships!

The years of pent-up shame burst, and tears began to spill down her cheeks—not the terrified tears of guilt and fear she had shed just moments before, but tears of joy and relief, tears of love and thanksgiving. She *was* loved despite any previous actions, loved not for what she had done but loved for who she was—a child of God!

There is power in love—power to change people, power to heal broken hearts, power to transform lives. God is love, and it is his plan to pour his love into our hearts to heal, transform, and rebuild each of us back into his original design for humankind (Rom. 5:5). But sadly, something obstructs that love. Something has prevented far too many good Christian people from experiencing that transforming power.

There Is Something Wrong

Have you ever been the first to recognize a problem? Have you ever known something was wrong before others around you saw it? Have you ever had the difficulty of identifying a danger when a superior, or some other expert, already determined no threat exists?

When I was in my second year of residency, I examined a patient who put me in just such a bind. A young man was admitted to my team on the psychiatry service with odd and peculiar behavior. I took a detailed history, but his presentation just didn't seem right. Sure, he had a strange look in his eyes; his thoughts were disconnected and confused, and his wife reported he had extreme mood swings with anger and aggressive outbursts. But he would also wake up in the living room after having gone to sleep in his bed with no recollection of actually moving from the bedroom. He had subtle, but nonspecific, physical findings suggestive of a neurological brain problem. So I ordered an MRI of the brain.

The problem was he had already been evaluated by the chief of neurology, had an EEG and CT scan of the brain, and was cleared by the senior neurologist in the hospital as not having a neurological problem. In those days, MRIs were new and very expensive and required the approval of the chief of neurology. My request for the MRI for my patient was denied because the neurologist who had already examined him believed the MRI was not warranted. Further, because I was a second-year resident, my assessment was not deemed to be as diagnostically accurate and reliable as that of the chief of neurology.

What was I to do? This young man was in my care, and I was convinced he had a neurological problem, not a psychiatric one, but I was not taken seriously. My faculty supervisor supported the need for diagnostic clarity and spoke to the chief of neurology about getting an MRI, but he wouldn't budge. This put everyone in a bind. But I wouldn't relent and kept pressing to get the MRI. My faculty supervisor struggled with what to do. Should she believe the neurologist or me? Should she order me to let the matter go or support me and potentially offend the neurologist by going over his head to the hospital commander?

My conviction was so strong, and my concern for the welfare of my patient so great, that I kept pressing my request until I convinced my supervisor there really was something neurologically wrong with my patient. Finally, she went to the hospital commander, who ordered the MRI. The MRI revealed a massive tumor invading both sides of my patient's brain. Reexamination of the CT scan, with the MRI findings in mind, revealed the tumor was there but was so large it was missed by both the radiologist and neurologist. My patient was immediately transferred from psychiatry to oncology and neurosurgery services.

Have you ever been in a situation like this, convinced you saw a problem, but those in authority didn't see it; or worse, having gone on record with a different view, those in leadership refused to even consider new evidence? I believe this happens all too frequently within Christianity. I think there is something wrong in Christianity, yet many in leadership defend the status quo.

Multiple studies document that domestic violence against women is no different in Christian homes than in non-Christian homes. While men suffer abuse from their wives about three times less frequently than wives from their husbands, the risk of being abused by one's wife is actually greater if a man marries a Christian woman than a non-Christian woman.[1]

There is something wrong in Christianity. America, the nation in which 70–82 percent[2] of people identify themselves as Christian, has the highest rate of teen pregnancy and abortion of any westernized country in the world. Thirty-four percent of American teenage girls will get pregnant before the age of twenty. Teen pregnancy in the United States is ten times that of Japan (where less than 3 percent of the population is Christian), four times that of France and Germany, and nearly twice that of Great Britain.[3]

There is something wrong in Christianity. Epidemiological surveys of the US population place the prevalence of alcohol-use disorders in the general population at 8.5 percent,[4] but according to the Barna group 28 percent of young Christians describe themselves as struggling with alcohol-use problems.[5] Other research shows no difference in rates of worry and anxiety among Christians as compared to the population as a whole.[6]

When comparing trends in Christian character, studies show that with each generation since World War II, character became more corrupt. When comparing the Greatest Generation (WWII generation), the Silent Generation, Baby Boomers, Generation X, and Millennials, a disturbing trend is revealed. From the Greatest Generation to Millennials, sexual misconduct increased from 3 percent to 21 percent, lying or cheating went from 3 percent to 22 percent, and not fulfilling one's responsibilities at work increased from 30 percent to 56 percent.[7] With a large portion of the population self-identifying as Christian, there is definitely something wrong in Christianity.

According to a national survey conducted by Proven Men Ministry and the Barna group, pornography use is no different among Christians and non-Christians. Sixty-four percent of US men view pornography monthly, and the rate among Christian men is the same. The ages of those who view porn at least monthly break down as follows: 79 percent of men age 18–30, 67 percent of men age 31–49, and 50 percent of men age 50–68. Fifty-five percent of married men view porn monthly compared to 70 percent of single men.[8]

There is something wrong in Christianity. We have all heard the distressing news reports of children who have been molested by a pastor or priest and of the subsequent cover-up by their religious institutions. Christianity appears to have no impact on reducing child abuse. Various studies have documented that 25–35 percent of women and 15–20 percent of men are molested before the age of twenty, and the rate of molestation in Christian homes is no different from that of the general population.[9]

There is something wrong in Christianity. Even though Jesus prayed for his followers to be united as one in love, mission, purpose, and message, and even though the apostle Paul predicted that the followers of Christ would be unified under one head—Jesus himself (John 17:20–23; Eph. 1:10)—according to the *World Christian Encyclopedia*, Christianity is fragmented into over thirty-three thousand divergent groups all too frequently arguing among themselves.[10]

And while many of these different groups argue over doctrine, ritual, and textual interpretation, perhaps the most distressing problem in Christianity is distorted ideas about God.

Distorted Ideas

Mara, depressed and anxious, came to see me. Laundry was undone. The kitchen was a mess. Her home hadn't been vacuumed in weeks, and even showering was a chore. She was not doing well. Her daughter had been diagnosed with cancer at age three and underwent chemotherapy, which had put the cancer into remission. But seizures developed from the chemo, and now, at age nine, a new cancer had occurred.

Mara looked at me with pain in her eyes and pleaded, "What did I do that God is punishing me? Why has God given my daughter cancer?" Mara's view of events is not unique.

Nate, referred to me by a friend, was overwhelmed with grief from the death of his son in a car accident. Nate couldn't understand "why God would take my son from me."

Sharon wanted to know why God would allow her husband to have an affair. "I prayed, but God didn't do anything. Why would God want this for me?"

When Christians come to believe that God, the One about whom Jesus said, "Anyone who has seen me has seen the Father" (John 14:9), would inflict cancer, kill children in car accidents, or cause husbands to cheat, we know, without a doubt, there is something terribly wrong in Christianity.

God in his foreknowledge warned that something would be wrong in Christianity near the end of time:

> But mark this: There will be terrible times in the last days. People will be lovers of themselves, lovers of money, boastful, proud, abusive, disobedient to their parents, ungrateful, unholy, without love, unforgiving, slanderous, without self-control, brutal, not lovers of the good, treacherous, rash, conceited, lovers of pleasure rather than lovers of God—*having a form of godliness but denying its power.* (2 Tim. 3:1–5)

These poor people, struggling with all the problems of the world, have a form of godliness but no freedom, no power to overcome. Paul is not speaking of atheists but of those who profess a belief in God, yet who have no power to live victoriously.

Shouldn't people who claim Jesus as their Savior, who strive to live like Christ, and who claim the indwelling of the Holy Spirit be people who abuse their wives, molest their children, attack their husbands, worry, be addicted, and view pornography less often than people who have not accepted Jesus Christ? In fact, should people who are like Jesus abuse their families at all?

Shouldn't they treat their families like Christ treats the church, sacrificing self for them (Eph. 5:25)?

Shouldn't people who claim their bodies are the temples of the Holy Spirit have less premarital sex than those who do not?

Shouldn't people who claim to have the peace that passes understanding actually suffer less anxiety than those who don't participate in God's peace?

Shouldn't those who have died to the world, who have crucified the flesh, who have the mind of Christ, and who have the new covenant promise of God's law written on their hearts visit porn sites less often than those who have not died to self?

Is it wrong to expect those who have been reborn by the Holy Spirit to be conformed to the image of God's Son (Rom. 8:29)?

Something *is* wrong in Christianity—and it is time for a remedy, a solution, a revitalizing power to infuse Christianity so that the followers of Jesus will no longer be patterned after this world "but be transformed by the renewing of" their minds (Rom. 12:2).

The purpose of this book is not to find fault with Christianity, any more than I wanted to find fault with my patient who had the brain tumor. But, just as I had concern for the welfare of my patient and had to accurately identify what was wrong in order to bring healing, so too I have great concern for my brothers and sisters in Christ, whom I see struggling and all too often not experiencing the freedom that could be theirs. This book is intended to help people identify and remove an infection of thought, a distortion of belief, and a corruption of ideas that have taken root in the hearts of far too many good Christian people—holding them in the bondage of fear, addiction, and violence—and to connect them to the life-transforming power of God's truth and love that will set them free. I have written this book to help people experience the promise of God—a heart renewed, with genuine peace and freedom—and to help them grow up into the full stature of sons and daughters of God. For, "we know that when Christ appears, we shall be like him, for we shall see him as he is" (1 John 3:2).

KEY POINTS FROM CHAPTER 1

- There is something wrong in Christianity.
- There is a remedy freely available that brings healing and transformation.

2

The Infection

As any doctor can tell you, the most crucial step toward healing is having the right diagnosis. If the disease is precisely identified, a good resolution is far more likely. Conversely, a bad diagnosis usually means a bad outcome, no matter how skilled the physician.

Andrew Weil

Hypertension—high blood pressure—has been called the silent killer. Today, it is undisputed that hypertension causes a host of medical problems, including headaches, stroke, renal failure, and heart failure, and that it ultimately leads to an early death if not treated. But medical professionals didn't always realize this. In fact, some doctors argued that hypertension was a made-up disorder that didn't need to be treated at all.

> The greatest danger to a man with high blood pressure lies in its discovery, because then some fool is certain to try and reduce it.
>
> J. H. Hay, 1931[1]

> Hypertension may be an important compensatory mechanism which should not be tampered with, even were it certain that we could control it.
>
> Paul Dudley White, 1937[2]

Because many medical professionals thought this way, tragic results occurred. Consider the true case of Frank.

Frank was diagnosed with hypertension in 1937 at the age of fifty-four. His blood pressure was 162/98 and was considered by physicians at the time to be "mild hypertension." No treatment was initiated.

By 1940, his blood pressure was running 180/88. In 1941, his pressure was 188/105; treatment was initiated with phenobarbital and massage, and he was encouraged to cut back on smoking and work. But his condition didn't improve.

By 1944, his pressure was running 180–230/110–140, and he suffered a series of small strokes. This was followed by classic symptoms of heart failure, so he was placed on a low-salt diet with hydrotherapy and experienced some improvement.

But by February 1945, his pressure was 260/145, and on April 12, 1945, he complained of a severe headache with his blood pressure measuring at 300/190. He lost consciousness and died later that day at the age of sixty-three. Perhaps you know him better as Franklin Delano Roosevelt, the thirty-second president of the United States.

The Heart War

Unrecognized problems can cause devastating results. But it is much worse when the professionals who are supposed to identify and treat the problem deny it even exists. I would suggest that a similar situation is occurring within Christianity today. An infection of thought has taken such deep root within Christianity that it is accepted by many as orthodoxy, yet it silently destroys millions of lives.

This infection of thought is the avenue to corrupt and ruined hearts. It obstructs God's healing power from transforming hearts. Worse, it actually hardens hearts. But before we explore how this single distortion has mutated into a multiplicity of various ideas that prevent many struggling people from experiencing the love that Christ longs for us to have, we need to clarify exactly what the *heart* is.

When I speak of the *heart*, I am not speaking of the pump inside our chests that circulates blood, nor am I referring to the brain. In Bible terms the heart represents one's core self, the inmost secret self, the place where one's true desires, affections, longings, beliefs, and identity reside—the core elements of one's individuality. It is our character, composed of all those elements, that make us the individuals we are.

Thus, the heart (our true self, our individuality, our character) is involved in all aspects of our lives. Our thoughts are an expression of our true selves, of who we are in our hearts:

- Immediately Jesus knew in his spirit that this was what they were thinking in their hearts, and he said to them, "Why are you thinking these things?" (Mark 2:8).
- Out of the abundance of the heart the mouth speaketh (Matt. 12:34 KJV).

While our thoughts are an expression of our hearts, they also influence and change our hearts—our true selves, who we are and are becoming:

- For as he thinketh in his heart, so *is* he (Prov. 23:7 KJV).

Humanity since Adam has had a corrupt, selfish, and fear-filled heart (sense of self):

- The LORD saw how great the wickedness of the human race had become on the earth, and that every inclination of the thoughts of the human heart was only evil all the time (Gen. 6:5).
- The heart *is* deceitful above all *things*, and desperately wicked: who can know it? (Jer. 17:9 KJV).

The plan of salvation is about healing the heart, renewing the character, and restoring God's perfection into the inmost being. Rebirth—transformation by God through the Holy Spirit—occurs in the heart; it is cutting out of our inmost being the values, desires, motives, beliefs, and attachments to worldly things and establishing our characters in harmony with God and heavenly things:

- Circumcise your hearts, therefore, and do not be stiff-necked any longer (Deut. 10:16).
- No, a person is a Jew who is one inwardly; and circumcision is circumcision of the heart, by the Spirit, not by the written code (Rom. 2:29).
- Love the LORD your God with all your heart and with all your soul and with all your strength. These commandments that I give you today are to be on your hearts (Deut. 6:5–6).

- I will give you a new heart and put a new spirit in you; I will remove from you your heart of stone and give you a heart of flesh (Ezek. 36:26).
- Let love and faithfulness never leave you; bind them around your neck, write them on the tablet of your heart (Prov. 3:3).

While the brain is not the heart—not the character—the brain is the platform upon which the heart (character) operates. Our hearts, our characters, would be analogous to a computer's software, which operates on the substrate of the hardware.

Our thoughts, then, are gateways to our hearts; they are avenues to access our inmost being and pathways of expression for our secret selves. Thus, the thoughts we think are powerful. What we think changes us, our beliefs alter us—physically, psychologically, relationally, and spiritually—for good or for ill, just as the Bible teaches: as a man thinks in his heart, so is he (e.g., Prov. 23:7).

A provocative study demonstrating the power of our beliefs to alter our physiology was conducted at Yale University and published in *Health Psychology* in 2011. Forty-six participants were enrolled in a study to evaluate their physical response to the consumption of two different shakes ingested two weeks apart. The participants were told that the first was a decadent, fat-filled sugary shake of 620 calories and that the second was a nutrient-rich healthy shake of 140 calories. Body ghrelin levels were measured in response to each shake. Ghrelin is a hormone released by the gut when we are hungry. As we eat and are satisfied the gut reduces the production of ghrelin and the blood level of ghrelin decreases. The brain registers this fall in ghrelin levels, and our drive to eat, our sense of hunger, falls.

Sure enough, the study documented that after the consumption of the 620-calorie decadent shake ghrelin levels fell and that they did not fall after the consumption of the 140-calorie healthy shake—but in each instance they were given the exact same 380-calorie shake![3] It wasn't the calories consumed that determined the body's response and the subsequent sensation of fullness; it was what the participants *believed* about what they were consuming that made the difference. This was a function of their heart. Not merely hearing what the shakes contained but believing it was what made the difference. What we think has the power to impact our beliefs—our inmost sense of self—and that has the power to change us. Our hearts (characters, deeply held beliefs, and core sense of self) have the ability to actually change our brains.

Mind, Heart, and Brain—What's the Difference?

What is the difference between the mind, heart, and brain? Often these words are used interchangeably, but they are not the same. The brain is analogous to a computer's hardware, the machine. It is the neurons, glia, neurotransmitters, and any aspect of the central nervous system that we can physically touch. The mind is analogous to a computer's software, the operating system and programming. For instance, if you are reading this book you have an English "software package." English (or whatever language one speaks) is not programmed into the DNA. A neurosurgeon cannot open the skull and touch "English" somewhere in the brain. If a person born in America to English-speaking parents is adopted at birth by a French-speaking family living in France, that child will grow up with a French "software package." The ability to learn a language is programmed into the DNA, but the specific language learned is not biologically determined. It is uploaded after birth.

Consider for a moment how you learned to speak (not read and write) your first language. Children automatically begin speaking the language that is being used in the environment in which they live. In fact, a child cannot choose to avoid learning that language. A child growing up in an English-speaking home cannot decide to learn German instead. Environment is where the software originates and gets uploaded into the hardware/brain. But such software systems, like our language, are so deeply embedded that, unless we purposefully learn a different one, we cannot even think without using them.

When was the last time you awoke and said to yourself, *I am going to think in English today*? Unless we are bilingual, we never make the choice to use our language; it is always there, always operating. And if like me you speak only one language, then everything you experience in life gets filtered through it. When your eyes perceive a plant with a trunk, green leaves, and apples on its limbs, you see a *tree*. You do not see a *baum* (German for tree). Think about it; the language you speak, which is not programmed into your DNA, which is not part of your brain structure, is so deeply a part of you that everything filters through it. However, the brain responds to the exercise of this language and creates a hardware platform for the uploading and maintenance of this software—language.

Do you think language is the only software that was uploaded into your mind in this way? Our spiritual views, our values, our moral compasses, our attitudes toward the opposite sex, our beliefs about people of other cultures and races, and how we understand the world around us are all uploaded in the same manner. When you see a deer, do you see a cute animal that triggers a smile, or do you see dinner? How does your software process the data?

Our minds are broader and more encompassing than our hearts. Another way to say it is that our hearts are part (a subsection) of our minds, part of our software. For instance, while our specific language is part of our minds and not our brains, our language is a software ability that our hearts (individuality) access and utilize. But our language is not part of our hearts (character). The language we speak doesn't determine whether we are fearful or courageous, kind or cruel, selfish or loving, honest or deceitful. The heart is our character, our true identity, our secret self, which is not biologically determined nor genetically programmed but developed through life experience and the choices we make. Therefore, our hearts—our characters— are part of the software. All the software together constitutes the mind; only that part that contributes to forming our core identities—our characters—is part of the heart.

Unlike the clumsy and crude computers we buy in stores, our brains are amazing machines built to adapt and change based on the choices of the mind and the desires of the heart. The brain is not prewired to play chess, read ancient hieroglyphics, do algebra, or fall in love with a specific person. However, if you choose to engage in any of these activities, the brain will create new components (neurons) and rewire itself to form new networks to enable you to learn and become proficient in that endeavor or to bond to a specific person. Master musicians begin at an early age to use particular motor skills and practice those skills for thousands of hours to be proficient in their instrument. Brain-imaging studies confirm that such choices result in larger, more developed brain regions that correspond with certain motor, auditory, and visuospatial abilities than brains of nonmusicians.[4] Our software (minds) changes our hardware (brains)! This is normal brain function. It is the way we were designed. And this is why it is so critical to form healthy belief systems—our beliefs do matter.

While we are free to believe anything we choose, not all beliefs are equally healthy. I once had a patient who believed cigarette smoking helped her lungs work better. While she was *free* to believe this, her belief was not as healthy as believing cigarette smoke actually damaged her lungs. Unfortunately, many people have confused the moral principle of liberty—leaving others free to choose their own spiritual beliefs—with the false idea that all spiritual beliefs are equally healthy. They are not! In fact, some spiritual beliefs are downright harmful.

University of Michigan researchers examined the impact of prayer on coping, mental health and adjustment, and overall well-being in the aftermath of traumatic events. They found that those survivors of the terrorist attacks on the New York Trade Towers on September 11, 2001, who prayed regularly had better psychological adjustment one year later. But when they examined Muslim refugees from Kosovo and Bosnia, they discovered not all prayer is equally healthy. Sixty percent of the Muslim refugees suffered from post-traumatic stress disorder, and 77 percent of these had practiced negative forms of prayer, such as praying for vengeance on their enemies. The Muslim refugees with positive forms of prayer, such as extending forgiveness and grace, had higher levels of psychological well-being, hope, and optimism.[5]

Epigenetics and the Brain

The brain is able to rewire itself because of alterations in how genes in the DNA are expressed. Genetic-expression changes occur based on environmental experience, whether from sub-stances (food, drugs, toxins), ideas, or relationships. This is known as epigenetic modification.

Every cell of a person's body has the same chromosomes (with the exception of individuals with rare genetic or chromosomal disorders), but bone cells are different from heart cells, which are different from retinal cells, which are different from skin cells. How is this possible? In each type of cell there are differ-ent instructions sitting above the genes telling which genes to turn on and which genes to turn off; this set of instructions is known as epi (above) genetics (the genome). While we cannot change the genes we inherit, we can change the instructions sitting above the genes altering how the genes are expressed. Thus, our software alters our hardware but within the limita-tions of what is available within our genetic makeup. A person born with a defective dystrophin gene (which is located on the X chromosome) will develop muscular dystrophy—a rare X-linked recessive disorder. No change in belief or thinking will result in that defective gene being fixed. Thus, while the software changes the hardware, it does so within the limitations of the available resources found within the inherited genome.

Even though the degree of change is fixed within certain limits, the capacity for change is massive. Recent studies have demonstrated that children with ADHD who participate in mindfulness meditation experience reduction in ADHD symp-toms and improved attention and focus.[6] This improvement has been correlated with changes in brain structure and connec-tivity that reduce error rate and improve processing accuracy.[7] Our minds—our preconceived ideas, beliefs, and values—filter the data input and alter the outcomes of who we are and are becoming.

Perception and the Mind

The brain does not make decisions—the mind does. The brain has hardwired reactions. When a person looks at a piece of art, the brain processes the shapes, colors, textures, and dimensions, but the mind interprets the meaning. Thus, different people viewing the same object (painting/sculpture) may see totally different things. A loud bang will stimulate the brain's alert circuitry causing a startle response, but the mind then interprets the event and draws a conclusion about the meaning—was it a car backfiring or the report of a gun? The interpretation of the mind determines whether one calms or becomes more apprehensive.

Consider a woman with corneal opacities or cataracts (opaque defects in the lens of the eye, the farthest point in the visual system away from the brain). A hundred yards away stands a Great Dane, but with her cataracts she perceives a lion and yells "lion." Is there something wrong with this woman's mind? Moving the problem back farther in the visual system, she has retinitis pigmentosa and again perceives a lion instead of a Great Dane. Does she have a problem with her mind? What if she has optic neuritis, inflammation of the nerves that carry the visual signal from the eyes to the brain, and she yells "lion" when she views the Great Dane—does she have a problem with her mind? What if she has a tumor in the occipital cortex of her brain and again perceives a lion instead of a Great Dane—does she have a problem with her mind?

The mind is dependent on the information it receives from the brain. Any physical event that impairs the functioning of the brain or the quality of information that comes to the mind will undermine the accuracy of the conclusion the mind forms, with a subsequent cascade of compounding problems. If this woman, with visual problems, thought a lion was coming toward her and began running down the street screaming at the top of her lungs, would she have a mental health problem? No, she would have a perception problem.

Just as damage to the hard drive of a computer will impair its functioning, regardless of how good the software is, physical disease that damages the brain will undermine the efficiency of the mind and cause the mind to form inaccurate beliefs that in turn determine which brain circuits fire, causing further brain changes. Diseases such as Alzheimer's, schizophrenia, and bipolar disorder are examples of brain-based disorders in which the originating problem is in the hardware, but they can lead to the formation of false beliefs and distorted thinking—disrupted software. Because the brain is changeable based on the beliefs, thoughts, and choices of the mind, faulty beliefs react back upon the brain causing further negative brain changes, and negative-reinforcing cascades can occur, which is one pathway of mental illness. A classic example of this bilateral reinforcement is obsessive compulsive disorder (OCD) in which there are brain-based problems that alter normal signal processing and cause heightened fear and urgency, leading to the formation of inaccurate beliefs. These beliefs activate the brain's stress circuits increasing anxiety and fear, and reinforcing loops of dysfunction occur. This is why, for OCD, the most effective treatment has proven to be interventions that address both brain problems and thinking patterns—medication and psychotherapy.

Conversely, just as a computer with the latest hardware will not function well if the software is corrupted with viruses, so too the human being with a healthy brain will not function well if the mind becomes corrupted with "software viruses"—distorted and unhealthy belief systems. The devastation is much more profound when the distortion reaches the heart (character). Believing a false report that a friend was killed in an accident will cause activation of stress circuits and inflammatory cascades, negative and distressing thoughts—the mind is infected with a falsehood. However, believing a lie about the self—as when individuals who have been abused believe lies such as I am ugly, I am gross, I am worthless, I am no good—is much more devastating: the corruption is not just in the mind (beliefs about the world around) but also within the core self (the heart). Further, a corruption in our thinking can and does cause negative changes in the brain and body. Unhealthy thought patterns activate the brain's stress circuits causing inflammatory cascades that, if not resolved, damage insulin receptors and increase the risk for diabetes mellitus type II, heart attacks, strokes, obesity, high cholesterol, depression, dementia, and other health problems.

Spiritual Warfare

In order to have an efficient mental computer, one needs undamaged hardware (brain), uncorrupted software (mind, including a healthy heart, a healthy sense of self operating on healthy principles), and a reliable energy source (blood supply from a healthy body). Possessing only two of the three results in a computer (person) that will not function. All three are required for an operational system.

Understanding this, we gain some insight into what spiritual warfare is. It is a battle for the core operating system—the heart!

For though we live in the world, we do not *wage war* as the world does. The weapons we fight with are not the weapons of the world. On the contrary, they have divine power to demolish strongholds. We demolish *arguments* and every *pretension* that sets itself up against the *knowledge* of God, and we take captive every *thought* to make it obedient to Christ. (2 Cor. 10:3–5)

If you have a war over arguments, pretentions, knowledge, and thoughts, where is the battlefield? In the mind. The battle between Christ and Satan is a war going on in the minds of God's intelligent creatures for our *hearts* over whom to trust, whom to give our hearts to. This is why Satan is known as the father of lies, because he works to infect our minds—our software—with ideas that corrupt its functioning and thereby obstruct the healing of our hearts (John 8:44). This is known in computer jargon as a virus!

Viruses and the Mind

Human beings can have hardware viruses. These are the physical viruses that we hear about in medicine, such as Zika, HIV, hepatitis A, B, C, the common cold, or influenza. Physical viruses damage the physical body and brain (the hardware) and require hardware solutions—medications or other physical interventions. In addition to actual physical viruses, the human brain (hardware) can be damaged by unhealthy practices (smoking, alcohol, unhealthy diet, malnutrition, and trauma). This is why Scripture teaches that the mature are to care for the body (the Spirit temple), because injury to the body damages the brain and will impair the functioning of the mind, making renewal of character more difficult.

Unlike HIV, hepatitis, or other physical viruses, software viruses are not physical. They are concepts, ideas, and ways of thinking that corrupt the mind, infect the heart—inflaming fear, doubt, and selfishness—and impair functioning. These viruses are more commonly known as lies, distortions, and falsehoods. Consider for a moment the damage that can occur from believing a lie—whether the lie is purposeful, accidental (misheard, misunderstood), or told by someone who actually believes the lie is true. The more deeply imbedded the lie, the more damaging it will be.

On the evening of January 31, 2016, the manager of the Morro Bay Burger King received an urgent phone call from a person stating he was from the Morro Bay, California, fire department. Sounding alarmed and with a commanding tone, the man explained that a dangerous methane gas leak had occurred and was filling the Burger King with lethal levels of this toxic gas and that immediate action was required. He ordered the manager to break out all the windows in the restaurant to ventilate the deadly fumes. Panicked, the manager instantly ordered his employees to break out the windows. But the windows were difficult to break, so the manager heroically drove his car through the plate-glass window, and the employees eventually succeeded in breaking the rest of the windows and saving the building from a devastating explosion.

Relieved, the manager called the fire department to proudly report his success and received disturbing news—no one from the fire department had made any such phone call! It was nothing more than a prank call by someone pretending to be a city official. The manager and his employees had inflicted over $35,000 of damage to his business—all because of a lie.[8]

What if someone told you a lie, which you believed, that your brother was molesting your five-year-old daughter. Just think of the damage—the pain, suffering, heartache, and conflict

all from believing this lie. Stress circuits would activate causing elevated heart rate and blood pressure. Your body's immune system would launch an inflammatory cascade, sleep
would be disrupted, and appetite suppressed—perhaps severe
enough to cause nausea and vomiting. Anger, fear, and other
negative emotions would likely be experienced leading to multiple internal conflicts—temptations to attack your brother,
verbally, legally, and perhaps physically. Could your heart become infected with hatred and vengeance? Could such a lie
harden your heart? Then consider the actions you might take
based on this lie—call the police, lodge a complaint, have your
brother arrested, or worse. Consider the family strife—and
what of your daughter? Would she be put through assessments,
questioning, and therapy? Lies, when they are believed, are
devastating!

What we believe changes us physically, relationally, psychologically, and spiritually. Understanding that Satan is the father
of lies (John 8:44) and that we are in a war over who we believe
God to be (2 Cor. 10:3–5), what is the single most destructive
lie that has infected Christianity and obstructed our ability to
experience God's love, thereby holding millions in the bondage of fear, violence, and addiction cycles? The answer: how
one understands God's law, which directly impacts how one
understands God's use of power and ultimately the kind of
being he is.

The Insidious Infection

When you hear the word *law*, what comes to mind? I have asked
thousands of people this question, and almost everyone answers
with "rules, regulations, or ordinances." They mention speed

limits, tax laws, or other man-made regulations. When I follow up and ask about God's law, most answer similarly, "God's rules, God's ordinances, and God's regulations."

But something quite profound happens when I ask, "What comes to mind when I say *law* of gravity, *laws* of health, or *laws* of physics?" Suddenly an entirely new concept of God's law is considered.

God is the Creator, designer, and builder of the universe. His laws are those on which the fabric of the cosmos is constructed and operates. Humankind cannot create space, time, matter, the substance of life, nor the parameters for healthy relationships. Human beings make rules and regulations; God constructs reality. God's ways are higher than our ways (Isa. 55:9).

When God built his universe, he constructed all reality to operate in harmony with himself. God is love and his designs (laws) are an expression of his character of love (1 John 4:8). God's laws are the protocols by which life operates, and Paul accurately writes, "For since the creation of the world God's invisible qualities—his eternal power and divine nature—have been clearly seen, being understood from what has been made, so that men are without excuse" (Rom. 1:20).

The Bible writers understood that God, as Creator, built the universe to operate in harmony with himself. He did not construct reality to be at variance with himself. Therefore, God's design law is an expression of his character of love:

- Love does no harm to a neighbor. Therefore love is the fulfillment of the law (Rom. 13:10).
- The entire law is fulfilled in keeping this one command: "Love your neighbor as yourself" (Gal. 5:14).

As Jesus said, all law is summed up in love for God and for our fellow man (Matt. 22:37–40). This love is not sentiment or emotionalism; it is functional, operational. Love is the very element, code, or principle that all reality is fabricated on. This wisdom has been known for millennia: "Whoever pursues righteousness and love finds life" (Prov. 21:21). They find life because life is built to operate only on the protocol of love. It would be like saying to a person in the desert, "He who finds water finds life." How does a life of love operate?

Functionally, Paul describes this law as love that "does not seek its own" (NASB) or "is not self-seeking" (1 Cor. 13:5). This means that love functions by the law of giving; it is selfless, not selfish.

A simple example of this law in action is respiration. With every breath we breathe out, we *give* away carbon dioxide (CO_2) to the plants, and the plants *give* back oxygen to us. Life is actually built on this law—if you want to live you must breathe. This is God's design for life, a perpetual circle of free giving. It is the law of love built into the fabric of reality by our God of love!

But you are still a free being. You can choose to break this law, this circle of giving, by tying a plastic bag over your head and selfishly hoarding your body's CO_2 to yourself. However, if you transgress this law, the result, or wages, of this rebellious choice is death (1 John 3:4; Rom. 6:23). This design—this law of giving—is the foundation of every living system: the water cycle, pollination, citric-acid cycle, nitrogen cycle (plant growth, digestion of plants, fertilization), economies, ecosystems, literally everything that lives—gives. And everything that doesn't give—dies!

When was the last time you got up in the morning and said to yourself, *Oh no, another day in which I have to breathe?* Do you ever get up and feel stressed by the fact that you have to breathe? No, you don't even think about it—unless you have severe lung disease. Only then is breathing difficult, so difficult for some that artificial respiration is required.

We are spiritually sick of heart and on God's artificial love-respirator. It is currently hard for us to love well; we need external help. But when God has his way in us, when God completes his plan to heal and restore us, it will be as easy to love others as it is to breathe! We were constructed by God to be conduits of love. Human beings were built to be the repository and showcase of God's law, because the law of love is a living law. It cannot be fully understood written on stone; it can only be truly seen when operating in a living being. In loving, we experience an infinite aspect of God's nature. When it comes to love, our capacity for growth is limitless.

Consider with how much of your heart you love your spouse. Did you answer *with all of my heart*? Then with how much of your heart do you love your firstborn child? What about your second, third, and fourth child? What about your parents and siblings? If you love each person with all of your heart, does your love for any one person diminish the love you have for others? No, in love we are able to expand and grow without limit; the more we love, the more capable we are of loving!

God wants to restore his design law of love in us in order to fix what's broken in us and free us from fear and selfishness, to put us back in harmony with him and restore his creation to perfection.

The law of love is not a rule; it is a design protocol built into the fabric of reality. God has many such design protocols or laws. We will explore a number of them throughout this book.

Evidence from History

When one understands God's laws as the design protocols on which life is constructed and operates, one realizes that deviations from them are incompatible with life. Further, one understands that deviations from God's law require the designer to heal and restore the deviant (sinners) to harmony with his design, for if he does nothing, death ensues. This is how the apostolic church understood God's law, and note how they functioned. They lived communally, sharing what they had to help others and trusting God with how things turned out. They refused to engage in physical conflict against Rome (state power) or any other religious group who believed differently than they did. They loved others and died as martyrs in the arenas of Rome, singing hymns and praising God—and the gospel spread throughout the known world in a generation.

But something changed in Christianity—what? What changed is how Christians understand God's law and, therefore, how they view God. While this infection began in the first century, it didn't become dominant in Christianity until Constantine's conversion. At that time, the understanding of God's law changed: from design law (law of love) to functionally no different from laws made by created beings—rules imposed and enforced by threat of punishment.

Eusebius, the first church historian, lived during Constantine's reign. In the book *Church and State from Constantine to Theodosius*, S. L. Greenslade summarizes how Christianity came to view God's law:

> There are no reserves in the stilted encomium [praise] with which Eusebius closes his history, no wistful regret for the blessings of persecution, no prophetic fear of imperial control of the Church.

His heart is full of gratitude to God and Constantine. And it is not only his feelings that are stirred. He is ready, with a theory, indeed a theology, of the Christian Emperor. He finds a correspondence between religion and politics. . . . *With the Roman Empire monarchy had come on earth as the image of the monarchy in heaven.*[9]

Unbelievably, in just a few hundred years, followers of gentle Jesus—the "Lamb of God," the One who refused to use any coercive power against his enemies but instead washed the feet of his betrayer and forgave his killers—were worshiping a god who functioned like the pagan power that murdered their professed Savior.

And to this day, Christianity has not freed itself from this insidious and destructive view of God and his law. Thomas Lindsay, in his book *A History of the Reformation*, not only documents this change in how Christians saw God's law but also observes how all of Western Christianity is still infected with this damaging imposed-law construct:

The great men who built up the Western Church were almost all trained Roman lawyers. Tertullian, Cyprian, Augustine, Gregory the Great (whose writings form the bridge between the Latin Fathers and the Schoolmen) were all men whose early training had been that of a Roman lawyer,—a training which moulded and shaped all their thinking, whether theological or ecclesiastical. They instinctively regarded all questions as a great Roman lawyer would. They had the lawyer's craving for exact definitions. They had the lawyer's idea that the primary duty laid upon them was to enforce obedience to authority, whether that authority expressed itself in external institutions or in the precise definitions of the correct ways of thinking about spiritual truths. *No branch of Western Christendom has been able to free itself from the*

spell cast upon it by these Roman lawyers of the early centuries of
the Christian church.[10]

Consider the vast difference between God's design law and imposed rules by created beings: human governments can pass laws to make tobacco legal; they can never pass laws to make tobacco healthy! God's laws cannot be changed by created beings because God's laws are the very parameters on which life exists. But sadly, the *idea* of God's law has been changed in the minds of Christians, and this change is so deeply embedded as orthodoxy that most people never even question it.

History confirms the devastating consequences of replacing design law with imposed law. Christianity went from gentle believers who lived communally and died as martyrs to violent people who marched in the Crusades with crosses emblazoned on their tunics, conducted the Inquisition at the direction of priests, and burned people at the stake who believed differently—all in the name of Jesus.

Yes, there is something wrong in Christianity. God's law of love—his design protocols on which reality is built to operate—has been replaced with a fallen human-law construct, and God has been falsely presented as a punishing dictator. This idea, above all others, is at the root of Christianity's impotence, its inability to connect to the power of God for real healing and transformation of the heart!

Throughout this book, we will examine how this one idea has penetrated every phase of Christianity, regardless of denomination, and altered our understanding of God and his methods and, all too often, diverted us from fulfilling our mission for him. And we will discover the truth that will set us free and open our minds and hearts to experience God's true power of love, which can transform us back to his original design—back to the perfection of love as revealed in Jesus.

KEY POINTS FROM CHAPTER 2

- An infection of thought has taken such deep root within Christianity that, by many, it is accepted as orthodoxy, yet it silently destroys millions of lives.
- What is this infection of thought? The idea of God's law changed from design law (law of love) to functionally no different from laws made by created beings—rules imposed and enforced by threat of punishment.
- God's law of love is the principle of giving on which life is built.
- God's law of love is a living law and can only be fully understood when operational in a living being.

3

Growing Past the Rules

We may brave human laws, but we cannot resist natural ones.

Jules Verne

It felt like a sauna. The air was thick, hot, and humid, already over 90 degrees at 6 a.m., and as the sun climbed in the sky, the temperature soared to unbearable intensity. It was the summer of 1987 at Fort Polk, Louisiana, and I was there doing my officers basic training with the US Army. As part of our training we were required to learn basic land navigation—how to find our way, with only a map and compass, through uncharted terrain to a specific location within a specified time period. We had to walk miles through wilderness with temperatures climbing above 100 degrees in high humidity, all while wearing our battle dress uniforms—combat fatigues, pack, and weapon.

After several hours in the heat, I began to feel strange. Our instructors had directed us to drink water at regularly scheduled intervals. They had cautioned us regarding the intense heat in Louisiana and the risk of dehydration. They had warned us of the life-threatening consequences of heatstroke—and I was feeling strange. I was hot, but no longer sweating. I was dizzy, fatigued, my vision was blurry, and I was nauseated. I suddenly realized I was in serious trouble. I was suffering from heat exhaustion, and if I didn't take action in a very few minutes, I could suffer heatstroke and death.

I found some brush and crawled under the branches into the shade. I mixed some sugar packets from my pack into water and made a dilute sugar-water solution, which accelerates hydration. And I slowly rehydrated myself.

But why did this happen to me? Why did I suffer with fatigue, nausea, and blurry vision? Did God do this to me? Was an angel dispatched from heaven to make me light-headed and cause my symptoms?

My basic training instructors had told us to drink regularly, but I had gotten caught up in my navigation and failed to drink enough. I had *disobeyed* my orders—was I being punished for my disobedience?

Perhaps you think my example is ludicrous, an extreme and unrealistic example of the tension between design law (in this case, laws of health) and imposed rules. But millions of people throughout history have suffered mental distress, psychological oppression, and spiritual abuse as a result of replacing God's design law with imposed law and have wrongly concluded that health problems are punishments from an angry god.

The Jewish religious leaders in Christ's day accused those suffering from leprosy of being under the curse and punishment of God. During the seven years from 1346 to 1353, the Black Death bubonic plague killed seventy-five- to two-hundred-million people. While most scholars today believe this terrible disease was caused by a bacterium, *Yersinia pestis*, carried by fleas, at the time the masses believed what their religious leaders told them—they were being punished by an angry god. I frequently see patients today who wonder why God gave them or a loved one cancer, schizophrenia, or some other debilitating illness.

God's laws are design laws. One type of those laws is the laws of health. What I suffered that summer in 1987 occurred simply because I violated the laws of health, and there are damaging consequences to violating God's laws. Unfortunately, not everyone views God's law as design law. Children don't understand how life is designed. They don't understand the principles of health and often need loving parents to provide rules to protect them until they grow up. Far too many people, however, struggle to grow up. Some even prefer to stay on milk.

Stuck on Milk

Time magazine shocked the nation with its May 20, 2012, cover of Jamie Lynne Grumet breastfeeding her three-year-old son. The internet, radio, and TV were abuzz with angry, shocked, and disgusted comments, while only a few expressed support. But why was this picture so sensational? What caused such an intense reaction? Bobbi Miller, quoted in a *CBS News* article, seemed to sum up the concern: "Even a cow knows when to wean their child."[1]

The outrage wasn't against breastfeeding; most people recognize and support the benefits of breastfeeding. The shock, the disapproval, was focused on the failure to know when it is time to get off the breast.

The writer of Hebrews expresses the same disapproval when Christians fail to be weaned from spiritual milk. In fact, he even suggests failure to do so prevents becoming righteous—growing up into Christian maturity:

> We have much to say about this, but it is hard to make it clear to you because you no longer try to understand. In fact, though by this time you ought to be teachers, you need someone to teach you the elementary truths of God's word all over again. You need milk, not solid food! *Anyone who lives on milk, being still an infant, is not acquainted with the teaching about righteousness.* But solid food is for the mature, who by constant use have trained themselves to distinguish good from evil. (Heb. 5:11–14)

God calls us to grow up, to mature, to develop *by practice* the ability to discern right from wrong—to develop critical reasoning skills by thinking things through and making choices. Life is all about choices—regular or diet coke, caffeinated or decaf, or perhaps water instead—which one and why? Ask her out or not, say yes to him or not. Visit the local church, go on a mission trip, pay pretax or posttax tithe—choices, so many choices. How do you know which is best?

Choices can be stressful, and everyone has within themselves a system for decision making, but have you ever noticed that some people consistently make better decisions than others? Why? Because some methods of evaluating options and forming conclusions are actually healthier and more mature than others.

What method do you use to determine what is right and wrong, good and evil (moral decision making)? Do you look to a higher authority—parent, teacher, political leader, pastor, priest, or deity—to tell you? Do you look for consensus among peers, or perhaps a code of rules or system of established laws?

Do you decide based on what is most likely to reward or least likely to cause pain? Or do you simply flip a coin and hope for the best?

Eric and Difficult Decisions

Eric was home Wednesday evening, June 16, 2010, when he noticed his wife, Aline, seemed to be suffering a stroke. Aline, a nurse, and Eric, an EMT, both worked at Erlanger Hospital in Chattanooga. Erlanger is the regional stroke center, and it is well known that if a person suffering a stroke can get to Erlanger quickly, the likelihood of reversal is very high.

Aline's face was drooping and her arm was numb. They lived about seven miles from the hospital, and Eric, understanding time was critical, decided to drive his wife rather than wait for an ambulance to be dispatched.

He picked her up, raced out of the house, and got her into the car. As he sped to the hospital, he spotted the posted speed limit of 35 mph. It was late and traffic was light. What should he do? Break the law or follow the legally posted limit? What was the *right* action to take?

Eric chose to speed. But then he came to an intersection with a red light. What should he do? Wait for the light to change to green or slow down, look both ways, honk his horn, flash his lights, and when traffic was clear break the law and go through the red light? What was the *right* decision?

Eric chose to go through two red lights. However, a police officer saw him and pulled in behind him with lights flashing and siren blaring. What should he do? He was more than halfway to the hospital; should he stop and take the time to explain or keep going and disobey the law that says to stop when a police officer indicates you need to pull over? What was the *right* action to take?

Eric kept going. When he got to the hospital, he jumped out of his car, ran around to the other side, and picked up his wife. The police officer shouted for him to stop and came up to physically try to restrain Eric. What should he do? Stop for an officer of the law or continue to carry his wife into the hospital? What was the *right* action? Eric shouldered past the police officer and carried his wife into the emergency room.

Eric was arrested and charged with assault on a police officer, disorderly conduct, reckless endangerment, two counts of traffic signals violation, and an expired registration.[2]

Did Eric do right or wrong? How do you know? It all depends on your level of development.

Seven Levels of Moral Decision Making

There are multiple stages of moral development, our ability to comprehend right and wrong. Dr. Lawrence Kohlberg is credited with pioneering research in defining six stages.[3] With insights from God's Word, I have adapted and expanded his work, provided examples from Scripture, and added a seventh level. Following are the seven stages of development in our ability to comprehend what is right and wrong correlated with evidence from Scripture:

1. *Reward and punishment*: The most basic level of understanding whether something is right or wrong is if we receive reward or punishment.

   This level of functioning is normal for small children and a necessary starting point in our learning. But when an adult operates at this level something is terribly wrong. This is slave mentality—don't think, don't understand, just do what the master says to avoid the whip. This is the level of the Nazi soldiers who put people in gas chambers. Why did they do it? They would be punished if they didn't, and it was right to do as they were ordered. This is ancient Israel as slaves in Egypt, doing what the master said to avoid punishment.

At level one, a ruler establishes his right to rule by displays of power and vengeance upon his enemies. He rules by threat of punishment and hope of reward. Mercy, or failure to punish, is seen as evidence of weakness, not morality, in level one mentality. People at this level see a God of mercy as a marshmallow God and insist God must use his power to torture and kill his enemies.

God meets people where they are. So with ancient Israel and the people of Egypt, he first established his credentials to rule by acts of punishment on the Egyptian gods and by mighty, spectacular miracles to demonstrate that the Egyptian gods were not gods at all. "I did this so that you might know that I am the LORD your God" (Deut. 29:6).

Level one decision making is so primitive it doesn't even require a brain; the mind is completely sidelined. Animals, plants, and bacteria avoid painful stimuli and grow toward rewarding stimuli. This level of functioning is not worthy of human beings created in the image of God. In fact, it is Satan's goal to reduce us to "unreasoning animals, creatures of instinct" (2 Pet. 2:12) operating at level one.

2. *Marketplace exchange*: Level two morality is the quid pro quo system of right and wrong; you do something in

exchange for something of agreed value in return. You scratch my back and I'll scratch yours, the let's-make-a-deal mindset.

In normal childhood development, children who are often powerless to force their way quickly learn to make deals. This is a positive step forward and healthy for small children to transition through.

Yet, for an adult, this is still an immature level of functioning. This is ancient Israel at Sinai, with the mentality of an eye for an eye and a tooth for a tooth and saying when the law was first read, "We will do everything the LORD has said" (Exod. 19:8; 21:24).

At level two, vengeance is a moral duty. This is the level of retributive justice. Those who do evil must be paid back with an equal amount of pain and suffering. To not return pain and suffering is considered immoral. Far too many people still make decisions at this level.

This level of understanding of right and wrong also manifests itself in the health-and-wellness gospel. If you perform the right rituals, attend the right church, or say the right prayer every day for thirty days, then God fulfills the bargain by giving you better health, more wealth, or expanding your territory. At this level, it is a simple business transaction with God: if you do right, you will be blessed by God; if you don't do right, you will not be blessed by God.

Level two development requires only the most minimal amount of mental awareness. Monkeys, dolphins, and dogs operate on this level—doing a trick to get a treat. Again, this is okay for small children but not worthy of mature beings created in God's image.

3. *Social conformity*: At this level, right and wrong are determined by community consensus. This is the child who says, "Everyone else is doing it." Right is deemed right by the approval of peers. Individual vengeance is not allowed, forgiveness is preferred, but group punishment is deemed just. If group punishment doesn't happen, social order is undermined.

   This was ancient Israel when they demanded to have kings. All the other nations had kings, so it must be right and Israel wanted them too. This was also manifested by ancient Israel collectively punishing those who didn't conform to the agreed-upon norm. Recent news stories of families stoning their daughters who marry outside their religion or caste reveal this level of functioning is still in operation today.[4]

   Level three decision making also doesn't require thinking, reasoning, or significant engagement in higher cortical activity. Many herd animals function like this, determining that the right way to go is the way the herd goes, even if it's right over the cliff.

   Following the herd, the group, or what's popular in culture can bring an emotional sense of security, but it doesn't develop the person into a son or daughter of God.

4. *Law and order*: At level four, right and wrong are determined by a codified system of rules, impartial judges, and prescribed punishments. At this level, individuals defer judgment to properly elected or otherwise constituted authority. Right is getting a proper pay or reward for good work and a prescribed infliction of punishment for breaking the rules. Authority figures are rarely questioned; "He

must be right—he is the president, the judge, the pastor, the pope."

Elementary school children operate at this level and find security, predictability, and peace in the rules. At this level, tattletales abound as children are intolerant of rule breakers and demand fairness, which is typically some imposed punishment. The black-and-white thinking of this level of operation leads to fragmenting into divergent groups or cliques who share a core set of group rules and who demean and criticize those who don't share their rules.

This was ancient Israel at the time of Christ—"We have a law!" the Pharisees proclaimed, as they sought to stone Jesus for healing on the Sabbath. The Jews in Christ's day were separatists who were intolerant of those who didn't keep their rules and obey their rituals.

This is much of our modern world too, with its codified laws, courts, prosecutors, judges, juries, and imposed punishments. Authority at this level rests in the coercive pressure of the state to bring punishment upon those who deviate from the established laws. At this level, police agencies and law enforcers are required to monitor the populace, search for breaches in the law, and inflict codified penalties.

This is the first level that requires the emergence of thinking but only minimal thinking—basic indoctrination and memorization of rules. One doesn't have to understand reasons for things. One only has to know the rules and obey them.

5. *Love for others*: Level five morality understands that right is determined by doing what is in the best interest of others,

realizing people have value in who they are irrespective of the rules. Wrong is when our actions are objectively harmful to others.

Right, at level five, is determined not by a checklist of rules but by doing what is actually helpful and beneficial for another. Individuals have inalienable rights as free moral agents and are valued for who they are. At level five functioning, African Americans are recognized to have value and are treated with equality, despite Jim Crow laws that discriminate against them. Circumstances dictate what action is most helpful to another, and that makes it right.

Parents who love their children may, in one situation, praise, hug, and kiss them, but in another circumstance shout commands to stop, with threats of discipline if disobeyed. Love motivates to protect, heal, and promote the welfare of the one loved, but circumstances dictate what action love takes at any given moment.

Jesus demonstrated this level of functioning when he touched lepers, spoke to women, socialized with tax collectors, healed on the Sabbath, and turned over money tables in the Temple. These were acts of love that violated the laws of the Jewish authorities. The Pharisees, operating at level four and below, wanted to stone him for breaking their rules.

Jesus illustrated this level of functioning with the stories he told, such as the parable about the good Samaritan who gave from his own resources to help another human being while ignoring social custom and religious law; or the story about the prodigal son who was restored to his place in the family despite leaving home and squandering his inheritance.

6. *Principle-based living*: Level six decision making understands the design protocols or principles on which life is
   constructed to operate and intelligently chooses to live in
   harmony with them. It is doing something not because a
   rule says to do so but because it is understood to actually
   work that way.

   Mature individuals recognize that governments can
   pass laws to make substances such as marijuana legal, but
   they can never pass laws to make them healthy. Thus, level
   six thinkers choose not to use such substances regardless
   of their legal status because they violate the laws of health
   and damage body and brain.

   This principled way of living is why mature individuals
   don't commit adultery, harbor resentment, or cheat on
   their taxes, for example. They understand all such activities
   violate the design for how our minds were constructed to
   operate. They disrupt neural circuits and not only cause
   guilt and shame, which warp the character and undermine
   peace, but also activate fear circuitry, which causes inflammatory cascades and damages our brains and bodies, resulting in pain and suffering to the one who commits such acts.

   Jesus lived in harmony with God's principles, revealing
   God's character of love in all he did. And after Pentecost
   the apostles lived in harmony with God's design, motivated
   to love God and others more than self. It is understood
   at this level that God says what is right because it is right,
   because it is the way things actually are. It isn't right simply
   because God said so.

7. *Understanding friend of God*: At level seven, a person not
   only has love for God and others, not only understands

God's design protocols for life, but also understands God's purposes and intelligently chooses to cooperate in fulfilling their role in his purposes. Jesus said to his disciples in John 15:15: "I no longer call you servants, because a servant does not know his master's business. Instead, I have called you friends, for everything that I learned from my Father I have made known to you."

Persons functioning at level seven understand the truth about God's character of love, his nature and design for life, the origin of evil, the nature of sin, the weapons of Satan, the original purpose for the creation of humanity, the fall of humanity into sin, God's working through human history, the purpose of the cross, and the ultimate cleansing of the universe from sin.

Jesus operated at this level, as will his bride, those who are ready for translation when Jesus comes again. The Scriptures describe those who are ready to meet Christ when he returns as being sealed on their foreheads with the seal of God, those who do not love their lives so much as to shrink from death (Rev. 7:1–3; 12:11). They live in the world with purpose to advance God's kingdom of love, not themselves, and to fulfill God's purposes utilizing God's methods.

The Bible teaches that love is the design protocol for life, the principle of other-centered giving on which life is constructed. Love for others results in such values as modesty, humility, and wise stewardship of money. Application of these values might preclude the purchase of expensive jewelry, flashy cars, or other items primarily for show and to promote self. A person functioning at level seven would have no problem living in harmony with such values. Persons functioning at level four and below, on the other hand, might make legalistic rules about appropriate dress for church, for example, but they might not even notice a flashy car. That's not on the list.

Dealing with people at level four and below explains the detailed instructions given in the books of Moses. Just as our state and local governments have laws for almost every situation, so too ancient Israel had a code of conduct covering almost every situation. However, when a person matures to level five and above, the law may be summed up in two statements: "'Love the Lord your God with all your heart and with all your soul and with all your mind.' This is the first and greatest commandment. And the second is like it: 'Love your neighbor as yourself.' *All the Law and the Prophets hang on these two commandments*" (Matt. 22:37–40).

When we love a person, we don't murder him, or steal from her, or covet what they have. When we live at level five and above, the rules are no longer needed, not because they were wrong but because the law of love is written on our hearts, and we would rather die than exploit others (Heb. 8:10).

This is God's goal for humanity—to restore his law of love in us, to re-create us in righteousness such that we love God and others more than self. This is what it means to mature in Christ, to grow in godliness, to receive the mind of Christ, and to be a partaker of the divine nature. But growth for many has been obstructed. Why? Because accepting the infection that God's law is functionally like human law—imposed rules—stops growth at level four. It results in spiritual failure to thrive, failure to grow to the full stature of children of God. Failure to thrive is a tragic situation. To watch a child fail to assimilate nutrition and slowly wither and die is one of the most horrible experiences a person can have. Are we equally horrified when newborn (reborn) babes in Christ fail to thrive?

Aunt Sandy

The failure to thrive reminds me of my aunt Sandy. I miss my aunt. Sandy was very special. She was fifteen when I was born, but she was like one of us. As a result of an anoxic brain injury she suffered at birth, she remained a child. My brother, sister, and I grew, developed, and advanced in our abilities, but Sandy did not. Her body grew, but her mind never did.

My siblings and I became independent, married, had our own homes and careers, and lived autonomously, but Sandy did not. She required supervision, direction, instruction, and an ongoing imposition of consequences in order to protect her from others and herself, not because she intended to do wrong but because she wasn't always capable of making wise decisions. She needed someone to do her thinking for her.

Sandy never learned to read and write, other than her own name. She was never able to plan proper meals, pay bills, go shopping, or drive a car. She couldn't problem solve and was easily confused by symbols, metaphors, and analogies.

I miss my aunt; she always brought smiles. But everyone knew her condition wasn't "normal," wasn't what God designed humans to be.

Growth in Christ is compared to our growing up as people. We are born into the world and grow physically and mentally, and we are to be reborn in Christ and grow spiritually. For those like my aunt, whose growth is impaired due to brain injury, God promises new brains when this mortality puts on immortality (1 Cor. 15:53). Though my aunt didn't grow cognitively, she did grow in her ability to love. She loved Jesus and she loved others, thus she lived at level five. I look forward to the day my aunt rises in newness of life, with a new brain and all the joys of discovery that await her.

If we fail to mature as Christians, then we too will require constant oversight and external threats to do what is right, because we cannot be trusted. We have a form of godliness but no power to overcome our sinful nature!

There are two general types of untrustworthiness. One type is the untrustworthiness of the person who chooses evil, such as the rapist, terrorist, and sociopath. Such persons have evil intent in their hearts and desire to exploit and harm others; they cannot be trusted. However, this is not the untrustworthiness of the majority of people. It was not characteristic of my aunt, nor was it the primary untrustworthiness to which Hebrews is speaking. The second type of untrustworthiness is caused by immaturity, the inability to carry out the task of wise decision making and self-governance. Immature persons cannot be trusted either.

Imagine you are the treasurer of your church, and you have five thousand dollars in cash to deposit in the bank Monday morning. You certainly don't ask a known thief to take it to the bank; this is the first type of untrustworthiness. What if your seven-year-old son offers to take the money to the bank. Would you trust him with the five thousand dollars? Why not? Not because of evil intent, but because of immaturity. Your son still needs oversight, direction, supervision, and protection.

Many Christians with good hearts are like the seven-year-old. They mean well, they want to do well, and they are sickened in heart when they mess up. But they have not matured, not grown up, and thus they remain as infants. They are still living on milk rather than solid food and cannot yet be trusted. As Hebrews says, they are "not acquainted with the teaching about righteousness" (5:13). God wants us to grow up into full maturity, to develop the mind of Christ, to have new hearts of love, and to manifest the fruits of the Spirit, the last being self-control. Failure to mature, when we are capable of doing so, means we don't become righteous; we are not healed; we are not restored to Christlikeness. Failure to mature means we stay focused on self, are fear-driven, and do not love!

Law of Exertion

There is a difference between my aunt's inability to grow and a person who possesses the ability but *chooses* not to grow. Many are stunted in their spiritual growth, in their ability to love, simply by failing to exercise their God-given ability to reason and think.

Jesus describes this group in the parable of the talents recorded in Matthew 25:14–30. Thinking concretely, a person may read this story and conclude it is primarily about money, investment, and fulfilling one's obligations to a superior. While such lessons are true and can be drawn from the parable, a deeper reality is being taught.

Jesus is the light who gives light to all people, meaning he is willing to lead us to maturity and help us see reality as it is. The deeper lesson of the parable of the talents is the unveiling of the law of exertion, which is another design law. God is the Creator and his laws are the protocols that the cosmos and reality are built on. One of these laws is the law of exertion, which simply stated is *strength comes by exertion*. If you want something to grow stronger, you must exercise it; as everyone knows, if you don't use it, you lose it. If you don't exercise a muscle group, an ability, or a talent, it will slowly wither away.

The landowner in the parable represents God—our Creator. The servants represent human beings. The talents represent the abilities with which we are endowed at birth, some with ten, some with five, and some with one.

When a person exercises their abilities, those abilities grow stronger. Those with musical talent who take lessons and practice, athletes who train, mathematicians who pursue higher education and challenge their thinking, artisans—craftsmen of every kind who exercise their craft grow stronger, more capable, and more proficient. Those with raw talent who neglect it will over time lose the ability they have, while those who exert themselves will not only develop their abilities but will also discover new skills they didn't previously possess.

The law of exertion is so self-evident that people as diverse as popes and fiction writers recognize its reality:

> All life demands struggle. Those who have everything given to them become lazy, selfish, and insensitive to the real values of life. The very striving and hard work that we so constantly try to avoid is the major building block in the person we are today.
>
> Pope Paul VI[5]

> Talent is cheaper than table salt. What separates the talented individual from the successful one is a lot of hard work.
>
> Stephen King[6]

This is God's design (the way life is constructed to work). Within the brain it is called neuroplasticity, the ability of the brain to change its structure based on use. Neural circuits that are being used will expand, make new neurons, and recruit other neurons, and the network grows ever more complex as the ability is utilized. Circuits that are not used are either never developed or pruned back and are eventually deleted. Thus, failure to use one's talents results in losing that talent.

This is not a punishment by God, as those operating at level four and below might suggest. It is not an infliction by the ruling authority to take an unused talent away. It is the unavoidable result of failing to exercise an ability. Those operating at levels six and seven understand God's design and realize that such a loss is a natural result of one's choices.

Because of how design law actually works, one cannot skip developmental levels. A baby cannot go from crawling to running; they must first learn to walk. Likewise, growth through the moral levels is progressive. As we comprehend and operate at one level, we are ready to proceed to the next level. And strength comes from exertion. Thus "we also glory in our sufferings, because we know that suffering produces perseverance; perseverance, character; and character, hope" (Rom. 5:3–4). Weight lifters know that lifting ten-pound weights increases muscle strength and enables them to move to twenty pounds, then thirty and beyond. One cannot start out lifting three hundred pounds. Likewise, our growth in spiritual maturity requires that we first master the basic levels, and then with perseverance we, step by step, mature in our comprehension, understanding, and functioning of the higher levels.

There is real danger in seeking to jump levels. Persons operating at level four and below may hear the call to live at level seven—a purpose-driven life. But a purpose-driven life is dangerous when one is immature. Those who operate on the reward-and-punishment level or with an eye-for-an-eye mentality and who aspire to jump to level seven will often misconstrue their purposes through their immature understanding—and in God's name burn people at the stake, shoot abortion doctors, protest with vile signs, or become suicide bombers. Those at level four and below, longing to have a purposeful life for God but not yet mature in their understanding of God's character and methods, often become the worst enemies of God's cause. Purpose without principles (level five and above) leads to destruction. Only by rejecting imposed-law constructs and returning to design law can we mature and become true partners with God in fulfilling his purposes.

Sadly, for many Christians development and growth has been impaired. In the next chapter, we will explore normal spiritual growth and development and the factors that contribute to spiritual failure to thrive.

KEY POINTS FROM CHAPTER 3

- There are different levels of moral understanding.
- Growth through the levels is progressive, and God calls us to grow and mature.
- Growth requires exertion; we must think for ourselves.
- We can fulfill God's purposes only when we understand and practice his methods and principles.

4

Spiritual Failure to Thrive

> When I was a child, I talked like a child, I thought like a child, I reasoned like a child. When I became a man, I put childish ways behind me.
>
> Paul, in a letter to the Corinthian church

Do you brush your teeth? What is the reason you do so? As an example of normal development, let's consider brushing one's teeth. Why is it right or wrong at the various stages?

1. *Reward and punishment*: It is wrong not to brush because the parent will be mad and the child will be punished. It is right to brush because the child will be praised.
2. *Marketplace exchange*: This is the child or parent who says, "I'll brush my teeth if you read me a bedtime story," or "Brush your teeth and I'll read you a bedtime story." Don't brush, no story; do brush, get story.

3. *Social conformity*: It's wrong not to brush because one will be teased at school; it's right to brush in order to be accepted.

4. *Law and order*: There is a family behavior contract with codified expectations and consequences. Don't brush and lose a privilege (e.g., no cell phone for a day). Do brush and maintain the privilege.

5. *Love for others*: Concern for others determines what is right and wrong. Realizing that going to the dentist and paying dental bills is both inconvenient and expensive for parents and desiring to reduce their burdens, the maturing child brushes his or her teeth.

6. *Principle-based living*: Individuals understand the second law of thermodynamics (even if they can't name it) that if energy isn't put into the system, it will decay. Therefore, they brush to live in harmony with how life is designed to function.

7. *Understanding friend of God*: Individuals not only love others and understand the law of thermodynamics but also realize they were made in God's image and the body is the temple of the Holy Spirit. Failure to brush would cause decay of teeth, increase risk of infection and sickness, and undermine their ability to fulfill God's purpose for their lives. Therefore, they brush as good stewards to maintain health and to be of greatest usefulness in God's cause, to be a good witness to others, and to demonstrate love for God and their fellow human beings.

Notice, people at all seven levels are brushing their teeth, but the *reason* they brush their teeth changes over time. *Only those operating at level five and above can be trusted.* Those at level four and below require oversight, supervision, threat, or coercive enforcement to continue on. Those at level four and below view law as imposed, and with no higher reason for brushing, they would stop the behavior if not for some authoritarian pressure. Furthermore, those operating below level five have little tolerance for those who break the rules. The focus is very self-centered: "If I have to brush my teeth, it isn't fair that Johnny doesn't." Not understanding God's design law and focusing only on the rules, level four and below thinkers almost always demand rule breaking be punished. Many at this level actually take pleasure in seeing another suffer, and even die, by the infliction of "just retribution."

For individuals operating at level four and below, God's law is not yet written on their hearts, not yet assimilated into their characters. But those at level five and above have moved from a self-centered orientation of right and wrong to an other-centered orientation. These individuals no longer see right and wrong as a system of rules coercively enforced to which they must comply but as an internal value and principle of action by which they desire to live. When they see someone break the rules, their hearts ache in love for the rule breaker because they know the deviant one is searing their own conscience, warping their own character, and—if not brought back to Christ for healing—destroying their own soul.

God, like a loving parent, reaches out to all his children regardless of their level of development. He meets people where they are and throughout human history has spoken to his children in a voice they needed to hear. Loving parents might notice the risk of being misunderstood that God took in order to reach his children at various levels of development.

Tricycles and Cars

Consider what you would do if you were sitting on your porch and saw your three-year-old daughter riding her tricycle and barreling straight toward the street and an oncoming truck. Would you sit back and relax, resting secure in the knowledge that you have already given her a rule not to leave the driveway and you expect obedience? What if she was giggling and not paying attention as she rode closer and closer to the street. Would you speak softly and gently, or would you yell? And if the sound of the plastic wheels on the concrete driveway was so loud she didn't hear you, would you yell louder? And if your daughter happened to be in a particularly independent mood and didn't follow your instruction to stop but kept going—what would you do then? Would you threaten, "If you don't stop you're going to get a spanking!"? If she does stop, do you spank her? What if she doesn't stop and is hit by the truck. Do you get out your belt to inflict "just punishment" for her disobedience?

What if neighbors were nearby and could hear you shout and threaten but couldn't see what was happening. Would you refuse to scream for fear of being misunderstood?

Why would you have a rule for your child to not leave the driveway in the first place? Do you have such a rule in order to dominate and control and exert a hierarchical command structure, or to protect the one you love, who, at her stage of development, is incapable of comprehending and keeping herself safe?

What is the problem if your daughter disobeys, rides into the street, and is hit by the truck? Is the problem that she broke your rule, and broken rules require just punishment? Or is the problem that her actions deviated from the laws of health and that she moved out of harmony with the stress tolerance limits of the human body, resulting in her little body being battered and broken?

Teens and Peers

Let's move the scenario. Your child is now fourteen and a freshman in high school. She has friends who were not raised to believe in God. Her friends tell her the rules you have set for her are old-fashioned, arbitrary, and restrictive. They tell her the only problem with breaking the rules is that you will get mad and punish her. If she just keeps you from finding out, there is no problem with breaking your rules because she won't get punished. Your daughter, having not yet moved past level four development, doesn't have any reason beyond the threats of punishment for her obedience. So she listens to her friends and begins smoking behind your back. She experiments with marijuana and alcohol, sneaks out and goes to parties, and shares her body before marriage.

Why is it wrong for your daughter to do these things? Is it because she is breaking your rules, and if you find out you will be required by justice to inflict punishment? Is the problem that she is breaking God's rules, and God knows and keeps an accurate list of our sins and will one day inflict just punishment? Or is it that she is breaking God's design protocols for life (God's law) and that all such actions are actually damaging to your daughter? She is not only destroying her physical health but also warping her character, searing her conscience, hardening her heart, and taking herself further and further away from God and his design of love. Her ability to hear and respond to the movements of the Holy Spirit is being impaired.

Do you speak differently to a fourteen-year-old than a three-year-old? Yes, but is your goal for them different? Is your love for them different? Is the reality on which life is built—the laws of health, physics, and morality—different for them at different ages? What is different? The way you approach them and teach them about how life actually works is different at each age because their level of maturity, their level of understanding, and their ability to comprehend are different.

Do you see this same process happening in Scripture? God is our loving Father, and we humans are his immature children. Just as a large family might have children ranging in age from infancy to adulthood, so too God has children across the entire range of moral development. And just as loving parents speak differently to their toddler, elementary-school child, high schooler, and adult child, so too God speaks the language his children need.

Should the adult child, when he hears his parent cooing and making baby sounds to his infant brother, regress and talk to his parent like the infant? Should the adult child, when she hears her parent telling her unruly teenaged sister, who doesn't want to listen, "because I said so," conclude that her parent doesn't want her sister to understand but only "do what I say"? Should the adult child, when he hears his mom yelling threats at the three-year-old riding her tricycle toward the street, run in fear of his parent and seek protection from her?

God and Unruly Children

God is our loving Father, and he speaks in love just what each person needs. The mature are those who have grown up and understand reality. They understand that we have deviated from

God's design and are in a terminal condition, dead in our transgressions and sins (Eph. 2:1), and that God is working, through Christ, to heal and restore us.

Do you see God's love when he thundered and spoke at Sinai because his children were heading toward a collision with idolatry, hedonism, and selfishness in their vilest and grossest forms, all of which would corrupt their minds, sear their consciences, harden their hearts, and destroy their souls? Can you stand beside Moses, who was called God's friend, and say in the midst of the thundering that they needn't be afraid (Exod. 20:20)? God didn't worry about what others, thousands of years later, would think if they only read his threats but didn't take the time to understand his passion to protect. He had children to save! But might people stuck at levels one through four of moral development read the Old Testament and misunderstand?

What if in the first scenario your daughter was riding her tricycle with a neighbor child who had just moved into the community. Both children are rolling toward the street, and the truck is heading right for them. You see an imminent collision if you don't do something. So, in love, with a heart desperate to protect and save, you yell and even threaten. Thankfully, both children stop. Then your daughter says to the neighbor child, "That's my mommy. I want you to meet her." Immediately, the other child says, "No way, she scares me." Your daughter scrunches her face, confused, and shakes her head while saying, "You don't need to be afraid of my mommy." What makes the difference? Your daughter knows you, even though you yelled, and knows you love her—the neighbor doesn't. This is why the Israelites were trembling at Sinai, but Moses was not—Moses actually knew God.

Could much of the problem people have with the God of the Old Testament be that far too many don't actually know him for themselves? Why? They don't know him because God is dealing not only with children who are struggling to mature and think but also with an enemy who is actively misrepresenting him, filling our minds with lies that undermine trust. Believing the idea that God is like Caesar, an imperial dictator who imposes rules and inflicts punishments, prevents far too many from moving from fear to love.

Many Christians remain infants, babes, not because of an *inability* to grow but because of an obstruction to their growth—false beliefs that trick them into choosing not to exercise the abilities they possess. What makes this spiritual failure to thrive so difficult to treat is that the underlying cause—the infection of thought that obstructs maturing—has become so deeply rooted in church discourse that it remains hidden. Like the human immunodeficiency virus (HIV) hides within cells of the body, this infection of thought hides within many diverse doctrines. And worse, some spiritual health-care professionals deny that this infection of thought is a problem at all.

Just like the fourteen-year-old in our earlier scenario, far too many people have accepted the lie that sin is merely a problem with breaking the rules of the one in charge. They fail to realize that God's law is design law, not imposed rules such as sinful human beings make. They don't realize that God's written law, his rules, the Ten Commandments, were included out of love for sinful humans who need protection from their immature selves, as a diagnostic instrument to help them see their terminal condition. Far too many people have concluded the Ten Commandments are functionally no different from the laws human beings make, imposed rules enforced by external threat and inflicted punishment. God wants his children to grow up, and the mature rise above level one through four thinking to actually understand how reality works.

Infant Formula

Hebrews confirms that the mature have trained themselves to distinguish good from evil—but how did they do this? They did it by "constant use" of solid food; in other words, they grew and matured by exercising their ability to think, reason, comprehend, and weigh evidence (Heb. 5:14). Then what prevents growing up? It is the refusal of solid food, the insistence on staying on infant formula.

What is infant formula in this illustration? Or stated another way, what according to Scripture is the religious formula that infants prefer?

Therefore let us move beyond the *elementary teachings* about Christ and be taken forward to maturity, not laying again the foundation of repentance from acts that lead to death, and of faith in God, instruction about cleansing rites [baptism/rituals], the laying on of hands, the resurrection of the dead, and eternal judgment. (Heb. 6:1–2)

Hebrews lists six elements of infant formula:

1. Repentance from acts that lead to death
2. Faith in God
3. Instructions about rituals
4. Laying on of hands
5. Resurrection of the dead
6. Eternal judgment

We will explore the first of these six elementary teachings in the remainder of this chapter and unpack others in subsequent chapters.

Repentance from Acts That Lead to Death

The first element of infant formula is viewing God's law not as design protocols but rather as imposed rules—dos and don'ts, the Ten Commandments, keeping track of deeds and sins, behavioral religion. This is the legal, punishment-oriented approach to understanding God. An example of one who maintained this approach is Eusebius, who believed God runs his government in the same way fallen human beings run earthly governments. This is level one through four thinking, which focuses on the act rather than the heart motive that led to the act.

Jesus taught the people of his day that this type of thinking is inaccurate. In Matthew 5, he says to them:

> You have heard that it was said, "You shall not commit adultery" [bad behavior]. But I tell you that anyone who looks at a woman lustfully has already committed adultery with her in his heart. (vv. 27–28)

> You have heard that it was said . . . , "You shall not murder [bad behavior], and anyone who murders will be subject to judgment." But I tell you that anyone who is angry with a brother or sister will be subject to judgment. (vv. 21–22)

They focused on acts, behaviors, and deeds; Jesus points them to the condition of the heart that leads to the acts. The immature stay focused on the deeds and fail to seek healing for the heart.

My friend Ty Gibson beautifully illustrates the problem of a relationship based on law in the following story:

Linda was eager to be married, to have someone special to spend her life with, but there were not many prospects on the horizon. Then one day she met "her" man. He treated her so nicely. He opened the door for her, held her hand as they walked, and pulled her chair out as she sat down. After months of courtship, Herman proposed. Joyfully, she immediately said yes, and they were married.

For the honeymoon Herman took her to a very nice place. They had a wonderful time, but all too quickly the honeymoon was over. Their first morning home Linda was awakened early at 5 a.m. by a bright light. She opened her eyes and there stood Herman saying, "Rise and shine. The honeymoon is over, and we need to get down to real life."

She noticed he was holding a piece of paper in his hand, and he presented to her the first of many lists to come. He had spelled out in great detail her responsibilities in two-week segments.

March 1–14:

5:30 rise and shower

6:00 begin breakfast; see attached menu

6:15 awaken Hermie-cuddles with a gentle kiss and turn on his shower

6:45 serve breakfast (do not forget grapefruit)

7:15 begin breakfast cleanup while husband brushes teeth

7:25 meet Hermie-cuddles at the door with appropriate jacket (be sure to pay attention to the weather), and say goodbye with a smile and a kiss

7:30 finish breakfast cleanup

8:00 free time

8:15 housecleaning; see attached cleaning supply list and detailed instructions

> M—north rooms
>
> T—east rooms
>
> W—south rooms
>
> TH—west rooms
>
> F—the garage

11:00 balance checkbook

12:00 lunch, whatever you like except marked items; check list

12:30 miscellaneous duties

> M—car maintenance and wash car
>
> T—dry cleaning and banking
>
> W—shopping
>
> TH—wash windows
>
> F—yard work

3:30 dinner prep; see attached menu

4:30 meet husband at door with kiss and hang up his coat

5:00 serve dinner

5:45 dinner cleanup

6:15 free time; see list of suggestions

6:45 draw Hermie-cuddles's bath

7:00 do next day's ironing

7:45 hand husband towel as he exits bath

8:00 neck and back massage for the man of your dreams

9:00 lights out, pleasant dreams sweetheart

Linda was given a new list with slight variations every two weeks without fail. As the years dragged on—and they were dragging—ten years into the relationship Hermie-cuddles dropped dead of an unknown cause. Linda's first reaction was to praise God! She didn't know whether to rejoice or grieve.

She made a vow that she would never, ever, get married again. But after three years of being single, she met a guy named Michael. He was like Herman in some ways. He opened the door for a lady to walk through. He was polite and courteous. He pulled out her chair as she sat and enjoyed holding her hand. And she kept telling herself, "No way, no way, no way." Then one day Michael popped the question, and she said yes.

They had a wonderful honeymoon. The first day back she woke up with a start at 5:30 a.m. and saw Michael standing at the end of the bed with a piece of paper in his hand. Immediately, she jumped into a karate stance, yelled "no way," and yanked the paper from him ripping it in two.

Michael, with a sad and surprised look, said, "Linda, that was a poem I wrote for you after you fell asleep last night."

As his words sank in, she felt bad about her reaction. She picked up the pieces and read his beautiful expression of love, and it broke her heart. While she was reading, Michael came in and served her breakfast in bed. And no list was forthcoming. Ten years passed being married to this wonderful man. One spring day while cleaning in the attic she came across an old shoebox filled with lists given to her by Herman the horrible.

She pulled out one of the lists and began to read. The strangest realization came over her. She said quietly to herself, "Wow, I do all of these things for Michael, and I never think about it."

When we serve a god operating at level four—law and order—love is crushed. We may obey the rules, but we are never transformed into the likeness of Jesus.

Believing that sin is a legal problem, a problem with bad deeds, would be like having pneumonia, with a fever, cough, and chills, and concluding the symptoms are the actual problem. Such an immature approach might lead one to simply treat the symptoms with acetaminophen, a cough suppressant, and a blanket. But failing to treat the underlying cause in need of healing, the person only worsens. This is what much of Christian teaching has done—attempted to treat symptoms while neglecting to cure the deeper problem!

When a person has a fever, cough, and chills, it is certainly appropriate that such symptoms are not ignored. It is good that people are taught such symptoms are undesirable and an indication something is wrong. Knowing something is wrong is what leads them to the physician, who looks past the symptoms to the underlying cause and prescribes a remedy to cure them.

This is why God gave the written law—to diagnose and protect his children from further infection, while he, through Christ, procured the remedy to cure us. Paul instructs Timothy on this very point: "We know that the law is good if one uses it properly. We also know that the law is made *not for the righteous but for lawbreakers and rebels, the ungodly and sinful*" (1 Tim. 1:8–9).

The ten-commandment law was given at Sinai. Why? Because it was needed as a diagnostic instrument and protective hedge for God's very immature, out-of-control children:

Through the law we become conscious of our sin. (Rom. 3:20)

I would not have known what sin was had it not been for the law. For I would not have known what coveting really was if the law had not said, "You shall not covet." (Rom. 7:7)

Just as children don't understand much about reality and need someone to instruct them, so too we sinners on earth cannot comprehend reality as it is, including God's original design for life and the reality of our own sin-sick condition, without someone to tell us. God has provided the written law for those operating at level four and below as a tool to reveal our terminal state of being so that we will realize our need to return to our designer for healing and restoration. As we mature, and God's design law of love is written again on our hearts, the written law is no longer needed for diagnosis (Heb. 8:10). Still, the written law does something more than diagnose: it provides protection, a "do not go into the street and play" boundary, while God finishes his work of restoring us back to his original design—beings who live in perfect accord with him and his law of love.

Is the law, therefore, opposed to the promises of God? Absolutely not! For if a law had been given that could impart life [remedy our sin-sick condition], then righteousness [restoration to God's design] would certainly have come by the law. But Scripture has locked up everything under the control of sin, so that what was promised, being given through faith in Jesus Christ, might be given to those who believe. Before the coming of this faith, we were held in custody under the law, locked up until the faith that was to come would be revealed. So the law was our guardian until Christ came that we might be justified by faith. Now that this faith has come, we are no longer under a guardian. (Gal. 3:21–25)

Here is my paraphrase of Galatians 3:21–25:

Is the written law, then, somehow in opposition to the promises of God? Of course not! The written law was simply a tool to diagnose our sickness and lead us to God for healing. If the written law could somehow cure the infection of selfishness and promote life, then healing would certainly have followed the giving of the law. But Scripture is clear: All humanity is infected with selfishness and is imprisoned by this terminal condition. It is by trust that we experience the only cure, the one promised—Jesus Christ, who was given to humankind as the Remedy to this terminal condition. Before Christ came we were quarantined by the written law, restrained from continual self-destruction until Christ procured the only true cure. So, then, the written law was provided as a safeguard to protect us and lead us to Christ—the Great Physician, so that we might be restored to unity with God by trust in and partaking of Christ. Now that trust in God has been restored and we are set right in heart, mind, and character and again practice God's methods, we no longer need the law to diagnose our condition or lead us back to God.[1]

Those operating at level four and below struggle to understand God's provision of the ten-commandment law. His design law, the law of love, was always in existence. The codification of his law of love written specifically for sinful humans was added later. Some will protest that to suggest such an idea is to undermine the law, but consider the example of Newton's first three laws of motion:

First Law: An object at rest remains at rest and an object in motion continues at a constant velocity unless acted upon by an external force.

Second Law: The sum external force **F** on an object is equal to the mass m of that object multiplied by the acceleration vector **a** of the object: **F**=ma.

Third Law: When one body exerts a force on a second body, the second body simultaneously exerts a force equal in magnitude and opposite in direction on the first body.

Now answer the following questions about Newton's laws:

- Are they real?
- Do they apply to our lives?
- Do they apply to everyone or only to those who hear about them and choose to believe in them?
- Are they rules we must obey or descriptions of how reality is built to function?
- When did they go into effect?
- If Newton had not written them down, would that mean these laws would not exist and thus would not be in effect?
- If we decide in committee to change the wording of the first law to read: "An object at rest remains at rest unless it receives permission from the proper church committee to move," does anything happen?

- In other words, can humans change these laws?
- Are these laws imposed laws or design laws?

Newton did not create or enact these laws; he merely described laws that were already in effect from the moment God created his universe.

The Ten Commandments are like this. They *describe* but do not establish God's law, just like Newton's laws *describe* but do not *establish* the laws of motion. God's design law was already in effect *before* the Ten Commandments were written. But human beings, with minds darkened by sin, failed to comprehend God's design of love, so God provided a distilled version of his law specifically written for the needs of fallen human beings. Paul confirms this in Romans 5 when he points out that death reigned from Adam to Moses, before the law was given, even in those who didn't break a specific command. Death reigned because the actual condition of humanity had changed and was now deviant from God's design, not because of legal problems with breaking laws that were not yet given.

Angels and the Law

This is further demonstrated by considering the angels who rebelled. Did those angelic beings in heaven sin? Yes, which means they transgressed God's eternal law. But did the angels have laws stating sins would pass down three and four generations or requiring them to honor their father and mother and not to commit adultery? And what about the Sabbath commandment? Consider how the Sabbath is measured—by the rotation of this planet in relation to our sun, which didn't exist until day four of creation week. But the angels were in existence long before this (Job 38:7).

Angels in heaven didn't have a copy of the Ten Commandments. But angels in heaven are still bound by the design parameters on which God constructed all reality to function—the law of love! The problem on earth today is that almost the entire world has accepted the lie that God's law is merely a list of imposed rules that operate no different from the laws that created beings enact. Rather than realizing the Ten Commandments simply codify—put into words—the eternal law of love that all reality is built on, far too many people view God as ruling his universe like a human dictator rules a nation. We must come back to reality—to God's design—and understand the true purpose of the Ten Commandments:

> Now, we know that the Ten Commandments are like a medical diagnostic instrument, identifying infection and exposing disease. It diagnoses accurately everyone who is infected with distrust of God, filled with selfishness and dying of sin, so that everyone who claims to be sin-free or free of selfishness will be silenced, and the entire world will recognize their need of God's healing solution. Therefore, no one will be recognized as having a healthy relationship with God and being like Christ in character by adhering to a set of rules; rather, it is through the Ten Commandments that we become aware of our sickly state of mind.[2]

God, like a loving parent, gave the written law, the rules, to help protect his earthborn children who didn't understand his design law and thus were in danger of "wandering out into the street" and destroying themselves. But now, Jesus has come. He has revealed the truth of God's character. He has lived out

God's law of love perfectly—in humanity. He has procured the remedy to our sin-sick condition. And through trust in him we can partake of his victory, so that "it is no longer I that live but Christ lives in me" (Gal. 2:20 NLT). We can receive a new heart and right spirit (Ps. 51:10). We can have the heart of stone replaced with a heart of flesh (Ezek. 36:26). We can have the law written upon our hearts (Heb. 8:10). In other words, we can have God-shaped hearts—hearts that are in harmony with God and love like he loves! Selfishness and fear can be cut out of our hearts and love restored within (Rom. 2:29). We can have the mind of Christ and grow up into the full stature of sons and daughters of God (1 Cor. 2:16; Eph. 4:13). God longs for us to grow up, to mature, to move past milk and ingest the flesh of truth and become his understanding friends (John 15:15)!

KEY POINTS FROM CHAPTER 4

- For individuals operating at level four and below, God's law is not yet written on their hearts, not yet assimilated into their characters. But those at level five and above have moved from a self-centered orientation of right and wrong to an other-centered orientation.

- God is our loving Father. We humans are his immature children, and just as a large family might have children ranging in age from infancy to adulthood, so too God has children across the entire range of moral development. And just as loving parents speak differently to their toddler, elementary-school child, high schooler, and adult child, so God speaks the language his children need.

- What makes this spiritual "failure to thrive" so difficult to treat is that the underlying cause—the infection of thought that obstructs maturing—has become so deeply rooted in church discourse that it remains hidden. Some spiritual health-care providers (clergy) deny the infection of thought even exists.

5

Law, Love, and Healing

It is one thing to recognize something is wrong; it is quite another to accurately diagnose the cause, and something much more profound to provide effective treatment.

Timothy R. Jennings

A few years ago I received an email with a link to a Christian talk show on which a Catholic priest and a Protestant theologian discussed the Eucharist and transubstantiation. They went back and forth over several points, then the Protestant honed in on the allegation that transubstantiation sacrifices Christ again and again whereas the Bible teaches Jesus died once for all.

To this the Catholic priest responded:

There are two elements to any sacrifice: the immolation and the offering. The immolation is a bloody death. The lamb is slain. What is precious about that is the life in the blood of the lamb that is precious and pays back God. That's how the Old Testament rituals used to work. The immolation happened once but the offering is something Christ does for all eternity. He is right now in the presence of the Father, in the holy of holies, in the eternal presence, offering himself to the Father for the forgiveness of our sins. . . . Christ isn't killed again and again and again, he is offered [in the Eucharist] in the same eternal presence as Christ offers himself.

The priest said it was by this *offering* of his sacrifice over and over again that the sins were paid for. So each time we sin, we must go to Mass in order to have the sacrifice of Christ pay the Father for that sin.

How do you think the Protestant theologian responded? He argued that Christ is in heaven, not offering his sacrifice to the Father over and over, oh no! He emphatically stated that Jesus is in heaven offering his *merits* to the Father over and over again to remind the Father that he has already paid for our sins.[1]

In the Protestant view, all human sins were placed on Christ at the cross and paid for there. When we pray for forgiveness, Jesus goes to the Father and reminds him of what Jesus has already done in paying for the sins and makes the *legal application* of his "merits" as the payment he offers to the Father into our individual accounts.

Do you see it, the deep infection of the imposed-law construct? Here we have two sincere people, both desiring to live in harmony with God through the victory of Jesus, arguing over whether Jesus is presenting his *sacrifice* or his *merits* to the Father to *pay for our sins*, yet missing the fact they are both worshiping a dictator god who requires some payment in order not to punish. Why do they think God needs a payment? Because they both accept the idea that God's law functions like human laws—imposed rules, and if God doesn't punish, then there is no justice. Their doctrine is based on the idea that we need protecting from God. Thus, trust in God is undermined and Christians, rather than being reconciled to God in heart and mind, are separated from God by beliefs that keep them fearful and distrusting of him.

Previously, we explored the seven levels of moral decision making in regard to teeth brushing. We observed that people at all seven levels brush their teeth, but also saw a dividing line between levels one through four and five through seven. Levels four and below are self-focused, operating out of fear—fear of punishment, fear of rejection, or fear of getting into trouble. These first four levels have a very self-referenced orientation toward their understanding of right and wrong. Levels five and above move the focus away from fear and self-protection to love for others and living for a higher purpose. This is maturing. This is growing up. This is what God is working to accomplish in us.

We have also identified that for many the infection of thought that has obstructed Christian maturation is the false belief that God's law is functionally no different from laws enacted by sinful human beings—rules imposed and then enforced by threats of punishment.

Examining the seven levels of moral development in light of the two law lenses (God's law, protocols upon which life is constructed, versus imposed rules), we can identify the dividing line between the immature and mature. Levels four and below are based on imposed law with inflicted punishment, whereas levels five and above are based on design law with punishment being the unavoidable result of deviating from how life is constructed to operate.

All too often, persons operating at level four and below misunderstand God's use of written law. They struggle to realize God added the written law as a diagnostic tool and protective hedge, just like loving parents have rules to protect their children until they grow up.

What happens if some never grow up? What happens if some cling to the rules and never grasp the reality behind the rules? What are the consequences for accepting the idea that God's law functions no differently than the laws human beings make?

When God's law is understood to be an imposed list of rules, the following doctrines result:

- Breaking God's imposed rules requires God to inflict just punishment, which is the death penalty.
- Justice is the infliction of punishment on the disobedient.
- God, not sin, is the source of inflicted suffering and death.
- God must be appeased/propitiated to avoid his anger, wrath, and inflicted punishment.
- Jesus died to pay our legal penalty to an offended God.
- God executed Jesus on the cross.
- God is the cosmic executioner who will one day kill all those who don't accept the legal payment Jesus made to him.
- God is the one from whom sinners must be protected.
- Scripture gets warped and doctrines are created that function to hide and protect us from God rather than reconcile us to him.

The imposed-law construct infecting Christianity embeds itself within almost every teaching of Christianity and subtly exerts its influence to keep the heart infected with fear, undermine trust in God, and keep good people trapped in cycles of fear, addiction, and abuse. People who live within the confines of a legal religion focus on a legal accounting of bad deeds, an adjustment of legal status in the heavenly court, and provision of a legal pass for expunging the record of their transgressions. This legal construct results in a form of godliness but is devoid of power to actually transform lives, heal minds, and re-create characters to be like Jesus. Such thinking leads religious people to act in horrible ways.

This was graphically demonstrated on October 14, 2015, with the stunning headline from *CBS News*: "Parents Beat Son to Death in Church 'Counseling Session.'"[2]

Multiple media outlets covered the story. The *National Post* reported:

> Two teenage brothers were brutally beaten in church—one of them fatally—in an effort by their parents, sister and other members of the congregation to force them to confess their sins and seek forgiveness, police said Wednesday....
>
> Lucas and Christopher Leonard, 19 and 17, were pounded with fists Sunday at the Word of Life Church when a "counseling session" meant to explore their spiritual state turned violent, Inserra said. They were beaten in the abdomen, genitals, back and thighs, authorities said.
>
> Lucas died and his brother was hospitalized in serious condition. Six church members—including the brothers' parents and sister—have been arrested.[3]

How could such a thing happen? Because of the imposed-law construct and the false belief that sin must be punished. But

God's methods are truth and love—truth to set free and love to heal and transform!

The Contrast

The contrast between design law and imposed law is stark:

DESIGN—LAW OF LOVE (LEVELS 5–7)	IMPOSED—IMPERIAL ROME (LEVELS 1–4)
Violations are incompatible with life.	Violations are not incompatible with life.
Violations require the designer to heal, fix, restore, lest death ensue (John 3:17).	Violations require the ruling authority to impose death and kill, lest unpunished rebellion ensue.
Christ's mission: to destroy sinfulness, destroy Satan, and restore mankind (Heb. 2:14; 2 Tim. 1:10; 1 John 3:8).	Christ's mission: to pay legal penalty to God, appease God, and propitiate his wrath.
The problem is sin in humanity.	The problem is anger in God.
The solution is heart change in humanity.	The solution is heart change in God.
Power is used to heal, bless, sustain, and restore. The Ruler (God) *gives* of himself to benefit his subjects (John 3:16; 13).	Power is used to subjugate, control, and coerce. The ruling authority takes from their subjects (taxes, military service, etc.) to support the state.
Presents truth in love and leaves those who disagree free (Rom. 14:5).	Those who disagree are tortured, imprisoned, and executed (e.g., the Dark Ages).
Loves one's enemies.	Kills one's enemies (e.g., the Crusades).
Wins loyalty with love.	Demands obedience by threat.

Which list above more closely summarizes the Christianity with which you are familiar? Sadly, according to a Baylor University survey of views of God in America, the predominant view of God is that he is authoritarian, dictator-like. Less than one in four see him as a God of love.[4]

Rwanda

This distortion about God is not restricted to America. The destructive results of rejecting God's law of love and worshiping an authoritarian dictator who imposes rules and punishes rule breakers were graphically revealed in Rwanda in 1994.

Over one million people were killed in four months, and the primary killing zones were churches! Fifty-six percent of the population was Roman Catholic, 26 percent Protestant Christian of various denominations, and 11 percent Seventh-day Adventist Protestants. This was an overwhelmingly Christian nation. In this desperate time, refugees ran to the churches for sanctuary. Church leaders would usher fleeing victims into the church buildings and then seek out militias to come into the churches and slaughter those hiding there. Clergy murdered members of their own congregations, and parishioners murdered their own clergy. In the aftermath of the genocide, pastors, priests, nuns, elders, deacons, and parishioners of every church group and denomination were tried and found guilty of war crimes. Timothy Longman, in his book documenting the horrors of this war, wrote:

> Believing that their actions were consistent with the teachings of their churches, the death squads in some communities held mass before going out to kill. . . . People came to mass each day to pray, then they went out to kill. In some cases militia members apparently paused in the frenzy of killing to kneel and pray at the altar.[5]

In researching what separated those who participated in the killing from those who helped protect the refugees, researchers discovered it came down to one factor: those with authoritarian God concepts participated in the killing, while those with loving God concepts protected the refugees— *regardless of denomination.*

In other words, those who worshiped a God of love protected the refugees, while those who viewed God as a dictator participated in the killing—*regardless of denomination.* It didn't matter on which day they worshiped, or how they were baptized, or whether they confessed sins to a priest or directly to God, or how they practiced Communion. What mattered was whether they saw God as love—the One who is the designer, or whether they worshiped a dictator—one who makes up rules and enforces them by imposed punishments!

When we operate at level four and below (which operate on imposed law), we are vigilant that the rules be kept. We are concerned with right doctrines, right definitions, and right beliefs and have little tolerance for those who believe differently. As a result, fragmentation occurs. Rather than seeing all humanity as one species, one group descended from one couple created in Eden, all suffering with the same sin-sickness, all in need of the same saving remedy—Jesus Christ—we fragment into different factions based on race, sex, religion, nationality, or dogma.

Love Unites

It is love and love only that unites, that overcomes rules, that transcends arbitrary laws, and that supersedes doctrinal differences. It is love that heals the heart!

On January 23, 1943, the SS *Dorchester* sailed from New York on its way to Greenland transporting over nine hundred soldiers for the allied war effort in World War II. Aboard were four chaplains: Methodist pastor George L. Fox, Roman Catholic priest John P. Washington, Reform Rabbi Alexander D. Goode, and Reformed Church in America minister Clark V. Poling.

During the early morning hours of February 3, 1943, the *Dorchester* was torpedoed by the German U-boat *U-223*. The men were desperate to escape the sinking ship, but the chaplains calmed them and helped organize the evacuation. When the supply of life jackets ran out before each man had one, the chaplains removed their own life jackets and gave them to others. They helped as many as they could into the lifeboats, and then, as the ship went down, the chaplains linked arms and began to sing hymns and pray for the safety of the men.

Grady Clark, one of the survivors, reported:

> As I swam away from the ship, I looked back. The flares had lighted everything. The bow came up high and she slid under. The last thing I saw, the Four Chaplains were up there praying for the safety of the men. They had done everything they could. I did not see them again. They themselves did not have a chance without their life jackets. [6]

The freezing waters didn't differentiate between Protestant, Jew, or Catholic. When Rabbi Goode offered his life jacket to a desperate soldier, it didn't matter what beliefs that soldier held—design law doesn't make distinctions between people. Doctrine didn't matter, liturgy didn't matter, Bible version didn't matter, denomination didn't matter. What mattered? Love! Selfless love, love that gives, love that seeks to help others. It is love that heals, love that unites—love that transforms the heart.

Spiritual Heart Disease

God's love is obstructed when we teach the imposed-law con-struct. Rather than being transformed, hearts are hardened by legal theologies. Consider the example of trying to evangelize a heroin addict who has been using dirty needles and now suf-fers from endocarditis (infection of the heart—the pump in his chest). He has broken both types of law: the laws of health (design law) and the laws of the land (imposed human law).

Does this addict want to be taken before the magistrate, have his misdeeds presented to the court, judgment rendered, and sentence imposed? Most likely not. In fact, won't the addict if caught and taken before the judge seek a representative to stand between him and the judge to "cover" over his "sins," while seeking to influence the court to be merciful? Sounds eerily like the argument of the Catholic priest and Protestant theologian over the Eucharist discussed earlier.

Or does this same individual, strung out, sick, and feverish, want to go before a doctor and have his misdeeds presented to him? The doctor would investigate much more thoroughly than the magistrate. The doctor would penetrate deeply within the hidden recesses of his being with ultrasounds, lab tests, X-rays, and MRIs, searching out every possible defect—and for what purpose? To heal and restore! Does this addict want the doctor to search and see all his defects and then render "judgment," what we call a diagnosis, and then pronounce "sentence," what we call a therapeutic treatment plan? Absolutely!

When we accept the lie about God's law and present him as the supreme magistrate, investigating records to pronounce legal findings and impose just punishments, we obstruct sinners from coming to God. We must come back to the truth about

God. He is our Creator, the designer, and his laws are the proto-cols on which reality is constructed. He is constantly seeking to heal and restore every defect in those who trust him. When we trust him, then we will pray like David of old: "Search me, God, and know my heart; test me and know my anxious thoughts. See if there is any offensive way in me, and lead me in the way everlasting" (Ps. 139:23–24); "Create in me a pure heart, O God, and renew a steadfast spirit within me" (Ps. 51:10).

Felix Manz

Swiss Reformer Felix Manz, who was martyred for his faith, understood that Christianity is infected with the imposed-law concept that destroys and that love and love only is the power of God to transform lives. Prior to his death he wrote:

> Alas how many are found . . . who boast of the Gospel and speak, teach, and preach much about it, but are full of hatred and envy. They do not have the love of God in them, and their deceit is known to all the world. . . . They hate the pious on the earth and obstruct the way to life and to the true sheepfold.
>
> They call upon the authorities to kill us, by which they destroy the very essence of Christianity. But I will praise the Lord Christ, who exercises all patience towards us. He instructs us with his divine graces and shows love to all men . . . which none of the false prophets are able to do. . . .
>
> It is love alone that is pleasing to God; he that cannot show love shall not stand in the sight of God.[7]

We are in a war for the hearts and minds of every person. God is working to restore his character and methods of love in all who will let him. But his healing love has been obstructed by the false law construct that puts God in the role of cosmic executioner rather than divine healer. In our next chapter, we will examine the evidence that demonstrates the pervasiveness of this devastating distortion about God across the landscape of Christianity.

KEY POINTS FROM CHAPTER 5

- The idea that God's law functions like human law has not only altered our understanding of God but also changed the way we conceive of sin (as a legal problem rather than a condition of being) and what Jesus came to achieve (to fix the Father's wrath rather than to fix the sinner's heart).
- Legal theologies have a form of godliness but are devoid of the power of love that transforms lives and renews hearts.
- It is love and love only that unites, that overcomes rules, that transcends arbitrary laws, and that supersedes doctrinal differences. It is love that heals the heart.

6

The Evidence

Facts are stubborn things; and whatever may be our wishes, our inclinations, or the dictates of our passion, they cannot alter the state of facts and evidence.

John Adams, argument in defense
of the British Soldiers
in the Boston massacre trials
(December 4, 1770)

When a doctor diagnoses a problem and reveals it to the patient—especially those still refusing to believe they have a problem—sometimes the patient feels uncomfortable or condemned or put down. Others, those who have known something was wrong but didn't understand what, are often relieved to discover what the problem is—now they have hope for a cure. Regardless of which type of patient the doctor is dealing with, the physician is not condemning, criticizing, mocking, or putting anyone down.

The doctor is not against the patient. The doctor is diagnosing with a heart motivated to heal.

The reason the doctor must expose the defect to the patient is because we cannot solve a problem, treat a condition, or rid ourselves of false beliefs until we first admit we have a problem that needs resolving. Likewise, the evidence presented here is not designed to condemn or make anyone uncomfortable; it is presented in order to expose an infection of thought within Christianity so that healing can occur. Further, this evidence is not intended to represent the official position of any one denomination, person, or group but to demonstrate that the infection of imposed law is common, deeply rooted, and accepted within Christianity as a whole.

Following are just a few doctrinal statements demonstrating that the infection of imposed law, with its false idea that God is the problem that needs fixing, can be found across the landscape of Christianity—regardless of denomination:

Roman Catholic theology:

What did Christ's suffering and death actually accomplish that allowed the Father to provide the human race with salvation? . . . Scripture teaches only that Christ became a "propitiation," a "sin offering," or a "sacrifice" for sins. . . . Essentially, this means that Christ, because he was guiltless, sin-free and in favor with God, *could offer himself up as a means of persuading God to relent of his angry wrath* against the sins of mankind. . . . Anger against sin shows the personal side of God, for sin is a personal offense against him. *God is personally offended by sin and thus he needs to be personally appeased* in order to offer a personal forgiveness. In keeping with his divine principles, his personal nature, and the magnitude of the sins of man, *the only thing that God would allow to appease him was the suffering and death of the sinless representative of mankind, namely, Christ.*[1]

Evangelical theology:

We affirm that the atonement of Christ by which, in his obedience, he offered a perfect sacrifice, *propitiating the Father by paying for our sins* and satisfying divine justice on our behalf according to God's eternal plan, is an essential element of the Gospel.[2]

Pentecostal theology:

The word "propitiation" properly signifies the *turning away of wrath by a sacrifice.* Thus it signifies *appeasement.* . . . According to Leon Morris: "The consistent Bible view is that the sin of man has incurred the wrath of God. That wrath is averted only by Christ's atoning offering. From this standpoint his *saving work is properly called propitiation.*[3]

Southern Baptist theology:

The wrath of God was satisfied. . . . All other understandings of the cross in the Bible are themselves dependent on *penal substitution.*[4]

An article by a Baptist pastor recently appeared in my local paper revealing this infection in layman's terms. The article was titled "God Isn't Looking at Us with an Angry Face."

Have you ever been burdened with the feeling that God is looking at you with an angry face? If you're like many people, you do. "God must be angry with me" or "I think God is punishing me" are statements I hear frequently as a pastor. . . .

And yet the Bible says that there is a way to know with absolute certainty that God is not looking at you with an angry face. . . . Look at the cross of Jesus. . . . Instead of turning his angry face upon us, *God turned his angry face upon his son. God's eyes flashed fire, his nose compressed like a spring under pressure and, with locked jaw and clenched teeth he poured out upon Jesus the wrath we deserve.* "For God so loved the world" (John 3:16).

Jesus, the sinless substitute, absorbed in himself every ounce of God's anger over our sin, fully and finally. Therefore, there is now "no condemnation for those who are in Christ Jesus" (Rom. 8:1). Can you believe it? No condemnation. No angry face. If you are in Christ Jesus—that is, if you are trusting in Jesus for salvation—you can be absolutely certain that God is not angry with you. You will still grieve God with your sin and experience his fatherly discipline, but God will never look upon you in anger. *All his anger has been spent in Jesus.*[5]

Seventh-day Adventist theology:

For a loving God to maintain His justice and righteousness, the atoning death of Jesus Christ became "a moral and legal necessity." God's justice requires that sin be carried to judgment. *God must therefore execute judgment* on sin and thus on the sinner. *In this execution the Son of God took our place, the sinner's place, according to God's will.*[6]

Why did *God the Father choose* a cross to be the instrument of death? Why did He not choose to have Christ instantly beheaded or quickly run through with a spear or sword? *Was God unjust in executing judgment on Christ with a cross* when He could have done it by beheading, a noose, a sword, a gas chamber, a bolt of lightning, or a lethal injection?[7]

One of the fundamental problems of the Moral Influence Theory is that it rejects the substitutionary nature of Christ's death.

The idea that *God had to kill the innocent* instead of the guilty in order to save us is considered a violation of justice.[8]

Mormon theology (which takes the idea of God requiring a blood payment a step further):

> Joseph Smith taught that there were certain sins so grievous that man may commit, that they will place the transgressor beyond the power of the atonement of Christ. *If these offenses are committed, then the blood of Christ will not cleanse* them from their sins even though they repent. Therefore *their only hope is to have their blood shed to atone*, as far as possible, in their behalf. ... And men for certain crimes have had to atone as far as they could for their sins wherein they have placed themselves beyond the redeeming power of the blood of Christ.[9]

> There are sins that men commit for which they cannot receive forgiveness in this world, or in that which is to come, and if they had their eyes open to see their true condition, they would be perfectly willing *to have their blood spilt upon the ground, that the smoke thereof might ascend to heaven as an offering for their sins; and the smoking incense would atone for their sins*, whereas, if such is not the case, they will stick to them and remain upon them in the spirit world.
>
> I know, when you hear my brethren telling about cutting people off from the earth, that you consider it is strong doctrine, but it is to save them, not to destroy them. ... And furthermore, I know that there are transgressors, who, if they knew themselves, and *the only condition upon which they can obtain forgiveness, would beg of their brethren to shed their blood that the smoke thereof might ascend to God as an offering to appease the wrath that is kindled against them*, and that the law might have its course.[10]

Accepting the imposed-law construct has caused some to present God in the role of cosmic torturer and to argue that to do so is only just.[11]

> Does hell serve a purpose? As much as we resist the idea, isn't the absence of hell even worse? Remove it from the Bible and, at the same time, remove any notion of a just God and a trustworthy Scripture. Let me explain.
>
> If there is not hell, God is not just. If there is no punishment of sin, heaven is apathetic toward the rapists and pillagers and mass murderers of society. If there is no hell, God is blind toward victims and has turned his back on those who pray for relief. If there is no wrath toward evil, then God is not love, for love hates that which is evil.
>
> To say there is no hell is also to say God is a liar and his Scripture is untrue. The Bible repeatedly and stoutly affirms the dualistic outcome of history. Some will be saved. Some will be lost.[12]

Misunderstanding Justice

Notice the logic progression, that justice requires the imposition and infliction of punishment. Why? Because imposed law has no inherent consequence and requires the ruling authority to inflict punishment. Accepting the imposed-law construct causes people to believe that if God doesn't act the role of cosmic executioner and punish, then there is no justice; everyone just gets away with sin. God becomes the problem, not sin. I can almost hear the evil one saying through this view, *If we could just get God under control, just get him some anger management*

*classes, then we could live eternally in sin, because there isn't any-
thing wrong with sin—sin doesn't harm or injure. It's God—he's
the real problem.*

This leads to bizarre evangelism practices, like the one I encountered recently. A person came up to me and handed me a
bill that looked like US currency. It had Ben Franklin's face on
the front and the blue security stripe across it, but the denomination was for one million dollars instead of one hundred. I
turned it over and read the following message:

> Here Is The Million Dollar Question: Will you go to Heaven
> when you die? Here's a quick test: have you ever lied, stolen,
> or used God's name in vain? Jesus said, "Whoever looks at a
> woman to lust for her has already committed adultery with
> her in his heart." If you have done these things, *God sees you
> as a lying, thieving, blasphemous, adulterer at heart, and the Bible
> warns that one day God will punish you in a terrible place called
> Hell.* But God is not willing that any should perish. *Sinners broke
> God's Law and Jesus paid their fine. This means that God can legally
> dismiss their case:* "For God so loved the world that He gave His
> only begotten [sic] Son, that whoever believes in Him should
> not perish but have everlasting life." Then Jesus rose from the
> dead, defeating death. Today, repent and trust Jesus, and God
> will give you eternal life as a free gift. Then read the Bible daily
> and obey it. God will never fail you. (emphasis mine)

This classic evangelism technique is entirely based on the
false imposed-law construct and as such is inherently contra-
dictory. In this view the problem is one's legal status. God views
the sinner as a criminal who deserves inflicted punishment,
rather than a sick person in need of healing. God is the source
of inflicted punishment and will torture the sinner for eternity

in hell, rather than the source of our healing and restoration. But don't worry because God loves us, and so he punished his innocent Son instead of the guilty and accepts the payment of his Son's blood in order to dismiss the legal charges against the sinner. Now we are supposed to trust this God who would otherwise torture us and who is so untrustworthy that he inflicts punishment upon an innocent while letting the guilty go free. Such a depiction not only misrepresents God and his law but actually undermines our ability to trust him.

Recently, I heard such distortions being promoted on nationwide Christian radio in the following discussion about Moralistic Therapeutic Deism. The guest was concerned that recent trends in Christianity misrepresent God to children by presenting him too compassionately and failing to present sin seriously. She said:

> I think we're actually manipulating children by not sharing with them the full truth. Jesus did not die on the cross just because I don't want to be separated from God. He died on the cross because somebody had to be violently . . . there had to be a blood sacrifice for the sin that I had committed because my sin is so heinous against a holy God. And the cross is a bloody, violent picture of how horrible our sin is. Now while we don't want to go into too much detail when they're young, we have to let them know that when Christ died on the cross it was a punishment, and if Christ doesn't take the punishment then we have to be punished. And I will be punished in a place called hell.

The host challenged his guest, asking her, "What about those listening who discount the idea of a wrathful, vengeful God?" She responded:

One end of the pendulum is we only talk about the vengeance and wrath of God, which is required because of his justice. The other extreme is we only talk about the love of God. . . . Go ahead and tell the children the truth, and as they get older you can go into more and more detail; but when they are younger, to say there is a God who created you and because he created you he owns you. You owe him your allegiance because he is worthy: He is your master. He created you. And when you do not think, live, feel, behave in such a way that gives him the glory and honor he is deserving of, that is called sin. It is cosmic treason. And when you sin, God must, because of his holy sovereign justice, punish you. And either we get in trouble and we take the punishment, or someone has to do it for us. And God out of his great love for us came as a man and lived a perfect life and died the perfect death and rose again to conquer sin and death. And in knowing that and accepting that Christ as God was our punishment [and] paid that penalty—and when I repent and receive Christ as that substitutionary atonement—then I enter into a relationship with God that lasts the rest of my life. . . . So what pictures are we giving children of this God who is worthy of our allegiance and himself paid a violent sacrifice for our debt?[13]

The entire construct of God being articulated on this nationwide Christian radio program is based on the idea that God's law is like human law—rules imposed. God, in this view, is the great dictator in the sky who must inflict punishment. This is level one through four thinking. The solution in this view is to have some innocent step in and be punished, *by God*, in our place and therefore protect us *from* God—from his anger and wrath. God is presented as the enemy—not sin.

But God doesn't work this way. And because God doesn't actually work this way, this distorted view of him and his law causes a disconnect that leads thinking people to reject Christianity. This penal view is often the root cause for so many of our young people leaving the church.

Imagine you were raised in a home in which, at a young age, your parents, because of their love for you, taught teeth brushing as a rule. You were told it was wrong not to brush, and punishment would be required if you didn't brush. Unfortunately, however, you never discovered any other reason for brushing your teeth than the threat of punishment. Finally, at eighteen you move out of your parents' home. Tired of all the rules and threats, you rebel against the clear teachings of your parents and stop brushing your teeth. At first, because of years of indoctrination, you watch very closely to see if anything bad happens. And after a couple of weeks of not brushing, and no punishment, you smile and tell yourself, "I knew those rules were ridiculous."

A couple of years later, you find yourself suffering in pain. You know something is wrong. You need help. So you humbly call your parents in distress, confessing you haven't been living like they raised you to live. You admit you have been breaking the rules, and you tell them that you are so sorry, but you don't know what to do. They direct you to an expert in helping people deal with such problems.

When you go to this expert and confess your failure to brush your teeth and cry out in pain, you are told to be of good cheer because a solution exists. You are told you have an "older brother" who came to earth and brushed his teeth perfectly and has a perfect dental record. If you will accept the legal tooth brushing of your older brother, then the record of his perfect teeth will be placed in your record. Further, if you perform the right rituals, you can request this "older brother" to plead to the heavenly dentist in your behalf, and when the heavenly dentist examines your records he will "declare" you have perfect teeth—even though you don't. All you need to do is accept by faith your teeth are legally healthy. You claim you do, but you leave in just as much pain, with just as much decay as when you arrived! You slowly get worse, all the while claiming you are legally healthy.

This is the false legal righteousness of imposed law, people with level one through four thinking—the immature—who are, as Hebrews says, not acquainted with actual righteousness. Why? Because they don't understand what is truly wrong. They are doing what they think is right. They don't want to be sick. They want to get well. But they have accepted the false legal diagnosis, based on the wrong understanding of God's law, and thus fail to mature and instead remain on spiritual milk. They focus on symptoms, acts, and misdeeds, and seek to address the symptoms rather than cure the problem.

Genuine righteousness is being set right in heart, mind, and character with God! It is a change in the inner man! It is experiencing the creation of a God-shaped heart within! The heart of fallen humanity is selfish, distrustful, fearful, unloving, and opposed to God or, as Scripture says, in "enmity" toward God (Rom. 8:7 KJV). But when the heart is changed from distrust, or being opposed to God, to trust, that person is "set right," is righteous or justified with God. It is an actual resetting of the heart motives toward God, not some legal accounting done in a heavenly court.

Scripture says, "Abraham believed God, and *because of his faith* God accepted him as righteous" (Rom. 4:3 GNT). In other words, Abraham trusted God, and *after* his heart changed from distrust to trust, *then* he was recognized as being right with God.

Why? Because he was right, he was actually set right with God, united with God, having a right heart attitude in actual state of being! And once he trusted God (was set right in heart, i.e., justified), in trust he opened his heart, and the Holy Spirit entered and healed, transformed, and renewed (sanctification—the law written on the heart). Again, actual transformation in the state of the living being!

As babes in Christ, we are vulnerable to having our understanding of God distorted. Why? Because we think like children about God's law, viewing things with level one through four comprehension. In this view, we feel so bad about ourselves we accept the lie that God is mad at us; because we punish ourselves in our own minds, we believe the lie that God wants to punish us; because we want to do something to make up for our badness, we believe the lie that God needs something done to him to make up for our badness.

Design Law and Justice

Design law sees it completely differently. Design law realizes that deviations destroy the deviant. Therefore, the just or right action to take with someone who breaks the law is to seek to rescue, deliver, heal, and restore. This is biblical justice. Biblical justice, which is based on God's design law of love, is not about punishing the oppressor; biblical justice is about delivering, healing, and restoring the oppressed:

- Defend the poor and fatherless; *do justice to the afflicted and needy* (Ps. 82:3 KJV).
- Wash yourselves clean. Stop all this evil that I see you doing. Yes, stop doing evil and learn to do right. *See that*

justice is done—help those who are oppressed, give orphans their rights, and defend widows (Isa. 1:16–17 GNT).

- *The* LORD *longs to be gracious* to you; therefore he will rise up to show you *compassion. For the* LORD *is a God of justice* (Isa. 30:18).
- This is what the LORD says to the dynasty of David: "Give *justice* each morning to the people you judge! *Help those who have been robbed; rescue them from their oppressors*" (Jer. 21:12 NLT).

Consider this: you walk in on a person who is attempting suicide. He or she has a rope around their neck and has just pushed the chair out from under their feet as you open the door. This person is breaking the law of respiration. What does justice require you to do to this *lawbreaker*? If you do what is right, what is just, what action do you take? Do you get out your belt to inflict punishment for disobedience to the law? Do you hold a trial, present evidence, and seek a judicial pronouncement? Or do you seek to deliver, to save? How? By removing the rope and restoring the person to harmony with the law. This is God's justice. He is constantly seeking to save. How? By restoring us sinners—we who are out of harmony with his design, we who are deviant from the law and thus dead in trespasses and sin—back into harmony with his law, his design for life. As the Bible says, in the new covenant, "I will put my laws in their minds and write them on their hearts" (Heb. 8:10). This is God's justice—the justice of love, the justice of design law!

In his book *America the Beautiful*, Ben Carson documents the justice taught in the Old Testament: "They focused on reparation to the victim rather than punishment or fines levied on the perpetrator."[14] Throughout human history, the good news about God and his actions to heal and restore are the same.

Charismatic author Derek Flood, in his book *Healing the Gospel: A Radical Vision for Grace, Justice, and the Cross*, states:

> *We think* that the gospel is rooted in the idea that *Jesus had to die to fulfill the "demands" of (punitive) justice.* This is an understanding of the atonement known as penal substitution, "penal" meaning punish, and "substitution" *meaning that Jesus is punished instead of us.* . . . What I propose is that the above *is not at all what the Bible teaches*, and instead is a result of people *projecting their worldly understanding of punitive justice* onto the biblical text. The New Testament, in contrast, is actually a critique of punitive justice. It presents it as a problem to be solved, not as a means to the solution. The problem of wrath (that is, punitive justice) is overcome through the cross, *which is an act of restoration—restoring humanity to a right relationship with God.* In other words, *restorative justice* is how God in Christ acts to *heal* the problem of punitive justice. Love is not in conflict with justice, *love is how justice comes about* because the New Testament *understanding of justice is ultimately not about punishment, but about making things right again.* [15]

Anglican theologian J. B. Phillips, known for his beautiful translation of the New Testament, writes:

> Jesus once declared that God is "good to the ungrateful and the wicked" (St. Luke 6:35), and I remember preaching a sermon on this text to a horrified and even astonished congregation who simply refused to believe (so I gathered afterwards) in this astounding liberality of God. That God should be in a state of constant fury with the wicked seemed to them only right and

proper, but that God should be kind towards those who were defying or disobeying His laws seemed to them a monstrous injustice. Yet I was but quoting the Son of God Himself, and I only comment here that the terrifying risks that God takes are part of His Nature. We do not need to explain or modify His unremitting love towards mankind.[16]

But what if the person you saved by removing the rope from around their neck is insistent in their disobedience and attempts over and over again to hang themselves, and eventually they are left to themselves and no one delivers them—what then? Is there a punishment for their disobedience? Is that punishment inflicted by the ruling authority? What happens if the deliverer "lets go"?

This is what happens to the wicked in the end. Those who run from God beg for the mountains to hide them from him, and God sadly lets them go (Rev. 6:16). He surrenders them to *their persistent choice* to separate themselves from the only source of life, and the result is ruin and death (Rom. 6:23; James 1:15; Gal. 6:8).

Some might argue my analogy fails because the verses above are talking about delivering victims from oppressors, not delivering oppressors from their misdeeds. Consider this scenario. You and your spouse have two children ages seventeen and nineteen. You, your spouse, and your seventeen-year-old have all accepted Jesus and are in a saving relationship with him. But your nineteen-year-old has not accepted Jesus and is currently living like the prodigal son, out in "wild living" wasting his life using drugs and alcohol. One day, you walk into your home and see your nineteen-year-old brandishing a weapon at your wife and youngest child, threatening them for money. While you are concerned for each member of your family, which one of them, at that moment, are you most concerned for? Who, in that situation, is in the greatest *eternal* danger? What happens to each person if your oldest child murders his family? Who needs delivering? If you intervene to deliver your wife and youngest, have you not just delivered your oldest from unimaginable damage to his heart, mind, and character?

Kent Whitaker and the Power of Love

Fortunately, I have never had to face such a terrible situation, but on December 10, 2003, Kent Whitaker did. I had the privilege of meeting Kent, and I heard firsthand about his unimaginable ordeal.

On one fateful day in December, Kent, his wife, and two sons, Kevin and Bart, went out to dinner to celebrate Bart's upcoming graduation from college. After a wonderful family dinner, they returned home. As the family approached the house, Bart ran back to the car to get his cell phone. When the rest of the family entered the house, a masked gunman jumped out and shot and killed Kevin and Kent's wife. He also shot Kent in the chest, but fortunately he survived. As devastating as the murders of his wife and son were, the worst part for Kent was yet to come—the police, upon investigation, discovered that Kent's surviving son, Bart, had been the one who arranged to have his family murdered so he could inherent the family money. I cannot imagine the depth of pain, heartache, and despair that Kent faced. Bart was arrested and tried for murder with the prosecutor seeking the death penalty.

If you were Kent, what justice would you want for Bart? What law lens do you view this tragedy through? Do you see only through imposed human law and seek punishment for Bart, or do you see through God's design law and realize Bart is sick of heart and mind and in need of healing and restoration? If you realize your son is sick of heart and mind, what do you want for your son—to be executed for his crimes or to be transformed in his character?

Kent understood his son was sin-sick and needed healing, and therefore he forgave his son and publicly asked the prosecutor not to seek the death penalty. But the prosecutor, an agent of the human imposed-law system, did what he thought was just and sought to punish; he sought the death penalty. Bart was found guilty and sentenced to death.

Kent stood by his convicted son, pouring his forgiveness and love upon him, visiting him in prison, and seeking his eternal healing. Bart eventually said, "If you can still love me and forgive me for all I have done, then I believe God can also." And, though still on death row, Bart gave his life to Christ.

In a forty-minute interview in 2012 with a KPRC Local 2 reporter, Bart confessed:

> I've made some really bad mistakes in my life. I was a very messed up young man. There are some people who are never going to get past that.
>
> I think about what I could have done every day. But those types of thoughts are really torture back here. I have to limit myself to the good I can do in the here and now, or otherwise I will break.
>
> If there's any way my mother and brother are watching me, I want them to be proud of the way I'm living now. That is foremost in my mind every minute of every day.[17]

Kent said that though he has lost his wife and younger son on this earth and will also lose Bart, he has peace knowing that

Bart will now be with them in heaven, and their family will be together for eternity. Such grace, such forgiveness, such love is only possible when we realize the truth about God and experience his love in our lives—when we come back to focus on design law and reject the fallen, human imposed-law construct. This is the goal. This is the God-shaped heart. This is the new covenant—having God's law of love written on the heart. Ritual doesn't matter, denominational affiliation doesn't matter, legal accounting doesn't matter. What matters? Love—transforming love that reshapes the heart, that casts out fear, that overwrites selfishness, that overcomes survival instincts, and that bridges the gulf between heaven and earth and connects us again to our Father of love!

The Four Questions

Keith Johnson is an online friend who has worked for years in prison ministry teaching inmates about God's design law, helping them to move past imposed-law constructs of right, wrong, and justice. He developed four questions to help them understand more clearly what justice is from God's viewpoint. Take a moment and answer each of the following questions for yourself:

1. What if I told you that your youngest child was murdered? Would you want mercy or justice *for* the perpetrator?
2. What if I told you that the murderer was your oldest child? Would you want mercy or justice *for* the perpetrator?
3. What if I told you that you are guilty of the murder of the only begotten Son of God? Would you want mercy or justice *as* the perpetrator?

4. What if I told you that you had a daughter, your only daughter, the apple of your eye, who has never given you a moment's grief. Tonight you happen to have a tux hanging in the closet because tomorrow, as her father, you are scheduled to walk your daughter down the aisle and give her away to someone of whom you approve. If you're the mother, you have a new dress hanging next to her wedding gown, a wedding you have been planning and preparing for since the first time you held her in your arms. But tonight, your daughter is at a bachelorette party with her peers, and they talk her into having "one for the road," the first ever in her life. Two, three, four, five, six, seven (drinks) later, while on her way home, she wipes out a school bus full of little children on their way to camp. Everybody aboard the bus dies in a fiery inferno, but your daughter survives. Do you want mercy or justice for your daughter? And . . . what do those who are related to the victims who were on the bus want?[18]

Human justice is based on human law, imposed rules, is motivated by selfishness, and seeks vengeance in the name of justice. The selfish heart has an ingrained sense of justice that in reality is nothing more than vengeance, which is easily exposed because such justice is sought only so long as it doesn't apply to them or theirs.

Justice in God's universe is entirely different. God's justice always seeks to deliver, heal, restore, set right, fix, and save everyone who will allow God to do so. It is the justice of love—the law of God on which God's government runs.

Consider the justice those grieving parents of the children murdered in Newtown, Connecticut, on December 14, 2012, would choose, if they had the choice: punishment for the perpetrator or resurrection and restoration of their children and restoration of a Christlike heart into the perpetrator? God's justice is the justice of love, and love always does what is right; if we let him, he will restore all that has been taken and more—he will set things right again (Joel 2:23–27)!

This is the power of God—the power to heal, to set free, to renew and restore, and to create God-shaped hearts—it is the power of love! God is seeking to heal, deliver, restore, and re-create his children back into harmony with his character of love. Thus, two thousand years ago Jesus read the words of Isaiah applying them to himself:

> The Spirit of the LORD is on me, because he has anointed me to proclaim good news to the poor. *He has sent me to proclaim freedom for the prisoners and recovery of sight for the blind, to set the oppressed free*, to proclaim the year of the Lord's favor. (Luke 4:18–19)

God Is for Us!

Review the statements of theology at the beginning of the chapter, and note how each of them teaches that God, in some way, is the one we must fear, the one who is the source of inflicted pain and suffering, the one we need something done to in order to avoid death. But this is not true. God is *not* like this. The Bible is clear on this point:

> If God is *for us*, who can be against us? He who did not spare his own Son, but gave him up for us all—how will he not also, along with him, graciously give us all things? Who will bring any charge against those whom God has chosen? *It is God who*

justifies. Who then is the one who condemns? No one. Christ Jesus who died—more than that, who was raised to life—is at the right hand of God and is *also* interceding for us. (Rom. 8:31–34)

Who is for us? Who is justifying us (which means setting us right with God)? God, our designer, is the one working to remove the rope of lies and selfishness choking us and restore us back into harmony with his design (law). And what does that word *also* mean? It means in addition to. Jesus is *also* interceding for us—in addition to whom? The Father! Christ does *not* need to plead to the Father for us or present his sacrifice or merits to the Father because the Father is already on our side! Jesus said so himself: "I am *not* saying that I will ask the Father on your behalf. No, the Father himself loves you" (John 16:26–27). The Father was in Jesus working to reconcile the world back to himself (2 Cor. 5:19).

This battle between two views of God is *the* battle that has been raging from the beginning. Augustine was fighting it in his day: "Does this mean then that the Son was already so reconciled to us that he was even prepared to die for us, *while the Father was still so angry with us that unless the Son died for us he would not be reconciled to us? . . .* The *Father loved us* not merely before the Son died for us, *but before he founded the world.*"[19]

God longs for us to come back to a true knowledge of him. For "this is eternal life: that they know you, the only true God, and Jesus Christ, whom you have sent" (John 17:3).

Jesus is in heaven eager to return for his bride—the church. *But he isn't coming back for a child bride.* He waits for his bride—his people—to mature, to grow up, to be like him in character. One factor that hinders Christ's bride from growing up is staying on the infant formula of "repentance from acts that lead to death" (Heb. 6:1). This is caused by the infection of the imposed-law construct that keeps people operating at level four and below thinking. Those who don't end up leaving the church all too often fall into addiction, violence, and repentance cycles but with no real victory. The good news is God is not like his enemies have made him out to be—he is our trustworthy friend and ever-present helper longing to heal all who will let him.

KEY POINTS FROM CHAPTER 6

- The human imposed-law construct infects all of Christianity regardless of denomination.
- Biblical justice is delivering the oppressed, *not* punishing the oppressor.
- Legal adjustment of one's account doesn't matter, what matters is love—transforming love that reshapes the heart, that casts out fear, that overwrites selfishness, that overcomes survival instincts, and that bridges the gulf between heaven and earth and connects us again to our Father of love.
- Christ is longing to return for his bride—the church. *But he isn't coming back for a child bride.*
- God is not the enemy we must fear—God is our Creator who longs to heal us from the terminal sin-condition that is killing us.

7

Love and Worship

> We might be wise to follow the insight of the enraptured heart rather than the more cautious reasoning of the theological mind.
>
> A. W. Tozer, *The Knowledge of a Holy God*

Sandi was torn, caught in conflicting emotions. She didn't know what to do or where to turn, so she went to her pastor.

Her pastor had had suspicions. Sandi's quick glances to her deacon husband before answering questions, her half smiles in his presence, and her frequent use of heavy makeup. But her pastor had no idea of the severity of the abuse.

Sandi taught grades one through three at the local denominational church school. She didn't want to get her husband in trouble. She didn't want to lose her marriage. She didn't want people to find out that her husband beat her. But she knew she couldn't go on like this. Something had to be done.

So she finally told her pastor, and he immediately confronted her husband and in no uncertain terms told him this must stop! He admonished her husband to get help, to get counseling, and encouraged Sandi to call the police if he hit her again. But despite the pastor's attempts, the abuse never stopped. After years of mistreatment, Sandi moved out and filed for divorce.

Her husband, hurt and angry, went to their church conference officials and complained that his wife was divorcing him without biblical grounds (something he claimed since he had not had physical intimacy with another person). And, he argued, she was unfit to teach in a Christian school for failing to uphold biblical standards on marriage—and the conference officials terminated her employment.

As you consider this true story, reflect on these questions:

- At what level was Sandi's husband operating?
- Was Sandi's action in divorcing her husband right or wrong?
- Did she have biblical grounds for her divorce?
- What about the conference officials—at what level were they operating?
- Was the action of the conference to terminate Sandi right or wrong?

Your answers will reveal much about the level at which you are currently operating.

The mature friends of God understand his law is the law of love, which is actually an expression of his character and the design protocols on which life is built to operate. As such, love is not self-seeking but other-centered. All God's creation is built to operate on this principle. Thus, whoever breaks the law in one point breaks it in all points, because all deviations from the law are failures to love (James 2:10). A man who beats his wife breaks the law of love and violates her trust—he betrays her. Another description for betrayal is that he commits adultery.

What is wrong with beating one's wife? The answer depends on the level at which one is operating.

1. *Reward and punishment*: It isn't wrong because he is stronger and as long as he isn't punished for it, it is right. It is only wrong if it results in his being punished.

2. *Marketplace exchange*: It isn't wrong; it is just and proper to give his wife the beating she deserves when she doesn't fulfill her side of the marital bargain. It would only be wrong if he beat her without proper cause.

3. *Social conformity*: It is only wrong if the culture says it is wrong.

4. *Law and order*: It isn't wrong, because broken rules require punishment. God gave us rules, and when they are broken justice requires God to punish. Jesus took our punishment, and if we want to be like God, we must punish a disobedient wife. This is how love teaches her to obey her husband.

5. *Love for others*: It is wrong because it fails to love her, to treat her as a daughter of God who has value as a person.

6. *Principle-based living*: It is wrong because it violates God's design for life and love. It violates the law of liberty, one of God's design protocols for healthy relationships. Love can only exist in an atmosphere of freedom. Further, God designed husbands and wives as coequals, and husbands are to treat their wives like Christ treats the church, sacrificing himself for her (Eph. 5:25).

7. *Understanding friend of God*: It is wrong because it not only violates God's design but also damages the mind, character, and conscience *of the husband*, destroys the individuality of the wife, misrepresents God as dictatorial, and fails to understand the purpose in the creation of woman. Man was created in God's image, and God said it is not good for man to be alone, so a helper was made for him—a helper to do what? To enter into the fullness of godlike love. Adam could not enter into the fullness of godlike love without someone for Adam to serve, to give of himself for—and Eve was created to be the recipient of Adam's self-sacrificial love. Then that love flows through her back to Adam in her selfless service to him. Adam and Eve in relationship with the Spirit were designed to live out God's law of love, the rulers of planet Earth—God's image in humanity.

Law of Worship

Studies confirm that spousal abuse rates are no different in Christian homes than in non-Christian homes.[1] How can this be? What prevents professed Christians from overcoming anger, rage, and violence against their families? The replacement of God's law with imposed law, which results in worshiping a punishing god—and we become like the god we worship.

One of God's design laws is the law of worship—by beholding we are changed. We actually become like the God we admire and worship. In psychiatry, this is known as modeling. This occurs due to the amazing ability of our brains to rewire based on the thoughts we think and the experiences of life. We were constructed by God to adapt and change based on the choices we make: worship a God of love and become more loving; worship an authoritarian god and become more abusive. The issue is not the moniker one gives their god but the character of the god one worships. This makes all the difference.

Every false god operates on imposed law, imposed punishment, and authoritarian rule, which results in worshipers who live in fear and ultimately end up abusing others in the name of their god. Only the One true God—the Creator—builds reality that operates on love, the design protocol for life, and has worshipers who sacrifice self for others. All other gods are imperialistic, threatening, authoritarian, and ultimately abusive.

In his book *Sun of Righteousness, Arise: God's Future for Humanity and the Earth*, Jurgen Moltmann documents that the authoritarian god is the predominant view found throughout human history:

> On the steles set up by Xerxes at the frontiers of his empire stood:
>
>> "I am Xerxes, the great king,
>> King of Kings,
>> King of the lands
>> in which all manner of men dwell,
>> the king of this earth far and wide."
>
> Rule over the world belongs to the one God in heaven; lordship over the different peoples and countries belongs to his image on earth: one God—one king—one universal empire. That is the religious idealization of power: the more power the more divinity. And so the earthly ruler is declared to be God. As the Son of Heaven, the Son of God, the God Emperor, he stands over against his subjects, and demands religious worship and absolute obedience.

The notion that the one God in heaven has to have the one rule on earth as his correspondence, and that the divine universal sovereignty has to be matched by political rule over the earth, is age-old political theology. We find it in the Chinese ideology of the emperor as the Son of Heaven, in Japanese state Shinto-ism, and in Persian, Babylonian and Egyptian mythos of rule. Echnaton's state, with its sun worship, is a good example of this political monotheism. Yet it was never more than a utopia, be-cause there was never a worldwide empire that went undisputed. An encounter—ironical in the context of world politics—took place in 1245 at the court of the Mongolian ruler Genghis Khan in Karakorum. Two Franciscans from Rome came before the Khan hoping to convert him. He responded:

Dei fortitude, omnium hominum imperator. Praeceptum asterni Dei: In coelo non est nisi unus Deus aeternus, super terram non sit nisi unus Dominus Chingus Chan, filius Dei. Hoc est verbum quod vobis dictum est. [The might of God, the ruler of all men. The precept of the eternal God: In heaven there is none but the one eternal God, upon earth there shall be none except the one Lord Chingis Chan, the Son of God. This is the word I say to you.]

The Franciscans took this answer of the Mongolian emperor back to "God's representative on earth" in Rome, who legitimated his religious power in a very similar way.[2]

But Jesus—"who, being in very nature God, did not consider equality with God something to be used to his own advantage; rather, he made himself nothing by taking the very nature of a servant" (Phil. 2:6–7)—overturned this dictator view of God. Jesus presented a God who is love, a God who uses power to serve rather than to be served, a God who gives for the good of his creatures rather than demands service by his creatures, a God who sacrifices self.

As Philip Yancey wrote:

> Because of Jesus . . . I must adjust my instinctive notions about God. Perhaps that lay at the heart of his mission? Jesus reveals a God who comes in search of us, a God who makes room for our freedom even when it costs the Son's life, a God who is vulnerable. Above all, Jesus reveals a God who is love.[3]

Our instinctive notions of dictator gods are based on human imposed-law constructs—gods of power who rule by coercion. This is level four and below thinking. This is immaturity. But Jesus overturns such ideas! Jesus reveals a God who presents truth in love and leaves his creatures free. The apostles, once freed from the false-god view, preached Jesus and him crucified and presented God's law as love—and the New Testament church grew (Rom. 13:10; Gal. 5:14; James 2:8).

But sadly, after apostolic times, Christianity gave up its hold on the selfless God of love. The church rejected the understanding that God is Creator and his laws are built into the fabric of reality and replaced this truth with an authoritarian god in the mold of Caesar, a dictator who demands worship on the threat of punishment. Moltmann continues:

> The Roman father of a family corresponded to the Roman father gods and to the later father of the gods, Jupiter, acting as a household priest. The Caesar was seen as the *pater patriae*, the father of his country, and ruled as priestly king of priestly father, the *pontifex maximus*. On the one hand these titles reflect the people's expectation of protection by the ruler, and on the other his unrestricted power: the father of his country is omnipotent—*pater omnipotens*. In Lactantius's writing about "the Wrath of God," we can clearly see how the Roman idea of the father has been transferred to the Christian God: the one

God is both Lord and Father, his power being fatherly and also supreme. "We should love him because he is the Father, but we should also fear him because he is the Lord. . . . In both persons he is deserving of worship. Who would not love the Father of his soul with a proper childlike reverence? Or who without punishment could disdain the one who as the ruler of all things has the true power over all?"[4]

When the God of love whom Jesus revealed is replaced with this dictator view, it is no surprise that Christian husbands abuse their wives just as frequently as men who have never heard of Jesus. Why? Because they are operating on the same imposed law. And just as an apple cannot avoid falling to the ground when released, so too our characters (our hearts) cannot avoid becoming like the god we worship—it is the law of worship!

Religious Children Are Less Altruistic

A recent study of 1,170 children from six countries—United States, Canada, China, Jordan, South Africa, and Turkey—found that children raised in religious homes were not as good at sharing and more likely to be punitive when compared to children raised in more secular homes. The author of the study said in an interview, "In our study, kids from atheist and nonreligious families were, in fact, more generous. . . . Together, these results reveal the similarity across countries in how religion negatively influences children's altruism. They challenge the view that religiosity facilitates pro-social behavior, and call into question whether religion is vital for moral development—suggesting the secularization of moral discourse does not reduce human kindness. In fact, it does just the opposite."[5]

When one understands the law of worship, such a finding is no surprise; it is the predictable and unavoidable outcome when the predominant worldview of God is that of an authoritarian dictator who operates on imposed law. This is a function of design law—the law of worship—by beholding we become changed. We really are transformed into the image of the god we worship. It is just as the prophet Jeremiah said, "They followed worthless idols and became worthless themselves" (Jer. 2:5). Or as Paul said, "Because those people refuse to keep in mind the true knowledge about God, he has given them over to corrupted minds" (Rom. 1:28 GNT).

Believing the wrong view of God can result in much more tragic outcomes than mere failure to share. In fact, there isn't anything much more dangerous than someone on a mission for God who doesn't actually know him!

In Pensacola, Florida, on March 10, 1993, Michael Frederick Griffin, a thirty-one-year-old professed Christian, after praying for the soul of Dr. David Gunn, forty-seven, stepped out of a crowd of protestors and shot him three times in the back, killing him in front of the abortion clinic where Dr. Gunn worked.[6] What kind of a god do you think Griffin was worshiping? Do you recognize the same authoritarian god as the ISIS fighters who beheaded twenty-one Coptic Christians in February of 2015?[7]

Such actions are exactly opposite of love, exactly opposite of the teachings of Jesus: "You have heard that it was said, 'Love your neighbor and hate your enemy.' But I tell you, *love your enemies* and pray for those who persecute you, that you may be children of your Father in heaven. He causes his sun to rise on the evil and the good, and sends rain on the righteous and the unrighteous" (Matt. 5:43–45).

Do you see God's design law in Jesus's statement? Immediately after Jesus instructs us to pray for our enemies, so that we can be like our Father in heaven, he provides examples of God's love in action. What examples did he provide? Sunshine and rain—design law! God's laws are the protocols on which the universe is actually constructed to operate. We are being called back to God, back to reality, back to unity with our heavenly Father and each other, and back to love—for that is the only way life is designed to exist. But sadly, many have exchanged the truth of God for a lie.

Modern Baal Worship

Over twenty-eight hundred years ago, the cult worship of Baal had infected Israel and become the dominant belief system and worship practice among the people God called his own. Baal worship was promoted by the king and political and religious leaders and was accepted as true by most of the nation. In order to combat this distorted belief system, God called upon the prophet Elijah to confront the false system of worship.

God, through the prophet Malachi, foretold that before Christ returns the people of God would again, like Israel twenty-eight hundred years ago, need the prophet Elijah to call them back to the worship of the true God: "But before the great and terrible day of the LORD comes, I will send you the prophet Elijah. He will bring fathers and children together again" (Mal. 4:5–6 GNT). Malachi's prophecy is a warning that prior to the second coming of Christ the world will face a similar crisis—a world in which religious and political leaders will lead the majority of humanity into believing a false version of God.

In order to understand Malachi's prophetic application for today, we need to understand what made Baal worship false. What was the problem with worshiping Baal? Was it simply a matter of using the wrong word, *Baal*, when worshiping God? Was it because they were not saying *Yhwh* (Yahweh)? Or was it something else?

> The Hebrew noun *ba'al* means "master," "possessor" or "husband." Used with suffixes, *e.g.* Baal-peor or Baal-berith, the word may have retained something of its original sense; but in general Baal is a proper name in the Old Testament, and refers to a specific deity, Hadad, the Semitic storm-god, the most important deity in the Canaanite pantheon.
>
> Yahweh was "master" and "husband" to Israel, and therefore they called him "Baal," in all innocence; but naturally this practice led to confusion of the worship of Yahweh with the Baal rituals, and it became essential to call him by some different title; Hosea (2:16) proposed *'îš*, another word meaning "husband."[8]

Obviously, the problem was not the syllables they spoke, as *ba'al* was one name used for the true God. Could this mean, then, that today people could be worshiping a deity they call "Jesus" but actually be holding to a distorted view of who Jesus really is? In other words, could people who call themselves Christians actually not be followers of Christ? According to Jesus, yes:

> Many will say to me on that day, "Lord, Lord, did we not prophesy in *your name* and in *your name* drive out demons and in *your name* perform many miracles?" Then I will tell them plainly, "I never knew you. Away from me, you evildoers!" (Matt. 7:22–23)

Here Jesus describes people who at the end of time will identify themselves as *his* followers, but he makes it clear they weren't following him. They might have been singing praises with the praise band to "Jesus," but their version of Jesus was not him.

Like Israel of old, who worshiped *ba'al*, God has foretold that his followers on earth will face a similar crisis before he returns. So, if it wasn't the word *Baal* that made their worship wrong, what was wrong with Baal worship?

Ancient, nonbiblical sources give varying degrees of information regarding Baal and the pagan pantheon, but there are some key elements common among them.

Baal was the son of El (i.e., *El*-ohim or *El*-Shaddai). He was the god of weather, often called "Almighty" and "Lord of the Earth." Baal was the god who brought rain, thunder, and lightning, who fertilized the earth, controlled the sun, and brought the harvest. Baal fought the great serpent leviathan as well as battled against Mot, the god of death. And most amazing of all, it was taught that Baal died in his battle with Mot and was resurrected from the dead to bring life to earth.[9]

So what was the problem with worshiping a god who was the "husband and protector of Israel," the son of El, who controlled the weather, who brought rain, sunshine, and blessed with full harvest, who warred against the great serpent and death, who died and was resurrected to bring life to the earth? What was wrong with this god? What was Elijah opposing? What made Baal worship false?

Baal was an authoritarian god who required appeasement! Worshipers had to do something to or for their god in order to get blessings from Baal. As Scripture says: "So the prophets prayed louder and cut themselves with knives and daggers, *according to their ritual*, until blood flowed" (1 Kings 18:28 GNT).[10]

According to *Tyndale Bible Dictionary*, worshipers had to engage in a multiplicity of behaviors, including human sacrifice, in order to induce Baal to provide the blessings they desired. This was powerfully demonstrated in Elijah's confrontation with the four hundred fifty prophets of Baal, who prayed, danced, and cut themselves trying to meet the demands of their false god.[11]

Baal has persisted through history, becoming Zeus to the Greeks, Jupiter to the Romans, Thor to the Norse people, and Jesus Christ to Christians who worship an angry god who imposes rules, inflicts punishment for disobedience, and requires the blood of a human sacrifice in order to propitiate his wrath.[12] Thus, God, looking through the corridors of time, foretold that Elijah would be needed again to call his people back to worship our Creator God, who is not like Baal!

Are we worshiping the true God as revealed in Jesus—a being of infinite love and tenderness? A being who "so loved the world that he sent his only Son" to save us? Or do we worship Baal, an imperial dictator god who requires human sacrifice in order not to punish? Do we fail to mature, to grow up, because we, like ancient Israel, have been duped into worshiping a god infected with imposed-law concepts? Has our ability to become a faithful bride to our heavenly groom been impaired by teachings that incite fear? Have we as Christians taken the gospel of the kingdom of love to the world, or have we instead spread the infection of a Baal-like dictator god who imposes rules and punishes rule breakers?

When we worship a god of absolute power, who we believe functions like Caesar with imposed laws that require infliction of punishment, we become like that god and ultimately end up abusing the ones we say we love. But when we worship the one true God, who most certainly has absolute power but is like Jesus in character—who when he received all power used it to serve, to wash dirty feet, to heal, to bless, and not to be served—then we become like him and love our families more than ourselves.

It is time for the truth about God to go forth in the world! It is time for the people of planet Earth to prepare to meet Christ! It is time to throw off the false Baal-god concept and embrace the truth that Jesus revealed!

To the people of God in all walks of life, I invite you to throw off the imposed-law construct, embrace God's design law of love, and rise up and promote the truth about God just as Elijah did. Elijah's challenge—"If the LORD is God, follow him; but if Baal is God, follow him" (1 Kings 18:21)—rings out today.

If God is like Jesus revealed him to be, then serve him, but if God is a dictator god, a being who like Baal must be propitiated, then serve him. The question is, who will *you* serve?[13]

KEY POINTS FROM CHAPTER 7

- The law of worship is a design law—we become in character like the god we worship.
- Worship a God of love, and we become more loving; worship a dictator god, and we become more abusive.
- There isn't anything much more dangerous in the world than someone on a mission for God who doesn't actually know God.
- God is not like Baal—a god who requires sacrifice to appease him. We must reject the dictator, punishing views of God and return to worship the God of love—the God Jesus revealed.

8

Love and the Institution

A legalist is not someone who places divine law above all else. A legalist is someone who places human law above all else.

Rob Rienow, *Limited Church: Unlimited Kingdom: Uniting Church and Family in the Great Commission*

As sad as Sandi's story is (see the previous chapter), it gives us insight into why there is so much division within Christianity. Why did the conference officials act as they did? Because they were operating on imposed law—rules enacted requiring enforcement. They failed to see the true sin-sickness in the heart of Sandi's husband. This happens for a variety of reasons. First, persons who operate at level four—law and order—are concerned about rules, right definitions of doctrines, enforcement of policy, order in the church, and conformity to authority, and they gravitate toward administrative leadership positions in organized systems. As a result, many institutional churches have their leadership positions heavily weighted with people operating at level four. Second, human organizations operate on imposed law and the survival-of-the-fittest principle of the world—just like pagan Rome; they do not operate on design law. As such, the leadership of organizations all too frequently is motivated by fear rather than love—fear of damage to the organization rather than love for lost souls.

The conference officials were afraid of setting a precedent of employing individuals who divorced their spouses without sexual adultery. They made a decision to protect the institution at the expense of one of God's children. This is not new. Two thousand years ago the leaders of God's organized church on earth did the same thing: "You do not realize that it is better for you that one man die for the people than that the whole nation perish" (John 11:50). Better to kill an innocent than allow damage to the institution.

And throughout church history, *every* denominational church institution has sacrificed souls to protect their system. Organizational cover-up of child molestation in order to protect the institution has been well documented in the media, but at what cost? The exploitation and injury of more innocents; members disfellowshiped in order to maintain standards; organizations fractured and split over various interpretations of Scripture. Why? Because they are stuck at level four and below, thinking that proper definitions matter, rather than focusing on reality—the restoration of God-shaped hearts in people!

Christ confronted this problem repeatedly and taught that what really matters is a change of heart. In the parable of the good Samaritan, who is recognized as being right with God? It is not the priest nor the Levite, those who had the *right* doctrinal definitions, who participated in the *right* religious rituals, who attended the *right* worship programs, and who worshiped on the *right* day. No! It was the Samaritan, who as far as we know never sacrificed at the Temple or kept the Sabbath or ate a kosher diet. What did the Samaritan have right? He had love in his heart—he had a God-shaped heart!

The Samaritan gave of his time, energy, and resources to help another, with no expectation of return. This is love! This is God's goal. This is what Jesus taught: "As I have loved you, so you must love one another. By this everyone will know that you are my disciples, if you love one another" (John 13:34–35). We are truly followers of Christ only if we have hearts that love. Nothing else will suffice—no ritual, no doctrinal definition, no legal adjustment. Love is the lifeblood of God's universe, and only those who have such love are genuine members of God's family. This is why the Bible says, "Whoever claims to love God yet hates a brother or sister is a liar. For whoever does not love their brother and sister, whom they have seen, cannot love God, whom they have not seen" (1 John 4:20).

When the woman at the well asked Christ who was worshiping in the right place, her people or the Jews, Christ told her: "The true worshipers will worship the Father in the Spirit and in truth, for they are the kind of worshipers the Father seeks" (John 4:23). Those who have God-shaped hearts, who have been renewed in their inner being, are the true worshipers of God.

The church is supposed to be like a loving family, whose healthier members seek to help those who are sick: "Brothers and sisters, if someone is caught in a sin, *you who live by the Spirit should restore that person gently*. But watch yourselves, or you also may be tempted. *Carry each other's burdens, and in this way you will fulfill the law of Christ*" (Gal. 6:1–2).

What law is being fulfilled? The law of love—the principle of giving—the law of life in God's universe. This can only happen when we reject the imposed-law construct and come back to worshiping God as Creator and designer, and when we understand his laws are the protocols of life itself!

All too often churches get trapped into organizational survival and run their system like human governments with codified rules of behavior. We must remember that in God's plan of salvation, institutions are not saved—people are! When we forget this and focus on saving institutions, we lose members. Instead of focusing on healing hearts, loving others, and reaching the lost, the imposed-law infection of thought indoctrinates members into a system of behavioral conformity more concerned with belonging to the *right* institution, maintaining its authority, and ensuring rule enforcement than healing God's children.

Oswald Chambers recognized this problem:

> Reconciliation means the restoring of the relationship between the entire human race and God, putting it back to what God designed it to be. This is what Jesus Christ did in redemption. The church ceases to be spiritual when it becomes self-seeking, only interested in the development of its own organization. The reconciliation of the human race according to His plan means realizing Him not only in our lives individually, but also in our lives collectively. Jesus Christ sent apostles and teachers for this very purpose—that the corporate Person of Christ and His church, made up of many members, might be brought into being and made known. We are not here to develop a spiritual life of our own, or to enjoy a quiet spiritual retreat. We are here to have the full realization of Jesus Christ, for the purpose of building His body.[1]

We can only fulfill God's purpose of living in love and being conduits of God's love to help heal others by returning to design law. When we do so, then we see reality in harmony with God's view—that all the misdeeds, the sins, and the bad acts we at times commit are merely symptoms of hearts that are out of harmony with God's design (Matt. 5:21–22, 27–28). Sinners are understood to be like children who, sick with cholera, have fever, vomiting, and diarrhea; the sickness ravaging them causes a terrible mess. The symptoms are ugly, smelly, and revolting, something we dislike and don't want to get close to. Yet, sick children are treated compassionately as persons in need of healing, not judgmentally as people in need of punishment or expulsion from our fellowship.

What would happen if you offered a remedy to a person with cholera and they refused to take it? They would get worse; they would suffer more and eventually die from their unhealed condition. Inflicted punishment is not needed. But when we fail to mature past level four thinking, instead of seeing sins as symptoms of sick hearts in need of healing, we too often view sins as bad deeds requiring infliction of punishment. Rather than seeking to heal the sin-sick person, we too quickly sacrifice the person to protect the institution.

Linda—Love or Leave

In 2013 the story of Kat Cooper and her mother made national news. Kat, a police officer in Collegedale, Tennessee, sought partner benefits for her female life partner. During the hearing with the city commission, Kat's mother, Linda, sat next to her daughter. Linda did not give testimony or speak at the hearing;

she merely sat by her daughter's side giving maternal love and support to her daughter.

In the aftermath of the hearing, Linda, along with two other family members who also attended the hearing, were called to appear before their church one Sunday morning. The church leadership gave Linda and her two other family members an ultimatum, according to the local newspaper: "They could repent for their sins and ask forgiveness in front of the congregation. Or leave the church."

According to reports, the church officials said the sin that warranted such drastic action was Linda sitting in support of her daughter while her daughter sought partner benefits. In the minds of those church leaders, homosexuality is a sin, and a heterosexual mother, who spoke no words in support of homosexuality but sat in loving support of her child, must be punished.

Ken Willis, a minister at the church, told local reporters, "The sin would be endorsing that lifestyle. . . . The Bible speaks very plainly about that."[2]

What the Bible speaks plainly about is love! God is love and we are to love others as he loves us. When Jesus was confronted with a woman caught in the very act of sexual sin, how did he treat her? With love, grace, compassion, and forgiveness; he sought to heal her not punish her. But we can act in love only if we mature past the penal-law system of thinking. We must have hearts that love people more than institutions. If you think your church organization is immune to focusing on institutional protection, consider which of the following people would be permitted to serve on your church's leadership team:

- A confessed murderer who has lived the past several decades on the run, hiding from authorities? Remember Moses?

- A man who cheats his own brother and lies to his own father? Remember Jacob?
- A man who visits prostitutes? Remember Judah?
- A man who sets up shrines to pagan gods and even participates in human sacrifice, murdering one of his own sons? Remember Solomon?
- Someone who publicly denounces Jesus Christ with cursing and swearing? Remember Peter?

When we operate under the imposed-law construct rather than seeing sickness in need of healing, we see crimes in need of punishing; rather than seeking to save people, we obstruct God's healing plan. But when we understand that sinfulness is a condition of a heart that is in need of healing and sins are symptoms of that condition, then we realize that all humanity is infected and all suffer with symptoms, "for all have sinned and fall short of the glory of God" (Rom. 3:23). The question is not who sinned or who has suffered with symptoms; the question is, who is partaking of the remedy?

God does not look on the outward behavior, the symptoms merely. God looks upon the heart—who is partaking of the remedy, who is willing to open their hearts to him for healing and restoration (1 Sam. 16:7). This is all that matters—who can be transformed by love to have a God-shaped heart. This is the amazing story of Scripture—that God takes people deformed in character, bruised and battered by the ravages of sin, and fully heals and restores all who trust in him! This is design law, not imposed law.

If the conference officials to whom Sandi's husband complained were operating at level seven, they would not only have retained Sandi in her employment but would also have lovingly confronted her husband on the sickness (selfishness) in his heart. They would have reached out in love to help him. They would have held him accountable and recommended that the local church remove him as deacon until such time that he received professional help and demonstrated the ability to love others more than himself. But they failed to recognize the selfishness pervading the man because they were focused on institutional protection. I have seen far too many hurting souls like Sandi and Linda, battered, bruised, and tossed aside by church leadership focused on protecting the institution. It is time we come back to Christ—come back to love—God's design for our being!

Division in Christianity

Human institutions always run on imposed law and coercive tactics. They are motivated by fear not love—fear of failure, fear of financial ruin, fear of lawsuits, fear of bad publicity— and take actions that sacrifice members for the institution's survival. This leads to evangelism practices that focus on indoctrinating members into loyalty to the institution rather than loyalty to Christ. Leaders are afraid to allow those who haven't first overcome "sin" in their lives to be members with voting rights in the institutional church for fear the church will be corrupted. But this is not how the apostolic church evangelized.

The New Testament church preached Christ and him crucified, and converts were baptized into Christ immediately upon conversion. Consider Philip and the eunuch, or the three thousand baptized when Peter preached. But the common practice in many institutional churches today is quite different. Today, when people accept Christ and their hearts are filled with his love, the joy of his grace, and the relief of guilt removed, rather than baptizing them immediately into a new life with Jesus, some institutional systems instruct converts to pray the sinner's prayer. Then they are placed into indoctrination classes in which they are required to learn certain mantras, swear certain allegiances, agree to certain creeds, and give up all behaviors that don't meet with that organization's standards. Only after they have cleaned up their lives enough to meet a certain level of behavioral conformity are they permitted to be baptized. All too often, by that time, their love for Jesus and the joy of salvation have been replaced by fear, guilt, cold formalism, and an oppressive burden of works—all based on the false law construct. Why? Because the institution must be protected from sinners corrupting its standards, but such organizations become unsafe zones for struggling people.

Consider Patience and Prudence, members of the same church. They grew up in the same community, attended the same parochial schools, both married Christian men, and both have sons near the same age. Patience's son is named Rob and Prudence's son is named Jude.

Jude from an early age is a good boy, obedient, on time, always dresses neatly, speaks politely, gets good grades in school, helps his teachers, and is noted for his sharp and quick mind. He is elected class president, serves on the debate team, helps with mission trips, and works closely with school and church leaders. Being so well spoken, he is often called upon to read Scripture in church. He is bright and well liked. Eventually, he graduates college and becomes a member of the world church leadership committee and is involved in forming church policy.

Rob, on the other hand, struggles from an early age. He is talkative in school, plays tricks on other students, skips classes, doesn't do his homework, and gets very poor grades. Occasionally he gets in arguments and fights. His mother prays and prays, talks with him, and disciplines him, but it doesn't seem to help. In adolescence, he begins drinking, drops out of school, hangs out with the wrong crowd, and is soon burglarizing homes and stealing as a profession. He is eventually caught and, as a repeat offender, is imprisoned for his crimes.

Back at church, Patience frequently runs into Prudence, who never fails to mention how wonderful her son is doing. She speaks of his latest accomplishments and smiles proudly as she recounts his value at headquarters. Then, with contrived concern, Prudence looks Patience in the eye and asks about Rob's latest troubles and expresses how sad she is that Rob has caused her so much grief.

Which mother would you rather be? Which of these two children would you rather is yours?

Now, as Paul Harvey would famously say, for the rest of the story: Jude is better known as Judas, and Rob is better known not as "The Robber" but as "The Thief on the cross" who accepted Jesus as his Savior. Now which child would you prefer is yours? Which child turned out to be the truly successful one?

What is the point of this story? It is only and always about the heart, not the long list of symptoms (sins) with which we have struggled. Have we partaken of Jesus and been renewed? This is the question; this is the issue.

But children (newborn babes in Christ) are easily confused and divided because they operate at level four and below, focus on rules and get stuck on metaphor, and fail to see the reality of design law. They actually think the form of baptism, or dress, or diet, or day of worship is what matters. They fail to realize that it has always been, and always will be, about transformation of the heart! Paul had to deal with such immaturity threatening to fragment Christianity in his day:

> Brothers and sisters, I could not address you as people who live by the Spirit but as people who are still worldly—mere infants in Christ. I gave you milk, not solid food, for you were not yet ready for it. Indeed, you are still not ready. You are still worldly. For since there is jealousy and quarreling among you, are you not worldly? Are you not acting like mere humans? For when one says, "I follow Paul," and another, "I follow Apollos," are you not mere human beings? (1 Cor. 3:1–4)

Paul understood that all humanity suffers from the same sin-sick heart condition and is in need of the same remedy provided by Christ. This confusion persists. John Wesley had a dream that he died and came to the gate of heaven. There are various versions of his account, but it generally goes like this. He was anxious to know who had been admitted, so he questioned the keeper:

> "Are there any Presbyterians here?"
> "None," replied the keeper of the gate.
> Wesley was surprised. "Have you any Anglicans?" he asked.
> "No one!" was the reply.
> "Surely, there must be many Baptists in Heaven?"
> "No, none," replied the keeper.
> Wesley grew pale. He was afraid to ask his next question:
> "How many Methodists are there in heaven?"
> "Not one," answered the keeper quickly.
> Wesley's heart was filled with wonder. The angel at the gate then told Wesley that there were no earthly distinctions in

heaven. "All of us here in heaven are one in Christ. We are just an assembly who love the Lord."

Wesley was then taken downward, downward to the entrance of Hell. He met the keeper of the gate there.

"Have you any Presbyterians here?" asked Wesley.

"Oh, yes, many," answered the keeper.

Wesley stood still, "Have you any Anglicans?" he asked.

"Yes, yes, many," answered the keeper.

"Are there Baptists in there?" Wesley continued to ask.

"Of course, many," replied the keeper.

Wesley was afraid to ask the next question. "Are there any Methodists in Hell?"

The keeper of the gate grinned. "Oh yes, there are many Methodists here."

Wesley could hardly speak. "Tell me, have you any there who love the Lord?"

"No, no, not one, not one," he answered. "No one in Hell loves the Lord!"[3]

It is love that matters. Love is the key; love is the basis of life! God is love, and only those restored to love will be in heaven! Wesley was profoundly impacted by his dream, and it helped shape his theology. John Wesley later described what it was that set a Methodist apart from other religious people:

"What then is the mark? Who is a Methodist, according to your own account?" I answer: A Methodist is one who has "the love of God shed abroad in his heart by the Holy Ghost given unto him;" one who "loves the Lord his God with all his heart, and with all his soul, and with all his mind, and with all his strength." God is the joy of his heart, and the desire of his soul; which is constantly crying out, "Whom have I in heaven but thee? and there is none upon earth that I desire beside thee! My God and my all! Thou art the strength of my heart, and my portion for ever!" . . .

If any man say, "Why, these are only the common fundamental principles of Christianity!" thou hast said; so I mean; this is the very truth; I know they are no other; and I would to God both thou and all men knew, that I, and all who follow my judgment, do vehemently refuse to be distinguished from other men, by any but the common principles of Christianity,—the plain, old Christianity that I teach, renouncing and detesting all other marks of distinction. And whosoever is what I preach, (let him be called what he will, for names change not the nature of things,) he is a Christian, not in name only, but in heart and in life. He is inwardly and outwardly conformed to the will of God, as revealed in the written word. He thinks, speaks, and lives, according to the method laid down in the revelation of Jesus Christ. His soul is renewed after the image of God, in righteousness and in all true holiness. And having the mind that was in Christ, he so walks as Christ also walked.[4]

What matters is not proper definitions of doctrine or right enactment of ritual, but love—the proper treatment of others! When we understand God's law is love, and love is functional—is the protocol of life—then we can look past the imposed human-law concepts that divide and fragment and finally enter into the unity of love! As Jesus prayed, "I pray also for those who will believe in me through their message, that all of them may be one, Father, just as you are in me and I am in you" (John 17:20–21).

The solution is quite simple: we must reject the imposed-law construct—purge it from our books, catechisms, doctrines, creeds, and fundamental beliefs—and return to design law. We must return to worship our Creator God—he who made the heavens, earth, and sea and all that is in them. We must then realize that every human being is suffering with the same condition of heart and mind and in need of the same remedy provided by Jesus Christ. Only with Jesus is victory over sin in our lives possible. Only by partaking of Christ can a person be renewed in love. We must realize the problem with sin is not a legal problem but an actual condition of being out of harmony with God and his design for life!

Church leadership needs to refocus away from protecting institutional holdings and toward administering God's love and grace into the hearts of people. For those who cannot get past their fear of what will happen to the organization if we baptize people who haven't yet overcome their addictions, left their unmarried living situation, changed their diet, or quit the job that keeps them from weekly worship services, I would suggest we simply decouple baptism into Jesus Christ from joining a denominational institution. When a person accepts Jesus Christ, baptize them into the body of Christ at the earliest possible moment, like the eunuch who said to Philip the day he gave his heart to Jesus, "Look, here is water. What can stand in the way of my being baptized?" (Acts 8:36). And then, after rebirth in Christ, ask the new convert which organizational church group they would like to affiliate with. They can join an organization with which they fit best—based upon where the Holy Spirit leads them.

All of this being said, we must also acknowledge that, in their right place, organizations are useful and serve important functions. They are helpful for:

- Pooling of resources to accomplish shared mission (church schools, hospitals, orphanages, funding missionaries, publishing houses, etc.)
- Operating facilities for local community to flourish (worship centers, Christian concerts, weddings, social events, picnics, funerals, holiday celebrations, etc.)
- Providing resources to the community (counseling for the hurting, food for the hungry, clothing for the poor, housing for the homeless)
- Facilitating cultural expressions of love and worship

Perhaps most importantly, organized churches are the place where the mature help the immature grow in godliness. Just as babies born into the world are to have loving homes in which they are raised, so too the church is to be the loving home for newborn converts to Christ to grow, develop, and thrive. But organizations are not saved—people are saved. And as Oswald Chambers said, when church organizations become self-promoting, they fail to fulfill their purpose.

We cannot experience unity, at-one-ment, with God and each other as long as we stand on the ever-shifting sands of imposed law. We will never be united under one head, Jesus Christ, as long as we cling to human-law constructs. The infection of imposed law has resulted in the terrible fracturing of Christianity into tens of thousands of different groups arguing among themselves as to who holds the right doctrines or understanding of Scripture.[5] Accepting the lie that God's law is merely imposed rules opened the door for people to think that different interpretations of his law are actually possible.

When we come back to design law, differences evaporate and unity results.

Design Law and the New Testament Church

The New Testament church understood the distinction between imposed law and design law. When the immature were struggling with whether to require gentile converts to adhere to the imposed rules of a symbolic system, the church leaders said, "Instead we should write to them, telling them to abstain from food polluted by idols, from sexual immorality, from the meat of strangled animals and from blood" (Acts 15:20). These instructions are not imposed rules but are the wisdom of design law.

Food polluted by idols:

- An idol cannot change the nutritional quality of the food. Therefore, eating foods offered to idols does not pollute the body. Paul makes this clear in Romans 14.
- The issue they were addressing is the design law of worship—by beholding we become changed. As we discussed in chapter 7, this is called modeling. What we believe has power over us: truth heals and sets free, lies damage and enslave. Don't allow your minds to become contaminated by giving any credence to idols. Thus, don't eat food polluted by the *idea* that it is a bounty given you by a false god.

Sexual immorality:

- God designed relationships to operate on love and trust. When sexual intimacy occurs between husband and wife, as God designed, healthy bonding occurs. The brain actually rewires, and reward circuits are heightened for one's spouse. This is design law—how our biology is actually built to work. Deviating from this design is damaging to the mind, body, and relationships.

- It is a violation of design law, altering brain circuitry, inflaming selfish and fear circuits, thus obstructing healing of mind and character.

Meat from strangled animals or blood:

- It also violates design law—the laws of health.
- Humans are not designed to eat meat, and the blood carries waste products, stress hormones, and various inflammatory factors. Eating raw meat and drinking blood increases disease risk, and when the body is unhealthy the mind is compromised.

The New Testament church rejected the imposed-law rules and focused instead on living in harmony with God's design law for life. When we have accepted the lie that God's law is simply a list of rules, we believe they are subject to change with time and place. Good Christian people fall into the trap of arguing back and forth over trivial points, oblivious to the fact they are all worshiping the same dictator god. We then teach our children ideas of God that drive a wedge between them and God.

What would Christianity look like if the various denominations came together and pooled their resources for one single purpose—to spread the healing love of Christ into the hearts of people on earth—and stopped working to build their institutions by membership drives, often at the expense of other Christian organizations? This division and fracturing of Christianity into tens of thousands of various sects is the predictable and unavoidable result of replacing God's design law with human imposed law. I invite you to reject the imposed law and embrace God our designer and Creator and his design protocols of love!

KEY POINTS FROM CHAPTER 8

- Correct doctrinal definitions are meaningless without the restoration of God-shaped hearts in people.
- We are truly followers of Christ only if we have hearts that love—nothing else will suffice, no ritual, no doctrinal definition, no legal adjustment. Love is the lifeblood of God's universe, and only those who have such love are genuine members of God's family.
- Only those who have God-shaped hearts, who have been renewed in their inner beings, are true worshipers of God.
- When we operate under the imposed-law construct, rather than seeing sickness in need of healing we see crimes in need of punishing, and rather than seeking to save people we obstruct God's healing plan.
- God does not look on the outward behavior, the symptoms merely. God looks on the heart—who is partaking of the remedy, who is willing to open their hearts to him for healing and restoration.
- When we understand God's law is love, and love is functional—is the protocol of life—then we can look past the imposed human-law concepts that divide and fragment and finally enter into the unity of love.

- The problem with sin is not a legal one but an actual condition of being out of harmony with God and his design for life.
- We cannot experience unity, at-one-ment, with God and each other as long as we stand on the ever-shifting sands of imposed law.
- We must reject the imposed-law construct—purge it from our books, catechisms, doctrines, creeds, and fundamental beliefs and return to design law. We must return to worship of our Creator God—he who made the heavens, earth, and sea and all that is in them.

9

Rituals, Metaphors, and Symbols

The single biggest problem in communication is the illusion that it has taken place.

William H. Whyte

As a child, I attended a church that had great programs for children. In the children's division was a cool table about four inches deep with a removable wooden top. Beneath the top were several inches of beautiful white beach sand. We children loved to go to the sandbox, get out the Bible toys, build Bible scenes, and stage Bible events. It was a great way to help children learn. But the sandbox was not reality; it was only a teaching tool filled with symbols and toy representations of a larger reality.

Children need toys, dolls, and sandboxes to help them learn. God has used many "sandboxes" throughout history. But some people have gotten stuck in the sand, stuck in the illustration and lost in the metaphor and fail to understand the reality behind them.

The symbol TREE is not a tree. It is a symbolic representation of a tree. It would be quite a serious problem if people confused the symbol TREE for the real thing and began planting giant letters in their yard hoping to obtain fruit. You may laugh at this simple illustration, but letters are not the only symbols of reality. Ancient cultures used hieroglyphics or pictograms to symbolically represent a larger reality. Scripture is filled with such imagery, but many have made the mistake of clinging to the symbol and failing to embrace the reality to which the symbol, metaphor, illustration, or parable points.

For metaphor, simile, parable, or illustration to have any meaning, there must be a cosmic reality to which it points. *If there is no reality behind the example, then it is no longer metaphor or parable—it is fantasy.*

Several years ago I had the opportunity to discuss my views on salvation with a group of theologians who were ardent proponents of legal/penal atonement. After several cordial meetings and polite discussions, the group circulated a paper that alleged their view was richer, deeper, and more biblically holistic than the view I put forth. They acknowledged that the healing perspective I presented is taught in Scripture, but they argued it is only one metaphor among many and that by focusing on it I deny the rich beauty of all the other metaphors of Scripture, such as legal, ransom, lost and found, and others.

These well-meaning people have denied reality. They have suggested that healing, restoration to actual righteousness, recreation into true godliness, is not real—it is only metaphor. Such arguments obstruct maturing, obstruct healing, obstruct God's plan, and keep good people trapped in symbolism rather than growing up to embrace reality. Eternal healing and restoration to God's original design for humankind in Eden is not metaphor—it is real!

The writer of Hebrews tells the believers it is childish to constantly be thinking of rituals, which are only symbols of a larger reality, that have no power to heal. He challenges them to leave symbols behind and grow up to mature, reality-based understanding. And how do they mature? "But solid food is for the mature, who by constant use have trained themselves to distinguish good from evil" (Heb. 5:14). It is by practice! A concert musician trains by practice. A person will never become a master violinist by listening to the stereo twelve hours per day—they must practice! Likewise, a person will never become a master thinker by listening to others; at some point each person, if they want to mature, must practice thinking for themselves. Let's review a few of these Bible rituals, symbols, and metaphors, seeking to understand the reality to which they point.

Communion

Moral developmental level one through four thinkers are vulnerable to almost superstitious beliefs about communion, that there is some magic, some supernatural process, or cleansing in the ritual itself. As if the wine and bread were of some other substance than any other wine and bread.

History confirms that the doctrine of transubstantiation—the idea that the elements of Communion (Catholic Eucharist) transform into the literal flesh and blood of Jesus—came about because of the inability to see the reality behind the metaphor. For over eight hundred years, no one in Christianity, from peasant to pope, ever taught the doctrine of transubstantia-tion. But in 831 Frankish abbot Paschasius Radbertus released a paper titled *De corpore et sanguine Christi* (Concerning Christ's body and blood). According to former Secretary of Education and historian William Bennett, "Radbertus concluded that since God is truth and cannot lie, Jesus' declaration that the elements of the bread and wine used in communion were his body and blood must be taken literally. For Radbertus, the consecration of the elements mystically transformed the bread and wine into the physical body and blood of Jesus Christ."[1] Radbertus was unable to see past metaphor. He had forgotten that Jesus often used illustrations, parables, and metaphors that were not to be taken literally but pointed to a larger reality. Yet billions of people remain stuck, believing an idea that has its origin in the concrete thinking of a ninth-century abbot.

Level five through seven thinkers realize that when Christ told his disciples to "do this in remembrance of me," he was not merely setting up a ritual but also saying that every time you meet together and share a meal, remember me. Just as food and drink nurture your body, it is by partaking of me, by internalizing me into your hearts and minds, that your souls are nurtured. And just as your body needs to be fed every day, so too your soul needs to feed on the truth and love found only in me—every day! Thus Jesus said, "Unless you eat the flesh of the Son of Man and drink his blood, you have no life in you" (John 6:53). He was not talking about cannibalism but the internalization and assimilation of his character, methods, and principles into the heart and mind as a new way of living.

Because children don't abstract well, they struggle to see past metaphors, parables, and symbols. A person thinking concretely might hear me clear my throat and say "Excuse me, I had a frog in my throat" and wrongly conclude I was eating amphibians.

The mind searches for meaning, and if the true meaning is not understood, then false meanings, fantasies, and superstitions arise. Have you heard the magician's phrase, *hocus-pocus*? Some believe this phrase originated in the Roman Catholic Latin Mass during the Dark Ages: when the Eucharist was presented, the priest would incant the words, *hoc est corpus meum* (this is my body).[2] The worshipers, who by and large did not speak Latin, began to think something magical was happening when the words were spoken. Anglican prelate John Tillotson wrote in 1694: "In all probability those common juggling words of *hocus pocus* are nothing else but a corruption of *hoc est corpus*, by way of ridiculous imitation of the priests of the Church of Rome in their trick of Transubstantiation."[3]

Such spiritual immaturity does not mean uneducated. The best-educated minds in Christ's day, the church leaders, the supreme court rulers, were spiritually immature and thought concretely. They failed to see the reality behind the metaphor of Christ's use of blood and flesh. They thought Christ was talking about food for the body and was teaching some form of cannibalism, and it offended them. Likewise, today, many do the same thing when they substitute one metaphor, flesh and blood, for another, bread and wine, but still fail to see reality.

John 1:1 says Jesus is the "Word," and when Jesus instructs us to ingest his flesh he is telling us we must ingest into our minds his Word—the truth about him, his way of thinking, and his design for life. This becomes to us the meat, the substance, the building blocks of our thoughts, ideas, and beliefs, which form our attitudes and shape our characters. When he speaks of drinking his blood, he is speaking of partaking of his life, his perfect character of love, such that we die to self and live to love God and others more than self. It is an actual, real-life transformation of the inner workings of our hearts and minds, where selfishness is replaced by love. We must be partakers of the divine nature and possess the mind of Christ (2 Pet. 1:4; 1 Cor. 2:16).

The wine and bread have no power; they are only symbols to stimulate our minds to think and then choose to partake of what is real. Devour the Word of God. Study Scripture, think about it, ask for the enlightenment of the Holy Spirit, and choose to comprehend it, believe it, and apply it to your life so as to be transformed by the renewing of your mind (Rom. 12:2). Open your heart to God and receive the renewing presence of the Holy Spirit—who takes the life (blood) of Christ and reproduces it in us (Gal. 2:20). Choose to give, to help, and to love others! This is ingesting the body and blood of Jesus.

But this requires we actually engage with God, turn on our brains, and enter into a daily trust relationship with him. For many it is much easier to do our own thing, go our own way, and rest secure in thoughtless rituals to fulfill some legal requirement. But such childlike thinking is unacquainted with righteousness.

Baptism

Have you ever seen good Christian people arguing over which method of baptism is right? Some even allege that if the ritual isn't carried out in the proper way or at the right place, you can't be saved.

Such arguments reveal a failure to see past metaphor to reality. Baptism by water is a symbol, an acted-out drama, a metaphor, and a way of demonstrating by behavior what is real. Water baptism has no power to save and heal and is not required for salvation. (Consider the thief on the cross who, after accepting Christ, died without water baptism yet was promised life in paradise, or all the saved from Adam to the time of John the Baptist who were never baptized in water.)

The Greek word *baptizmo* means to immerse. Water is a cleansing agent, a purifying substance, with which every human being who has ever taken a bath is familiar. Immersion in water symbolically represents the immersion of the heart/mind/character into God via the Holy Spirit. It is a complete and total surrender of the self into a trust relationship with God, in which self is submerged under the cleansing waves of love and truth emanating from God. In this submersion the mind and heart (character) die to selfishness and fear and are renewed with new motives, desires, insights, and perspectives, longing for more and more intimacy and growth in godliness each day.

This baptism—the immersion of the heart into God—is required for salvation because it is the application of Christ and all he achieved into the believer in Christ. This is rebirth, to which the water ritual only points or symbolically represents. (It's a powerful reminder of the beginning of a new life, as just prior to the birth of all babies a woman's water breaks.)

"Children," however, those at level one through four moral development, will focus on the ritual, living in fear of not having done it properly; or believing that having had the ritual they are legally secure, but never really considering what is going on in the heart. Thus, the person undergoing baptism, without experiencing the reality to which the ritual points—the immersion of the heart into God via the Holy Spirit—is unacquainted with righteousness, just as Hebrews teaches.

Jelly Beans—Red or Blue?

When symbolism is clung to in minds that remain infected with imposed-law constructs, not only is healing impaired but also division and fragmentation are incited. Imagine that during the Dark Ages, when the Black Death was ravaging millions, we had a cure (e.g., penicillin, an antibiotic that cures bacterial infections) and wanted to teach people how to identify symptoms of the disease so they could take the medicine if the symptoms appeared. But because the masses could not read, the use of books, magazines, or flyers would do no good. Therefore, we devise a play, a little drama to act out what to do in case the sickness arises.

We have actors come on stage with red circles drawn on their skin; they act feverous and weak. Another actor playing the role of healer, perhaps in a white robe, sees the symptoms and pulls out a red jelly bean (symbolic of penicillin in its red capsule) and gives it to the sick ones. Then the red marks are washed off, and those who were formerly sick jump up and dance with joy. A simple play to illustrate a simple lesson: if you get these symptoms, take the remedy and you will get well.

As the years go by and the play is enacted from town to town, one group runs out of red jelly beans, so instead they use blue ones. But this is met with stern opposition from members of the original acting troupe who have always used red jelly beans. They insist that only red jelly beans are to be used because the penicillin capsules are red and red more closely represents the reality. Soon the two groups split and form separate acting companies, each claiming that only their play rightly teaches how to be saved from the plague. Does it really matter if the jelly bean is red or blue so long as the people take the actual antibiotic when the disease occurs? Or worse, what if people forgot reality and believed that there was some potency or power in the ritual, so they religiously—prayerfully—ingested jelly beans but failed to ever take the antibiotic? They would have a form of godliness but no power. This is exactly the state of Christianity today—stuck in forms of religion but devoid of the actual healing power of God!

One can easily imagine how the water ritual of baptism shifted from immersion, as some converts found themselves imprisoned and unable to be immersed. Having only a cup of water available they asked to be sprinkled to participate in the ritual as far as possible.[4] However, individuals stuck on the symbol and who have forgotten the reality to which it points have argued back and forth through the centuries over which symbolic form of baptism is right. Does it really matter whether a person is immersed or sprinkled, so long as their heart, mind, and character are immersed into the reality of Jesus Christ and they are reborn with character like Jesus? We must grow up past the symbols and enter into the reality to which the symbols point.

While we have already documented that people can experience baptism of heart and mind without going through the water ritual (thief on the cross), a more profound question is, Can people have a godlike heart (be baptized in heart by the Holy Spirit) if they have never had the gospel presented to them, if they have never read Scripture, if they have not heard about Jesus Christ?

Level four and below thinking focuses on rules and would argue no, a person must hear about Jesus and accept his legal payment on their behalf in order to be legally pardoned and thereby saved. But level five and above thinkers understand that cognitive knowledge is not necessary to be healed. A person doesn't have to understand how penicillin works to benefit from taking it. A person can even call penicillin "magic potion number one," but that doesn't change the objective quality of the antibiotic. And taking the antibiotic results in the same effects regardless of whether one knows how it works or not. What one *must* do if one wants to benefit from penicillin is take it.

But if penicillin was never developed, if it didn't exist, then no one could partake of it and no one could be healed by it.

The Bible is clear:

- Salvation is found in no one else, for there is no other name under heaven given to mankind by which we must be saved (Acts 4:12).
- Jesus answered, "I am the way and the truth and the life. No one comes to the Father except through me" (John 14:6).

Level four and below thinkers, those operating on imposed-law constructs, read these powerful verses and conclude that a person must hold to a certain confession, say a certain mantra, recite a particular prayer, or verbalize a specific word (name), and if one doesn't do so, then one cannot be saved.

But the mature understand God's design and how reality works. They realize that Jesus is the one through whom God worked out his purpose to heal and fix what Adam's sin did to humanity. Jesus partook of humanity terminal in sin and, in his human self, destroyed the sin-infection and cured the condition. Thus Scripture says of Jesus, "*Once made perfect*, he became the source of eternal salvation for all who obey him" (Heb. 5:9).

What does this mean, *once made perfect*? Wasn't Jesus always perfect? Jesus was always sinless, but Bible perfection means maturity. Once Jesus, as a human, developed a perfect, mature, righteous human character, destroying the infection of sin that causes death (2 Tim. 1:9–10), he then became the source of salvation—the remedy to sin.

Thus, Jesus is the only remedy to sin, and only those who partake of him will be healed, renewed, and transformed to be like him in character. They will have the heart of stone removed and a heart of flesh put in, circumcision of the heart by the Holy Spirit, the law of love written on their hearts and minds, and the mind of Christ. All of this is possible only because of what Jesus Christ achieved.

But, just as in taking penicillin, one doesn't have to have cognitive knowledge or perform certain rituals to benefit from taking the remedy for sin. What is necessary for salvation is to partake of Jesus—*whether one verbally uses the syllables* JE-SUS or not.

This gives us insight into what Jesus means when he says,

> And so I tell you, every kind of sin and slander can be forgiven, but blasphemy against the Spirit will not be forgiven. Anyone who speaks a word against the Son of Man will be forgiven, but anyone who speaks against the Holy Spirit will not be forgiven, either in this age or in the age to come. (Matt. 12:31–32)

If a person rejects a lifesaving brand-name medicine because someone told them that the medicine is poison and will kill them, even though it is exactly what they need, but they accept that very medicine in its generic form, what will happen? They will get well!

If a person rejects Jesus (brand name) because they have been told lies about Jesus or have such strong cultural biases they cannot see Jesus in his true light, but they accept the Spirit of truth and love (generic version—remember Jesus is the way and the truth and the life, the Word made flesh), valuing the principles of truth, love, and freedom—what will happen in their heart? The Spirit will heal and restore them to unity with the God of love!

But if the person who is sick rejects the only doctor who possesses and is able to administer the medicine, then what happens? They will surely die. This is what happens to those who reject the Spirit.

If a person finds the Spirit of truth and love reprehensible—such that they think honesty, fidelity, and truthfulness are weak and despicable, and love for others is cheap sentiment, and they reject such principles and motives—yet claims belief in God and the blood payment of Jesus, what happens in them?

Blasphemy against the Holy Spirit is not merely saying that one doesn't believe in the Trinity or in the Holy Spirit; it is the functional rejection of the presence of the Holy Spirit who brings the perfection that Jesus wrought into our internal worlds (hearts and minds)—the perfection of truth, honesty, integrity, love, fidelity, and so on. Rejecting this and choosing evil is the true blasphemy of the Spirit, and there is no healing for this.

Some may ask: Why then do we take the gospel to the world and preach Christ if this is true?

Let me give an analogy. Penicillin is an antibiotic discovered from mold. It is true that sometimes ancient cultures would treat wounds with moss or other materials that contained mold, and the molds secreted penicillin, and such individuals either avoided infection or had infections resolved.

Because it is true that people can benefit from naturally oc-curring penicillin, does that mean we should not produce and distribute penicillin, and teach people about its benefits and how to apply it to those with infections? Just because people can find God's character revealed in nature and benefit from the working of the Holy Spirit in their hearts doesn't mean that restoring hearts to God's design of love isn't much more effective when the truth is presented in its full light. And this is the core issue—restoring hearts back to God's design for life, hearts that love.

As John Wesley understood, there are no denominations in heaven—when Christ returns only two groups will be found:

- The wheat and the tares
- The sheep and the goats
- The pure woman and the harlot
- The fruitful vine and the withered vine
- Those wearing the wedding garment and those who are not
- The righteous and the wicked
- The saved and the lost
- The healed and those who remain dead in trespasses and sin
- Those with God-shaped hearts and those with hearts like Satan

Aslan and Emeth

C. S. Lewis taught the same unifying truth in the last book of the Chronicles of Narnia series when he described a Calormene soldier named Emeth and his encounter with Aslan the lion. Emeth was a worshiper of Tash and as a result was terrified when he came face-to-face with Aslan. But Aslan's response?

Son thou art welcome. But I said, alas Lord I am no son of thine but the servant of Tash. He answered, Child all the service thou hast done to Tash I account as service done to me.

I questioned the Glorious One: Lord, is it then true that thou and Tash are one? The Lion growled and said, It is false. Not because he and I are one, but because we are opposites, I take to me the services which thou hast done to him. For I and he are of such different kinds that no service which is vile can be done to me, and none which is not vile can be done to him. Therefore if any man swear by Tash and keep his oath for the oath's sake, it is by me that he has truly sworn, though he know it not, and it is I who reward him. And if any man do a cruelty in my name, then, though he says the name Aslan, it is Tash whom he serves and by Tash his deed is accepted.

Emeth questions once more:

Lord, I have been seeking Tash all my days.

Beloved, said the Glorious One, unless thy desire had been for me thou shouldst not have sought so long and so truly. For all find what they truly seek.[5]

It is about a God-shaped heart, not ritual and not institutional affiliation. Thus, Paul writes to the Romans:

It is not those who hear the law [scripture] who are righteous in God's sight, but it is those who obey the law who will be declared righteous. (Indeed, when Gentiles, who do not have the law [scripture], do by nature things required by the law, they are a law for themselves, even though they do not have the law. *They show that the requirements of the law are written on their hearts*, their consciences also bearing witness, and their thoughts sometimes accusing them and at other times even defending them.) (Rom. 2:13–15)

What does the law require? Healing, transformation, to have selfishness removed and perfect godly love restored. Why? For the same reason that the law of respiration requires we breathe—it is how life is actually built by God to operate. Paul is saying that these gentiles have been healed and renewed, and the law is written on their hearts, which is the new covenant experience: "*This is the covenant* I will establish with the people of Israel after that time, declares the Lord. *I will put my laws in their minds and write them on their hearts*. I will be their God, and they will be my people" (Heb. 8:10).

The gentiles whom Paul is speaking about have never heard Scripture, have not yet known the name of Jesus, yet they have the law written on their hearts. How? Because God's divine nature has been understood from what he has made so that men are without excuse (Rom. 1:20). God is Creator. His laws are the design laws that all reality functions on. Thus nature reveals the law of love—the character of God revealed perfectly in Christ.

Nancy Pearcey, in her book *Finding Truth*, calls God's truth revealed in nature *common grace*:

> Common grace functions as a constant testimony to God's goodness. When Paul preached to a Gentile audience in an area that is now Turkey, he used an argument from common grace: God "did not leave himself without witness, for he did good by giving you rains from heaven and fruitful seasons, satisfying your hearts with food and gladness" (Acts 14:17). The regularity of the natural order allows humans to grow food, raise families, invent technology, and maintain some level of cultural and civic order. All human endeavors depend on God's common grace.[6]

When people who have never had God's Word presented to them see in nature the truth about God's character of love and respond to the movement of the Holy Spirit on their hearts by opening their hearts in trust to God, the Holy Spirit takes *what Christ achieved* (like spiritual penicillin) and applies it to their hearts, and they are healed, renewed, and transformed in love—but still only through the remedy achieved by Christ.

And just as you can tell who among a group of sick individuals has partaken of penicillin, because those who partake of the remedy get well, so too we can discern who among us has partaken of Jesus Christ—regardless of their current religious affiliation. How? "By this everyone will know that you are my disciples, if you love one another" (John 13:35).

Greater Love

Such love shocks the world. It is alien to the natural heart and is found only in God who through Jesus Christ pours his love into our hearts (Rom. 5:5). Any person who loves selflessly is able to do so *only* because of the love of Jesus Christ being reproduced in them. Such love was seen on January 13, 1982.

It was cold. The Potomac River was covered in solid ice when Air Florida Flight 90 crashed into its frigid depths just outside Washington, DC. Horrified, onlookers watched as the twisted wreckage slowly sank below the water, doubtful that anyone could survive. But one by one, six people crawled out of the wreckage into the freezing waters. They initially clung to the tail of the plane, crying in the agony of broken bones and freezing limbs for someone to rescue them.

So close, just forty yards to the riverbank, but chunks of floating ice surrounded them and cut them off from shore. People tried to help. Ladders were laid over the ice, but they could not cover the distance; rags, belts, and clothes were tied together and dangled from the 14th Street Bridge, but the desperate survivors were out of reach.

Twenty minutes after the crash, as the sun was going down and hope seemed lost, suddenly out of nowhere a rescue helicopter appeared. A life ring was dropped right into the hands of one of the survivors and he was pulled from the water. And then something amazing happened—love burst forth. The ring was dropped to the next person, but rather than seek the safety of the helicopter he passed the ring to the person next to him. The chopper lifted her to safety, then wheeled back and dropped the ring to the man again—and again he gave the ring to another, and then to another, and he did so even when he was getting so weak that he must have known he would not survive, because when the chopper roared back he was gone. The man had vanished below the ice.

Arland Williams, a forty-six-year-old federal bank examiner, thought of others before himself.[7] This is not natural. This is not the way of survival-of-the-fittest, but such love is the way of Christ. "This is how we know what love is: Jesus Christ laid down his life for us. And we ought to lay down our lives for our brothers and sisters" (1 John 3:16). Such love is only possible through the achievements of Jesus Christ being applied to the heart, mind, and character of people.

On April 16, 2007, love again revealed itself. For Jewish professor Liviu Librescu, the day started out like so many others, off to classes at Virginia Polytech Institute with lectures to present and questions to answer. But at 9:45 that fateful morning everything changed. Seung-Hui Cho, a South Korean–born undergraduate student, entered the building in which the professor taught and continued his shooting rampage that killed thirty-two and wounded seventeen others. As the gunman approached

Professor Librescu's class, the professor ran to the door and held it shut while Cho attempted to enter. In spite of being shot through the door, the professor managed to keep the door closed long enough for all but one of his twenty-three students to escape. Professor Librescu was shot five times, dying when a bullet struck him in the head.[8] Such love is not natural—it is supernatural. It is the love of God, perfectly manifested in Jesus Christ, being reproduced in the sinner.

Jon Blunk, Matt McQuinn, and Alex Teves demonstrated Christlike love by shielding their girlfriends from gunfire. On July 20, 2012, the three young men had taken their girlfriends for a late-night screening of *The Dark Knight Rises* at the Century 16 movie theater in Aurora, Colorado. When a gunman dressed in tactical clothing entered the theater and began shooting, Blunk, McQuinn, and Teves covered their girlfriends with their bodies, protecting them at the cost of their own lives.

Blunk's girlfriend, Jansen Young, McQuinn's girlfriend, Samantha Yowler, and Teves's girlfriend, Amanda Lindgren, all made it out of the bloodbath with only minor injuries thanks to the selfless actions of their boyfriends.

Reporting on Jon Blunk, the *New York Daily News* wrote:

> "He's a hero, and he'll never be forgotten," a tearful Jansen Young told the Daily News of Blunk. "Jon took a bullet for me."
>
> She was too distraught to speak more, but her mother called Blunk, 25, who had two young children from a previous relationship, "a gentleman."
>
> "He was loving, the kind of guy you want your daughter to be with, and ultimately, she's alive because of this, because he protected her," Shellie Young said. . . .
>
> As the black-clad killer burst into the theater and unleashed tear gas and a torrent of indiscriminate gunfire, Blunk selflessly

protected his girlfriend. He pushed Jansen on the ground and under her seat, then threw his body on top of her, the mother said. "He was 6-feet-2, in incredible shape, which is why he was able to push her down under the seats of the theater," the mother said. "He pushed her down on the floor and laid down on top of her and he died there."[9]

Self-sacrificial love is not natural to the sinful human heart. Our natural desire is to protect self. Whenever we see selfless love in action, we can know that the power, the remedy of Jesus Christ is at work and hearts are being transformed. When we see self-sacrificing love in action, we can know that characters are being immersed and cleansed and people are being baptized into the reality of God's kingdom of love. This is the reality—the real baptism—the washing and cleansing of the mind from fear and selfishness and the rebirth in love and truth. As Scripture says, "He saved us through the washing of rebirth and renewal by the Holy Spirit" (Titus 3:5). We must leave behind satisfaction with metaphor and symbol and move forward to experience the full reality of God-shaped hearts as members of God's kingdom of love!

KEY POINTS FROM CHAPTER 9

- For metaphor, simile, parable, or illustration to have any meaning, there must be a cosmic reality to which it points. *If there is no reality behind the example, then it is no longer metaphor or parable—it is fantasy.*
- Christian maturity requires we move past metaphor to understand and live in harmony with the reality to which the metaphor points.

- The reality is that all humanity is sin-sick in heart and in need of the same healing remedy found only in Jesus Christ.

- Self-sacrificial love is not natural to the sinful human heart. Our natural desire is to protect self. Whenever we see selfless love in action, we can know that the power—the remedy—of Jesus Christ is at work and hearts are being transformed.

10

The Little Theater

Good teaching is one-fourth preparation and three-fourths pure theatre.

Unknown

All Bible metaphors, parables, illustrations, similes, object lessons, and rituals point to the same cosmic reality—God's character of love, his design law of love, and his plan to heal and restore his children back into unity with himself.

One of the most misunderstood illustrations found in Bible imagery is the Old Testament Jewish sanctuary and ritual service. There is not one aspect of that entire economy that is to be taken literally. Every element is symbolic of a larger cosmic reality.

In order to understand the meaning, one must first accurately decode the symbols. Consider Einstein's famous equation: $E = mc^2$. Energy (E) is equal to the mass (m) of any given matter multiplied by the speed of light squared (c^2). But if one doesn't know what the symbols mean, then the equation is meaningless. And worse than not understanding the meaning is to misunderstand and then begin teaching false meanings. Not only is the true meaning still not understood, attributing a false meaning to the symbols stops the search for the true meaning and makes it more difficult to comprehend the truth when it is presented.

This is what Christ meant when he said to the religious leaders in his day: "Woe to you, teachers of the law and Pharisees, you hypocrites! You travel over land and sea to win a single convert, and when you have succeeded, you make them twice as much a child of hell as you are" (Matt. 23:15). The converts were once the children of hell because they lived in ignorance and didn't have the truth. But now, they had two hurdles to overcome. They still needed to receive the truth, but thanks to the religious teachers their minds were now darkened by a false belief system—twice the obstruction.

Failure to correctly interpret the symbols of the sanctuary service has resulted in terrible misunderstandings about God, his design law, and his plan to heal and restore.

I was listening to Christian radio the week before Easter 2016 when someone called in and asked the two guest theologians to discuss the purpose of animal sacrifices in the Old Testament Jewish system. Their answers are further evidence of how deeply the infection of imposed law has penetrated Christianity:

> First theologian: There has to be punishment with death for sin, and so in Leviticus 17 when the animal sacrificial system is being established it says this, Leviticus 17:10–11, "Any Israelite or any alien living among them who eats any blood—I will set my face against that person who eats blood and will cut him off

from his people. For the life of a creature is in the blood, and I have given it to you to make atonement for yourselves on the altar; it is the blood that makes atonement for one's life." See blood represents life and there has to be the punishment of death for sin, so therefore an animal had to take the punishment and give its life—its blood—so that the offerer could live. That was the substitution. What my former professor used to call the exchange of life. The animal dies, the person lives. And so that's the reason for the Old Testament sacrifice for atonement.

Second theologian: A couple of things in the New Testament. In Luke's gospel it talks about how on the night that he was betrayed and Jesus was having the Passover meal, "and in the same way *He took* the cup after they had eaten, saying, 'This cup which is poured out for you is the new covenant in My blood.'" That is, it's the death of Jesus that comes about because of his blood loss among other things, his blood loss as well is the thing whereby he was our atoning sacrifice. His death is required for us as well in order to save us. Paul talks about it in Romans 5:9: "Much more then, having now been justified by His blood, we shall be saved from the wrath of God through Him." And so it's very much the same principle. In the Old Testament, the death of an animal was required to take care of the human sin problem and now we have not the death of an animal but of the very Son of God who dies for us. And so his loss of blood is the thing whereby he succumbed on our behalf.[1]

I hope that by this point in the book you can discern that this entire construct is predicated on the idea that God's law functions like human law, a system of rules imposed requiring punishment. The writer of Hebrews tried to help the New Testament church break out of such thinking by reminding them that "the gifts and sacrifices being offered were *not able to clear the conscience of the worshiper.* They are only a matter of food and drink and various ceremonial washings—external regulations applying until the time of the new order. . . . But those sacrifices are an annual reminder of sins. *It is impossible for the blood of bulls and goats to take away sins*" (Heb. 9:9–10; 10:3–4).

Animal sacrifices could never—at any time in human history—take care of the sin problem because they could not cleanse the conscience, transform the heart, and renew the character, which are required to save sinners. God has had his spokespersons telling us this throughout our entire history:

- "The multitude of your sacrifices—what are they to me?" says the Lord. "I have more than enough of burnt offerings, of rams and the fat of fattened animals; I have no pleasure in the blood of bulls and lambs and goats . . . wash and make yourselves clean. Take your evil deeds out of my sight; stop doing wrong. Learn to do right; seek justice. Defend the oppressed. Take up the cause of the fatherless; plead the case of the widow" (Isa. 1:11, 16–17).
- With what shall I come before the Lord and bow down before the exalted God? Shall I come before him with burnt offerings, with calves a year old?

  Will the Lord be pleased with thousands of rams, with ten thousand rivers of olive oil? Shall I offer my firstborn for my transgression, the fruit of my body for the sin of my soul? He has showed you, O mortal, what is good. And what does the Lord require of you? To act justly and to love mercy and to walk humbly with your God (Micah 6:6–8).

But perhaps Hosea puts what God wants, what he has always wanted and been working to achieve, most succinctly: "I want your constant love, not your animal sacrifices. I would rather have my people know me than burn offerings to me" (Hos. 6:6 GNT).

If the animal sacrifices could not save, then what was the purpose of the Old Testament sanctuary service?

The Great Stage Play

The entire Levitical system was a drama, a play, an acted-out production—a little theater. The system was given to a group of uneducated former slaves who didn't know how to read and write. So, on a grand scale, God directed them through Moses to build a very impressive stage (sanctuary/temple) and sew intricate costumes and provided them with a very detailed script. The children of Israel were the cast, the acting troupe, to act out in recurring yearly cycles God's plan to heal and save humanity, his plan to re-create human beings back to his original ideal. If this idea of a stage play is new, consider Paul's description to the Corinthians, "It seems to me that God has put us who bear his Message on stage in a theater in which no one wants to buy a ticket" (1 Cor. 4:9 Message).

Salvation—receiving a God-shaped heart (being reborn)—was not dependent upon acting in the play. One did not have to be a member of the acting troupe (Israel) in order to be saved. To be saved one only had to experience the reality to which the enactment was pointing. Consider Naaman, Melchezidek, Jethro, the widow who sheltered Elijah—all saved though none participated in the Levitical system. However, a person could join the troupe and become part of the cast if they desired—for example, Rahab and Ruth. And once a member of the cast (part of Israel), one was expected to follow the script. If a cast member refused to follow the script, or should we say the Script-ure, the member was removed from the stage.

What does the director of a Broadway play do if an actor persistently goes off-script and refuses to be corrected? Won't the director eventually remove that actor from the play—take them off the stage? This is what God did to many people in Old Testament times when they refused to follow the script; he removed them from the stage. Such removal did not necessarily mean they were eternally lost, only that they were no longer in the play. At other times, the entire cast had gotten so far off-script that God permitted the play to be shut down and the stage to be torn down (seventy years of captivity). While the play was in recess, God's faithful few were still being saved but without acting in the little drama. (Daniel and his three friends didn't sacrifice at the temple.)

Eventually, after learning some painful lessons, the actors returned home, rebuilt their stage, and started reenacting the play again. Esther and Mordecai didn't return home and apparently never participated in temple sacrifice, yet God did not abandon them. Why? Because God is concerned only with the reality to which the play pointed, and Esther and Mordecai participated in that reality—a trust relationship with God. By the time Jesus was born, however, the actors (Jews) had once again gone so far off-script that when he—the Source of all truth, the fulfillment of all the symbols—stood before them, they not only didn't recognize him but also rejected and killed him. So God once again put an end to the play, had the stage torn down, and began directing new helpers to take the true remedy that Christ achieved—the reality that the play only pointed toward—to the world.

With this in mind, let's consider some of the symbols in that Old Testament drama and seek the reality to which the symbols point. It is not the purpose of this book to do an exhaustive review of the sanctuary imagery but merely to demonstrate the fact that the symbols point to a larger reality. And by understanding the reality to which they point, we can experience a deeper and more meaningful experience with our amazing God.

The theme of the drama is this: humanity is separated from God by sin, and God is working through Christ to bring humanity back into unity with himself by restoring in our hearts his character of love. This is the view when one looks through the lens of design law—understanding God as Creator. However, since the corruption of Christianity with the infection of imposed law, many wrongly view the sanctuary drama as a system of legal payment and appeasement.

The Camp

The layout of the camp depicted the separation of humanity from God and his goal for reconciliation. At the center of the camp was the sanctuary, with the Most Holy Place—the dwelling place of God. Around the sanctuary the nation of Israel camped. They were organized into their various tribes with three tribes on each of the four sides of the sanctuary (symbolizing human beings from the four corners of the earth). The Levites camped *between* the rest of the tribes and the sanctuary. (The tribe of Joseph was divided into two, Ephraim and Manasseh, thus twelve tribes camped around the sanctuary with the Levites in between.)

What is the reality that this symbolism depicts? Sinful humanity is alienated and separated from God. However, God has come down to earth to "tabernacle" (take up residence) with humanity in order to reconcile humanity to himself. Jesus is the temple—the center, the connecting link, the unifying power, the source of love and life. As Jesus said, speaking of his body, "Destroy this temple, and I will raise it again in three days" (John 2:19). The temple ultimately represents Jesus who came to live with us and restore us to unity with his Father. The Levites represent the priesthood of believers who have partaken of Christ and go out into the world to share the gospel, the knowledge of God, with the unbelieving world (represented by the twelve tribes), bringing the world back into unity with God. Thus they camp between the temple and the rest of the tribes.

Moses represented Christ in his preincarnate form. Moses spoke to God face-to-face, left God's presence to confront the ruler of Egypt and deliver the people of Israel from bondage, and established the sanctuary depicting the plan of salvation. Christ in heaven spoke to his Father face-to-face, left heaven and came to earth to confront the ruler of this sinful world and deliver humanity from the bondage of sin (in the wilderness Jesus confronts and defeats Satan directly), and established his sanctuary here on earth. Speaking of Jesus, Zechariah prophesies:

> Tell him this is what the LORD Almighty says: "Here is the man whose name is the Branch, and he will *branch out from his place and build the temple of the LORD*. It is *he who will build the temple of the LORD*, and he will be clothed with majesty and will sit and rule on his throne. And he will be a priest on his throne. And there will be harmony between the two." (Zech. 6:12–13)

So Moses represents Jesus in his preincarnate state, planning with the Father and implementing the plan of salvation.

The lamb (sacrificial animal) represents Christ during his thirty-three and a half years here on this earth. As John the Baptist said of Jesus, "Look, the Lamb of God, who takes away the sin of the world!" (John 1:29).

The blood of the lamb (sacrificial animal) is symbolic of the life. Leviticus tells us, "For the life of a creature is in the blood" (17:11). And what did the blood do in the animal? It circled; the blood circulated. It makes up our circulation as well. What a perfect symbolic representation of the law of love in action—the principle of never-ending giving. Even in our modern day, the circle continues to represent never-ending love. This is why wedding *rings* are given as a physical representation of love. In a vision, Ezekiel saw the throne of God, which is symbolic of rulership and government, and upon what was the throne resting? A moving circle, inside a turning wheel, inside a rotating circle—God's government is built upon the living law of love! This is what the blood represents. The blood of the sacrificial animal represents the perfect, sinless life of Jesus who loved perfectly.

The high priest represents Christ after his resurrection and ascension. "Therefore, since we have a great high priest who has ascended into heaven, Jesus the Son of God, let us hold firmly to the faith we profess" (Heb. 4:14).

The reality behind these symbols is Jesus!

The Court

The outer court contained the brazen altar and the laver, both made out of bronze.

In order to understand the meaning of the symbols, we need to determine how we are viewing them and the general lesson being taught. Are we looking at these things through the lens of the penal imposed-law model or the healing design-law reality?

What, in general, is the lesson that the sanctuary teaches? It is reconciliation with God, God's plan to save humanity from sin. In light of this, let's consider the following questions.

What problem did sin cause that the plan of salvation is designed to fix? When Adam and Eve sinned, was God changed? Was God's law changed? Or was humanity changed? Is sin a defect in God or God's law, or a defect in humanity?

So when we look at these symbols, are we interpreting them in ways that suggest something is being done to God and/or his law (as the penal view teaches), or do we realize they all teach how God, through Jesus, heals and restores humankind back into unity with himself (as the design view teaches)?

The Brazen Altar

The altar was constructed out of shittim wood, which was symbolic of corruptible humanity, and overlaid with bronze, symbolic of our defective condition being judged or diagnosed as terminal.

Thus, the bronze altar represents the starting point in the salvation process. The first step in any healing process is admitting we have something wrong. The bronze altar is the place of "judgment" or diagnosis, where we acknowledge something is wrong and that we are powerless to cure ourselves. Therefore, we are in need of an external remedy or Savior. This is the first step, where we all must fall down and acknowledge our condition, our sinfulness, and our need of a Savior. The bronze altar is step one in the salvation/healing process.

The animal was slain by the hand of the sinner, not the priest, and the blood was poured out at the base of the altar and then applied to the horns of the altar. This represents a sinner coming to Christ and being reborn—a complete cleansing of the heart as the foundation of salvation or healing. The blood applied to the horns represents the beginning of character transformation—the life (righteousness) of Christ is reproduced in the believer. Our thoughts are brought into harmony with his, and we experience new desires in the heart. Jesus himself instructed that the reality of these symbols was applying them within the believer: "Very truly I tell you, unless you eat the flesh of the Son of Man and drink his blood, you have no life in you. Whoever eats my flesh and drinks my blood has eternal life, and I will raise them up at the last day. For my flesh is real food and my blood is real drink" (John 6:53–55).

Additionally, the inner fat of the sacrificial animal, the fat *hidden within* the animal around the organs, was removed and burned on the brazen altar. This represents the work of Christ in taking our sinful condition on himself and destroying the infection of fear and selfishness. He did this when he was tempted to save himself but didn't give in to those temptations. Christ was tempted in every way just as we are, yet without sin (Heb. 4:15). And we are tempted by our own evil desires (James 1:14). In other words, we have temptations that come from within. And Jesus was tempted like us. In Gethsemane, he experienced powerful human emotions to act to save himself. But instead of giving in to such a selfish temptation, Jesus gave himself in love. "No one takes my life away from me. I give it up of my own free will" (John 10:18 GNT). By this choice to love, with his human brain, despite the temptation to act in self-interest, Jesus destroyed the infection of fear and selfishness and restored

God's law of love into humanity. This is symbolized by cutting away and burning the fat of the inner organs.

Throughout Scripture, the burning of the fat is described as an "aroma pleasing" to the Lord (Lev. 4:31; 17:6; Num. 18:17). Now we can understand why. It is symbolic of the burning away of the carnal nature, the selfish desires, the infection of sin within God's children. If your child was dying of leukemia and was given chemotherapy, and the chemo burned away the cancer cells saving your child, would you be pleased? God is immensely pleased when sinfulness is burned out of the hearts, minds, and characters of his earthly children!

The horns of the brazen altar represent the power of sin in our lives, the defects of character that are in need of removal and transformation by the work of God through Christ in our lives—represented by the application of the blood to the horns. "To the arrogant I say, 'Boast no more,' and to the wicked, 'Do not lift up your horns. Do not lift your horns against heaven; do not speak so defiantly'" (Ps. 75:4–5).

The fire in the altar represents God the Holy Spirit. Before the blood was applied to the altar, the fire represented the working of the Holy Spirit to bring conviction and draw sinners to conversion. After the blood was applied, the fire represented the Holy Spirit working in the new convert to bring transformation, consume the desires and motives of the carnal nature, and regenerate a Christlike heart.

God said immediately after Adam and Eve sinned, "And I will put enmity between you and the woman, and between your offspring and hers" (Gen. 3:15). Ever since, the Holy Spirit has been working in the hearts and minds of sinners to convict of sin and draw us back to himself. And when the truth is presented, the Holy Spirit is there to enlighten and sink it deep in the heart:

"Were not our hearts burning within us while he talked with us on the road and opened the Scriptures to us?" (Luke 24:32). And when we respond to the truth and open our hearts in truth, the Holy Spirit is there to burn out defects of character and create God-shaped hearts of love within us: "They saw what seemed to be tongues of fire that separated and came to rest on each of them. All of them were filled with the Holy Spirit and began to speak in other tongues as the Spirit enabled them" (Acts 2:3–4).

The Laver

The laver represents the washing by the Holy Spirit, which cleanses, empowers, and equips God's saints for ministry. The laver was constructed out of the mirrors the women brought out of Egypt (Exod. 38:8). This aptly represents the purpose of God's Word to expose our defects and diagnose our condition (James 1:22–25). The water is symbolic of God the Holy Spirit, which filled the laver and cleanses and empowers believers. "He saved us through the washing of rebirth and renewal by the Holy Spirit" (Titus 3:5); "Christ loved the church and gave himself up for her to make her holy, cleansing her by the washing with water through the word, and to present her to himself as a radiant church, without stain or wrinkle or any other blemish, but holy and blameless" (Eph. 5:25–27).

Only the priests and the high priest washed in the laver, which aptly symbolizes that only the believers in Christ are cleansed by the Spirit, value the truth revealed in the Word, and are equipped to carry out God's purposes.

We find this theme of washing with the Word of God to cleanse our characters carried over by Jesus in the foot-washing service. Our feet symbolize our journey through life. Naked feet symbolize truthfully revealing our life journey to our brothers and sisters in Christ. Washing by another symbolizes others, directed by the Holy Spirit, using God's Word, methods, and principles to help us clean up our journey, removing the impure practices from our lives so that we experience cleansing of character. Washing others' feet reveals our willingness to help others, who reveal their life journey by sharing how they have gotten themselves dirty with sin, to clean up their lives and characters by the application of God's Word, methods, and principles.

The Vessels That Carried the Blood from the Sacrifice to Application Points

The vessels represent believers who take to the world the truth about God and the character of Christ in their actions and deeds, in the way they live, and in preaching the gospel message. "But the Lord said unto him, Go thy way: for he [Paul] is a chosen vessel unto me, to bear my name before the Gentiles, and kings, and the children of Israel" (Acts 9:15 KJV); "But in a great house there are not only vessels of gold and of silver, but also of wood and of earth; and some to honour, and some to dishonour. If a man therefore purge himself from these, he shall be a vessel unto honour, sanctified, and meet for the master's use, *and* prepared unto every good work" (2 Tim. 2:20–21 KJV).

The Daily Priests

The daily priests, dressed in their white robes and entering the Holy Place, represent the priesthood of believers—those who have been renewed in heart to have Christlike character and who minister the gospel to the world. Jesus said, "Peace be with you! As the Father has sent me, I am sending you" (John 20:21). They carry out their duties for God within the church. Peter wrote, "You also, like living stones, are being built into a spiritual house to be a holy priesthood, offering spiritual sacrifices acceptable to God through Jesus Christ" (1 Pet. 2:5). They are enlightened for ministry to others by the Word of God (light from the lamp) from the ministry, preaching, and teaching of others and the study of the Word of God for themselves, ingesting its truths (eating the showbread). In a trust relationship with God, they open their hearts to him and receive the character of Christ partaking of the divine nature (drinking the wine). As their hearts burn within, they pour out their love, praise, and concern for fulfilling God's will to the Father (incense burned on the altar).

The white robes worn by the daily priests represent the perfect character of Christ reproduced within the believer.

> Now Joshua was dressed in filthy clothes as he stood before the angel. The angel said to those who were standing before him, "Take off his filthy clothes." Then he said to Joshua, "*See, I have taken away your sin,* and I will put fine garments on you." Then I said, "Put a clean turban on his head." So they put a clean turban on his head and clothed him, while the angel of the LORD stood by. (Zech. 3:3–5)

> Then one of the elders asked me, "These in white robes—who are they, and where did they come from?" . . . And he said, "These are they who have come out of the great tribulation; they have washed their robes and made them white in the blood of the Lamb." (Rev. 7:13–14)

The Holy Place

The Holy Place, covered in gold, represents the true church cleansed and perfected by the righteousness of Christ with his pure golden character of love (Rev. 3:18). The door represents Christ our door, our gate, the way back into unity with the Father (John 10:7; 14:6). Through the door, the light of the lamp shone out into the courtyard. This represents Christ the light that shines out from the church into the world and enlightens all men (John 1:4, 9).

The Lampstand

The lampstand represents the Word of God—the written and living Word: "Your word is a lamp for my feet, a light on my path" (Ps. 119:105).

The entire lampstand was made of pure gold. It had a central stand and six branches. The central stand of the lamp represents Christ. The six branches represent the church, human beings (six being the number of a man) united with Christ—the central stand—making a total of seven lamps, the number of perfection. We are only perfected and able to shine light when we are united with Christ.

The bowls on the lampstand represent the hearts of believers in which the Word and Spirit burn, re-creating godlike character and shining heavenly light as a witness for God. The bowls connected to the lamp are like branches connected to the vine.

The almond flowers carved on the lampstand represent the fruit of the Spirit that are manifest in the church.

The high priest, and only the high priest, trimmed the wicks each morning and evening, symbolizing Christ working in our hearts to trim away defects of character so we can shine more brightly for him.

> You are the light of the world. A town built on a hill cannot be hidden. Neither do people light a lamp and put it under a bowl. Instead they put it on its stand, and it gives light to everyone in the house. In the same way, let your light shine before others, that they may see your good deeds and glorify your Father in heaven. (Matt. 5:14–16)

The oil in the lampstand represents the Spirit of God. "So Samuel took the horn of oil and anointed him in the presence of his brothers, and from that day on the Spirit of the LORD came powerfully upon David" (1 Sam. 16:13).

The Table

The table represents Christ. It was made of wood, covered in gold, aptly symbolizing Jesus our incarnate God, who took humanity (wood) upon himself and perfected it (gold) and from whom we receive all spiritual nurturance (bread).

The table had a border or crown on it, measuring a hand-breadth high, the only measurement in the sanctuary that wasn't in cubits. The border surrounded the twelve loaves and represents God's protective hand around his remedy for his people.

The twelve loaves represent Christ, who is the bread of life. "Then Jesus declared, 'I am the bread of life. Whoever comes to me will never go hungry, and whoever believes in me will never be thirsty'" (John 6:35). The loaves were made out of fine flour with no lumps and no leaven, representing the purity of Christ without sin. Incense was placed on top of the two stacks of loaves, and every Sabbath the priests would join with the high priest, who would burn the incense on the golden altar, and then they would eat the loaves. This symbolized believers coming together every Sabbath, in union with their High Priest Jesus, offering prayers and praise to God (incense), and partaking of the Word (bread).

The wine represents the perfect character, the sinless life of Christ. "Then he took a cup, and when he had given thanks he gave it to them, saying, 'Drink from it, all of you. This is my blood of the covenant, which is poured out for many for the forgiveness of sins. I tell you, I will not drink from this fruit of the vine from now on until that day when I drink it new with you in my Father's kingdom'" (Matt. 26:27–29).

The Golden Altar

The golden altar represents the renewed and purified heart of the saved. Prayers are offered from the converted, not unconverted, and incense was burned on this altar, not the brazen altar. "May my prayer be set before you like incense; may the lifting up of my hands be like the evening sacrifice" (Ps. 141:2); "And when he had taken it, the four living creatures and the twenty-four elders fell down before the Lamb. Each one had a harp and they were holding golden bowls full of incense, which are the prayers of God's people" (Rev. 5:8).

Incense also represents Christlike character lived out by the saints. The incense wafted out from the Holy Place over the camp of Israel as a sweet smell drawing the people to the sanctuary. The lives of God's saved are to be a sweet fragrance to the world, drawing the unsaved to Christ. "But thanks be to God, who always leads us as captives in Christ's triumphal procession and uses us to spread the aroma of the knowledge of him everywhere. For we are to God the pleasing aroma of Christ among those who are being saved and those who are perishing" (2 Cor. 2:14–15).

Fire in the golden altar represents the Holy Spirit working in the hearts of the saved to enlighten, transform, heal, and ennoble. "I baptize you with water for repentance. But after me comes one who is more powerful than I, whose sandals I am not worthy to carry. He will baptize you with the Holy Spirit and with fire" (Matt. 3:11).

The horns on the golden altar represent the remnant or vestigial defects of character, remaining elements of selfishness, and scars from sin in the hearts of the righteous who are being cleansed, healed, and purified by the continual partaking and application of Jesus via the work of the Holy Spirit. The horns of the golden altar are smaller than those of the brazen altar, symbolizing growth in righteousness and transformation of character.

When priests offered sin offerings, the blood was placed on the horns of the golden altar rather than the brazen altar, which was for the sacrifice of a nonpriest and symbolized the continual need for Christ's transforming power in the hearts and minds of believers. The golden crown around the golden altar represents the crown of victory received from Christ. There was no crown on the brazen altar as it represents the unconverted heart, not the victorious heart.

The Curtain

The curtain with the angels sewn upon it represents the lies of Satan, which separate us from God, and our carnal nature, which Christ assumed and destroyed at the cross.

The daily priests long to see God more fully, and they look toward the Most Holy Place, but something obstructs their view. A veil with angels sewn upon it obscures their ability to see God clearly. This veil must be destroyed so no barrier obstructs our reconciliation with God. And this veil was destroyed. The veil was the only element of that symbolic system that God destroyed when Christ died on the cross. This aptly symbolizes how Christ's death destroyed "him who holds the power of death—that is, the devil" (Heb. 2:14).

By destroying the lies of Satan and the carnal nature we inherit from Adam's fall, Christ opens a new and living way through the veil. "We have, then, my friends, complete freedom to go into the Most Holy Place by means of the death of Jesus. He opened for us a new way, a living way, through the curtain—that is, through his own body" (Heb. 10:19–20 GNT). By his death, "he destroyed death and has brought life and immortality to light" (2 Tim. 1:10). His body crucified—his death in our behalf—is the new and living way through the lies of Satan and through the sinfulness of fallen humanity that separates us from God. "And even if our gospel is veiled, it is veiled to those who are perishing. The god of this age has blinded the minds of unbelievers, so that they cannot see the light of the gospel that displays the glory of Christ, who is the image of God" (2 Cor. 4:3–4). Christ's death destroyed that veil, and now the light of the glory of God again shines into our hearts!

The Most Holy Place

The Most Holy Place represents the universe cleansed of sin and unified in perfect love and trust through the work of Jesus

Christ. The Shekinah glory represents God the Father who lives in unapproachable light (1 Tim. 6:16).

The angels on the lid of the ark of the covenant represent the onlooking universe who are watching things both in heaven and on earth as well as ministering to us on earth (1 Cor. 4:9; 1 Pet. 1:12; Heb. 1:14; Matt. 18:10). The box beneath the lid of the ark was made out of porous wood, covered completely in gold, and symbolized fallen humanity that though damaged by sin now has all corruption cleansed and all defects filled in by the perfect righteousness (gold) of Jesus Christ.

Three items were kept in the box, and they were procured in a certain order: manna, then the Ten Commandment law, and then Aaron's rod that budded. This symbolism is profound and has an amazing correspondence in reality.

The manna represents Jesus, the bread of life, who came down from heaven (John 6:48–51). In the salvation process we must first come to a knowledge of Jesus, partake of him, and then in trust open our hearts to him. When we do this, he writes his law upon our hearts and minds: "This is the covenant I will establish with the people of Israel after that time, declares the Lord. I will put my laws in their minds and write them on their hearts. I will be their God, and they will be my people" (Heb. 8:10). And when in trust Christ writes his law of love upon our hearts, then we who were dead in our trespasses and sin (Eph. 2:1) become alive in Christ and bring forth peaceable fruits of righteousness (Phil. 1:11) symbolized by Aaron's dead rod, which came alive and budded, blossomed, and produced almonds.

The lid of the ark was made out of solid gold, a fit representation of Christ's perfect character. It also was not given any dimensions, representing how he is boundless, without limit, in his love and ability to heal and restore. In Romans, Paul uses the

Greek word for the lid of the ark (*hilasterion*) to describe Jesus as the place and means of restoring sinners back into unity with God. "God offered him, so that by his blood he should become the means [lid] by which people's sins are forgiven through their faith in him" (Rom. 3:25 GNT).

Jesus is the connecting link that reconciles the entire universe back into unity with God. All holy beings are brought together into one accord via Christ—sinners redeemed (the box), unfallen beings throughout the universe (angels on the lid), and the Godhead (Shekinah) all united via Jesus (the lid): "He made known to us the mystery of his will according to his good pleasure, which he purposed in Christ, to be put into effect when the times reach their fulfillment—to bring unity to all things in heaven and on earth under Christ" (Eph. 1:9–10).

Read the Meaning

Now that we have spent time defining the meaning of the various symbols, we can interpret the meaning of what was being acted out. Let's examine the sin offering for nonpriest Jews and for a priest.

Sin Offering for the Nonpriest

The sinner would bring a sacrificial animal and confess their sin on the head of the animal, which rightly represents that sin is an issue of the mind. The repentant sinner, not the officiating priest, would then cut the throat of the animal. This simple illustration accurately represents that sin severs the circle of love and trust and results in death. Remember the life is in the blood, and the blood simply circles in the body, round and round it goes and life continues—unless something interrupts the circle (circulation). This is the law of love depicted—the principle of giving. Sin, however, breaks the circle of love, which is the design for life, and just as cutting the circulation of the animal results in death, so too breaking the law of love results in death. A straightforward and simple object lesson—no legal payment of blood involved.

The sacrificial animal represents Jesus who, though he was sinless, took our sinful condition upon himself (Isa. 53:4) in order to become our remedy: "God made him who had no sin to be sin for us, so that in him we might become the righteousness of God" (2 Cor. 5:21). Therefore, the shed blood of the animal represents the perfect sinless life, love, and character of Jesus— which cleanses from sin all who partake!

The blood is carried by the ministering priest in vessels; both the priest and vessel represent believers sharing the gospel message with others. The blood poured around the brazen altar represents the truth and character of Christ applied to the unconverted heart evoking a foundational change in motive from selfishness to selfless love. This is conversion—being won from distrust to trust in God. The blood applied to the horns of the brazen altar represents the life of Christ transforming the heart and overcoming sinful habits and traits of character.

The washing of the organs represents the cleansing of the inner man from lies about God by the truth of God's Word, the enlightening of the Holy Spirit, and the equipping with new motives. Separating the fat from the internal organs represents the destruction of the carnal nature, achieved by Jesus our substitute, and the freeing of our hearts (the inner man) from the domination of fear and selfishness. The burning of the organs represents the renewal of the inner man—the mind being re-created in Christlikeness—and the elimination of old habits and conditioned responses that are out of harmony with God's law of love.

The lamb's meat being eaten by the daily priests represents the internalization of Christ's character, truths, principles, and method, and the growth in spiritual strength as we minister the truth to others.

Sin Offering for a Priest

The repentant priest brings a sacrificial animal and confesses his sin on the head of the animal, representing that sin is an issue of the mind. The repentant priest (not the officiating priest) then cuts the animal's throat, representing that sin severs the circle of love and trust and results in death.

The sacrificial animal represents Jesus who, though he was sinless, took our sinful condition upon himself to become our remedy (Isa. 53:4; 2 Cor. 5:21).

The blood represents the perfect sinless life, love, and character of Jesus, which is carried by the ministering priest in vessels. Both the ministering priest and the vessel that carries the blood represent believers sharing the gospel message with others.

Thus far the process is similar between a priest and nonpriest, but now things change. The blood of the sacrificial animal is sprinkled before the veil, which represents the application of the character of Christ (the truth and love of Christ) within the church in order to remove any lies, correct any misrepresentations, and heal any wounds that obstruct our union with God when believers in Christ sin, thus healing the church. Remember that the veil represents lies about God and our fallen natures, both of which separate us from God. When Christians commit sin, they misrepresent the truth about God adding to the obstruction represented by the veil. Thus, the blood is sprinkled before the veil to represent the application of Christ's grace, love, life, principles, truths, and methods within the church revealing the power of Christ to overcome sin (Rom. 5:20).

Then the blood is placed on the horns of the golden altar, which represents the removal of residual defects of character from the heart of the repentant believer. (Note that the horns on the golden altar are much smaller than those on the brazen altar because believers in Christ have matured in character and their remaining resistance to God and character defects are smaller than those who don't know God.)

The remaining blood is poured out at the base of the brazen altar, which represents that when Christians are gracious and forgiving with each other, seeking to restore the sinner among us, we give witness to the power of Christ and him crucified to the unconverted world, thereby bringing others to repentance.

Separating the fat from the internal organs represents the destruction of the carnal nature and the freeing of our hearts (the inner man) from the domination of fear and selfishness. The burning of the organs represents the renewal of the inner man, the mind being re-created in Christlikeness, and the elimination of old habits and conditioned responses that are out of harmony with God's law of love.

Unity Is the Goal

Throughout the entire drama—theatrical stage play—there is one message being communicated: humans are separated from God by sin, but God through Christ has provided the remedy and is working to heal and restore those who are willing back into perfect unity with him! This is reality! Unity with God, healing from sin, and restoration to Christlike perfection are not metaphor but the goal, the prize that we seek. It is time to move past immaturity and enter into the reality of God's kingdom and universe of love.

Our growth, our healing, and our restoration to a God-shaped heart are hindered when we stay stuck on metaphor, insist on symbols, and persistently view God's Word through the imposed-law lens.

In our next chapter, we will continue our exploration of the elementary teachings described in Hebrews 6, pressing on toward ever-increasing maturation into true sons and daughters of God.

KEY POINTS FROM CHAPTER 10

- Failure to correctly interpret the symbols of the sanctuary service has resulted in a terrible misunderstanding about God, his design law, and his plan to heal and restore.
- Animal sacrifices could never—at any time in human history—take care of the sin problem because they could not cleanse the conscience, transform the heart, and renew the character, which are required to save sinners.
- Salvation is not dependent on acting in a ritual but on experiencing a God-shaped heart.

11

The Power of Love and Truth

All love is expansion, all selfishness is contraction.
Love is therefore the only law of life. He who loves
lives, he who is selfish is dying. Therefore love for
love's sake, because it is the only law of life, just as
you breathe to live.

Swami Vivekananda, in a letter dated 1895

Thus far we have identified that Christianity has been infected with an imposed-law construct that prevents good people from experiencing victory over addiction and violence cycles. Too many hurting people remain wounded and battered. Now it is time to expose how this imposed-law idea has led to a misunderstanding of the use of power and corrupted the truth about the sovereignty of God, resulting in millions living in fear of God rather than experiencing the transformative power of his love.

When you think of power, what comes to mind? Do you think physical might, energy, the power of arms? Most Christians agree that God is all-powerful, but they frequently struggle when bad things happen to good people. How can innocent children suffer if God is all-powerful? Under the imposed-law view, an all-powerful God imposes his will on his subjects. God makes things happen the way they do. If sickness happens—God is punishing. If disaster happens—God is destroying. According to livescience.com, 56 percent of Americans believe God is in control of *all* events on planet Earth, 44 percent believe natural disasters are caused by God, and 29 percent believe God punishes entire nations for the sins of a few people.[1] But as we move past the way sinful humans operate and see God through the lens of Jesus, we understand love never imposes or coerces; love wins the heart and love leaves free.

Redistribution of Wealth

In January of 2016, I was privileged to participate in the town hall meeting in Atlanta, Georgia, to discuss health-care policy in America. One of the other panelists argued that what is needed in the United States is for the government to impose a massive redistribution of wealth in order to provide equity in health care to the poor and disadvantaged. There was enthusiastic response from the audience to this idea.

Sitting on the panel, I was contemplating what God would have me say. Certainly Jesus spoke of caring for the poor. The story of the good Samaritan flashed into my mind. I was certain that greed was not in keeping with God's methods. I was confident that God would have people help the less fortunate, yet something was not right with this idea of government-mandated redistribution of wealth. How to communicate my concern without coming across as a selfish, white, upper-middle-class elitist? I thought through the lens of design law and realized what was wrong: the method being suggested was that of imposed law. While some of the panelists were focusing exclusively on governmental policies, I was thinking beyond policy to impacting the hearts and minds of people for God's kingdom. We cannot win God's cause by using the methods of human governments, so I shared the following ideas.

There are two general ways to redistribute wealth. One way is through charitable giving. Those with love in their hearts and who see the less fortunate freely choose to give of their resources to help the needy. This is God's method, taught by Jesus himself, built upon the law of love, the principle of giving: "*Freely* you have received, *freely* give" (Matt. 10:8).

In this method, those who give are blessed with ever-increasing love, grace, compassion, and Christlike character development in the act of giving. Give and it will be given back to you (Luke 6:38). The givers receive a blessing when they give from a heart of love. And those who receive the gift are blessed with thankfulness. Their hearts are warmed in appreciation knowing that what is given is not earned, is not a right, but is an expression of love for them. They realize that they are valued as people as others sacrifice to bless them. This inspires not only thanksgiving in their hearts but also a desire for the application of love in giving to others. It is by love that love is awakened in the heart. "We love because he first loved us" (1 John 4:19).

But there is another way to redistribute wealth—it is the way of earthly governments. The Bible describes these governments as ravenous beasts (Dan. 7). By coercive force, they can take from people not yet willing to give, forcing them to give their wealth to people whom someone else has deemed worthy of receiving those resources. In such a coercive system, those who have their property taken are cheated of the privilege of giving. Rather than love and compassion growing in their hearts, often resentment grows instead and a feeling of being exploited and taken advantage of. Such actions plant seeds of discord into the heart of those who are taken from and cause division rather than unity in society. Some who receive the redistributed wealth, rather than feeling appreciative and thankful, too often feel entitled, as if it is their right, and demand more and more from others. In fact, they often get angry and protest when more is not given, which only causes further division in society. Genuine unity is reached only when people freely choose to agree and participate. Successful government programs are those in which leaders have obtained agreement, a buy-in from the citizenry. When this happens, such tax and redistribution programs result in less conflict and greater harmony.

We as Christians will only win God's cause (to heal and transform hearts) through God's methods (the law of love) and not by the coercive methods of earthly governments. There is a reason that the church and state are to be separate. Human beings cannot create reality—space, time, matter, energy, life—thus, we create rules, and rules require coercive enforcement. The state always uses methods of coercion—even when their goal is good, such as helping those in need. The methods of the state will ultimately contaminate rather than heal the hearts of people who practice such methods. Jesus said, "My kingdom is not of this world. If it were, my servants would fight to prevent my arrest by the Jewish leaders. But now my kingdom is from another place" (John 18:36). If God's kingdom were based on imposed law, then his followers would use coercive tactics such as might and power. But God's kingdom is the kingdom of love, and love cannot be achieved by threat, intimidation, coercion, or command.

In the aftermath of this town hall meeting, I began to contemplate more deeply the various types of power and how they are used. I realized that having accepted the imposed-law construct and having believed God's law functions no differently than the laws sinful beings legislate, millions of people misconstrue God's power and thus the sovereignty of God.

It is my belief that God is sovereign—which means that he is supreme, the ultimate authority, the Being in charge, the One who originated not only space, time, matter, energy, and life but also law. God is sovereign, and his laws rule supreme over all creation. The confusion arises when we replace God's design laws with human imposed-law constructs, and instead of God's sovereignty being clearly seen, we obstruct it.

This misunderstanding has led to the classic conflict in Christian apologetics: How can a God who is love and who is all-powerful (sovereign) allow children to be molested, innocents to be murdered, evil to exist at all? The reason this question persists is because most people are stuck under a false law construct, thinking that God's laws function like ours and therefore all God has to do is use his might and power to punish the wicked and deliver the innocent. People think of God dealing with sinners as President George W. Bush dealt with those responsible for the September 11, 2001, terrorist attacks: "Whether we bring our enemies to justice or bring justice to our enemies, justice will be done."[2]

Human governments use might and power to coerce. But what is it that God actually wants from us? Does God want more than the obedience of a well-trained dog? Does God want more than the submission of a slave? Does God actually want our love and trust? As you answer these questions, consider which of the following types of power is capable of achieving God's goal for us and the impact each has on our relationship with him.

Coercive Power

Coercive power is the use of force, might, or strength to threaten, intimidate, or punish in order to pressure someone, who is otherwise unwilling, to comply with your will. Can God get what he wants from his creatures by the exercise of this type of power? Further, is the use of this type of power reliable in recruiting followers to one's cause?

This is the power used by level one through four thinkers, those who seek to avoid punishment, rejection, pain, and legal problems. Will the use of this type of power to obtain converts result in reliable, stable, trustworthy, and unshakable followers? Can one get loyalty by the use of threats? In other words, if you get people to follow you by using coercive power, do your followers stay true and loyal against all opposition? What will break coercive power and cause such followers to collapse, to give in, to betray you?

- A bigger threat
- A desired inducement
- Believing a lie
- Genuine love for someone or something else
- The hope of freedom

The use of coercive power does not result in transformed people who are reliable and trustworthy. In fact, coercive power is a violation of God's design law of liberty. Violate liberty in relationships and love is always damaged, the individuality of those dominated is slowly eroded, and a desire to rebel is instilled.

Consider a relationship in which the person you are attracted to begins to use coercive pressure on you: *Do what I say or else!* They begin exercising authority in an attempt to dominate you and take your freedom. When you go out to dinner, they don't ask what you would like; they order for you. They take your cell phone, close your email accounts, and inform you that you are forbidden from talking with your friends. When you go shopping, you are required to return with receipts to document how every penny was spent. If you were in such a relationship, would you love more or less? Would you want to stay or get away? And if you did stay, what would happen to your mind and your thinking? How long until you thought only through the lens of the one to whom you have surrendered?

Or what if the domination isn't as overt as physical threats and control; what if it is emotional instead? Don't do what your partner wants and they cry, stomp, pout, yell, slam doors, threaten suicide, or exhibit some other emotional outburst. You feel pressure to not upset them, to do what they want or else. What happens to love? What happens to your individuality?

One of God's design laws for relationships is the law of liberty—love can only exist in an atmosphere of freedom. This is testable and reproducible. Try it in any relationship and you will see that in every relationship in which liberty is violated love is damaged and eventually destroyed and a desire to rebel is instilled in the dominated person. If a person chooses to stay anyway, over time their individuality is eroded. Coercive power is not only destructive but is also a violation of God's design law and thus his character of love.

Imposed law always results in coercive power. God never uses coercive power because what God wants can never be achieved by it. God wants our love and trust, but one cannot achieve love and trust by threat and coercion. The Bible states, "'Not by might nor by power, but by my Spirit,' says the LORD" (Zech. 4:6).

The first type of power is coercive power. This type of power originates in Satan's government and is the primary method of the nations of this world. Such behavior is beastly!

Inducing Power

The next type of power is inducing power—the power of bribes, payoffs, promotions, money and advancement, praise and adoration. This is the power that appeals to level two and three thinkers, those seeking to make deals or who are concerned with acceptance by others. Does this type of power result in reliable, stable, trustworthy, and unshakable followers? Will people who follow you for what they can get stay loyal against all opposition? What will cause them to collapse and betray you?

- A serious threat
- A better payoff
- A lie
- Genuine love for someone or something else

The movie *The Godfather* made clear how these first two types of power operate: a deal you can't refuse—either take the payoff or you will be killed.

Deceiving Power

Yet another type of power is the power of lies—deception and fraud. Many don't realize it, but the power of lies is a stronger, more potent, and more reliable power than either coercion or inducement. Adherents who follow based on lies—if they truly believe those lies—will not be swayed by threats or bought by bribes. Consider members of cults or various terrorist groups, for example.

While lies are more powerful and reliable in achieving converts than threats or inducements, will such followers be faithful beyond betrayal? Will those who follow based on lies remain true in the face of all opposition? What will cause the deceived follower to collapse and betray you?

- Another lie that is believed
- The truth—when the truth exposes the lie, and they accept the truth and are set free (the truth may be revealed either by facts or experiences of life)
- Love for someone or something other than self

The Power of Love

The power of love—to be loved and to love others genuinely more than self—is the power operating in individuals at level five and higher of moral development. Does this power result in reliable, stable, trustworthy, and unshakable outcomes? Will those who follow based on love be loyal against all opposition?

Certainly, the power of love is greater than coercive force and inducing power. But there is one power that can and did break the power of love—that is, the power of deceit. Just remember Eden and the fall of our first parents.

To help people resonate with how powerful lies can be, I often use this example: imagine you are in a healthy, loving marriage in which you love and trust your spouse who loves and trusts you in return. Someone else you also love and trust, perhaps your brother or sister, comes to you and with tears in their eyes tells you the lie that your spouse is having an affair. They even show you pictures they have doctored on their computer to make it appear your spouse is with another. Now, while it is not true and your spouse is still loyal and faithful, *if you believe the lie* does something inside of you change?

Notice the cascade of destruction that comes from believing lies:

- Lies believed break the circle of love and trust.
- Broken love and trust result in fear and selfishness.

  I no longer trust you so I have to watch out for myself.
- Fear and selfishness result in acts of selfishness.

  I'm afraid you will give me a disease, so I'm moving out and going to the bank to get our money before you do.
- Acts of selfishness damage mind, body, and relationships— a terminal condition.

  Increased fear activates stress cascades, damages health, causes negative thought processes, and disrupts relationships.

I have used this example many times in my teaching and recently received the following (edited) email:

I "attend" your online Bible Study class most weeks and truly enjoy the discussions. I was raised in the church and attended church schools all the way through college.

Many weeks I listen with pain and understanding to your analogy of a person believing the lie that their spouse is having an affair—even though it is not true.

Several years ago, my (former) best friend told my husband that I was having an affair with a close family friend. This was untrue; however, my husband believed her, over my insistence (to this day) that I had been faithful, and our marriage spiraled into divorce. We ended with accusations, my husband screaming with a finger in my face, spyware on my computer, breaking into my email and Facebook accounts, tracking devices on my car, and him telling my children that I was a whore.

To make matters worse, my husband, who was not a church member, took his story to my local church pastors and key church members. I lost not only my marriage and my best friend, but my church family as well. Without the pastor ever speaking with me or counseling us, I was removed from teaching and ostracized within the church. I left and have never gone back. Unfortunately, this is one of the only churches in my area.

Even though years have passed and new pastors have rotated in, no one in that church has ever reached out to me or asked me to come back. They do, however, allow me to purchase items from their bookstore for a profit.

I was thinking about your analogy and had a bit of an epiphany. I think the reason my ex-husband was so ready to believe the lie was that he had so utterly neglected our marriage relationship that it was easy for him to believe that I would be unfaithful. We were married for 18 years, and in that time we had never gone on a "date night." I had never been given a birthday, Christmas, anniversary, or Valentine's gift, and several years he had forgotten my birthday altogether. He never planned anything for Mother's

Day or anniversaries and in general was not present in any of the activities that the children and I shared.

I think the reason we are so willing to believe the lie about God, is that we have so utterly neglected our relationship with Him. We don't know Him or His methods. Add to that the guilt that our religion places on us for making visible mistakes, and it is easy to believe that God will strike us dead if we don't obey the rules.

I have since remarried and my new husband has the arduous task of slowly dismantling my emotional baggage. What a blessing to have a gentle man who understands when a kind word and a small touch make me break down in tears. And his church reaches out to me weekly. This week, they somehow found out that my daughter had graduated from high school. The pastor showed up at our door and asked that the church be allowed to honor her and present her a gift on Sunday—and she has never even been there. The love I feel from that church family was never and still is not present in my own church.

If we are to be known by our love, I fear my church will be sorely underrepresented at the end of time.

What a sad but powerful story and one with incredible insight. Yes, I think the root problem is that we don't know God, and our failure to actually know him, to spend time with him, makes us more vulnerable to accepting lies about him—and lies believed break the circle of love and trust. We must come back to the truth about God and experience the transforming power of his amazing love!

The Power of Love and Truth

There is one power that cannot be broken, and that is the power of love combined with truth. Truth and love combined result in something impenetrable! This is why the Holy Spirit is known as the Spirit of truth and love. This is why at Pentecost the disciples saw two streams of fire—the fire of truth and the fire of love.

Lies cannot defeat understood and experienced truth; fear cannot overcome love founded upon truth! Only those who are partakers of God's nature of truth and love, which is received through the indwelling Spirit of truth and love, are transformed into beings who are unshakable. They are sealed of God, which is the state of being so settled into the truth and love of God in both understanding and experience that they cannot be moved. These are individuals operating at level seven.

Christian de Chergé, a French Catholic monk and the Trappist prior of the Tibhirine monastery in Algeria, knew the difference between imposed rules and God's love. He knew his life, his identity, and his individuality were safe with Christ—even though his body was not. In 1993, with the rise of radical Islam, Father de Chergé knew that his life was in danger. But rather than leave Algeria, he chose to stay and continue his witness to the love of Jesus Christ. On May 24, 1996, he was beheaded by Muslim radicals. Anticipating his death, Father de Chergé had left a testament with his family to be read upon the event of his murder. The testament reads in part:

> If it should happen one day—and it could be today—that I become a victim of the terrorism which now seems ready to encompass all the foreigners living in Algeria, I would like my community, my Church, my family, to remember that my life was given to God and to this country. I ask them to accept that the One Master of all life was not a stranger to this brutal departure. I ask them to pray for me: for how could I be found worthy of such an offering? I ask them to be able to associate such a

death with the many other deaths that were just as violent, but forgotten through indifference and anonymity. . . .

I should like, when the time comes, to have a clear space which would allow me to beg forgiveness of God and of all my fellow human beings, and at the same time to forgive with all my heart the one who would strike me down. . . .

My death, clearly, will appear to justify those who hastily judged me as naïve or idealistic: "Let him tell us now what he thinks of it." But these people must realize that my most avid curiosity will then be satisfied. This is what I shall be able to do, if God wills—immerse my gaze in that of the Father, to contemplate with him his children of Islam just as he sees them, all shining with the glory of Christ, the fruit of his Passion, filled with the Gift of the Spirit, whose secret joy will always be to establish communion and to refashion the likeness, delighting in the differences.

For this life given up, totally mine and totally theirs, I thank God. . . . And you also, the friend of my final moment, who would not be aware of what you were doing. Yes, for you also I wish this "thank you"—and this "adieu"—to commend you to the God whose face I see in yours.

And may we find each other, happy "good thieves," in Paradise, if it pleases God, the Father of us both.[3]

This is love, founded upon truth, that cannot be moved. This is the shape and nature of the heart when God has his way within!

What, then, is God's sovereignty? It is God constantly sustaining the operation of his universe, maintaining the laws on which all reality is built to function, and using his power to heal and fix all deviations from his design—but only and always in harmony with his nature and character of love!

Restraining Power

I would be remiss if I didn't mention one other type of power—restraining power. Restraining power is that force exercised to restrain, restrict, reduce, impede, slow, and/or obstruct injury, pain, suffering, destruction, and evil.

Examples of restraining power include a parent restraining a child running toward the street; the Centers for Disease Control officials implementing a quarantine; mental-health professionals forcibly hospitalizing and medicating a psychotic patient; benevolent societies incarcerating those bent on exploiting others; and God holding back forces of evil to allow his healing plan to be realized.

Refusing to restrain in any of the cases above results in injury, pain, suffering, and damage to the one in need of restraint and often to others as well. A child hit by a car will certainly be injured, but what of the damage to the mind of the driver who had no time to stop? A person infected with Ebola not only needs treatment personally, but what about the suffering of other family members if the disease is transmitted to them? And not just the family, but what of the heart and mind of the one not restrained if their own child should die? Likewise, how much would Andrea Yates have preferred someone restrain her before her untreated postpartum psychosis resulted in her drowning her five children?[4] Not only are innocents harmed when those who commit crimes are not restrained, but also the hearts, minds, and characters of the criminals are warped, hardened, and seared.

Restraining power doesn't change the character of the one restrained. It is the action of an outside intelligence inserting itself into the natural progression of events to overrule the autonomous choices of another human being when the restraining power determines that failure to act would result in unreasonable harm to others or *the one being restrained*. Restraining power uses the least restraint, for the shortest duration necessary, seeking to return the one restrained to full autonomy as soon as possible.

Love uses restraining power. God has used restraining power and continues to do so, but what God cannot do is overwrite the mind and choices of his children, which would result in the destruction of individuality. The only way God can heal a person, restore a mind, and reconstruct a heart is with the voluntary cooperation of that person. We must actively choose to cooperate with God, to agree with him. We must "be fully convinced in [our] own mind" (Rom. 14:5) in order to be transformed. This is the only way that love and truth can heal and restore. Yet, because restraining power cannot transform the heart, there comes a time when restraining power lets go. Parents who restrain rebellious children know that at a certain age parental restraint must end. The Bible speaks of a time when God lets go of his restraint, when there is no more that he can do (Rev. 7:1–3; 22:11).

There is a terrible tension in Christianity, the tension between rules and love, the tension between saving institutions or saving souls, as we'll see in the next chapter.

KEY POINTS FROM CHAPTER 11

- As we move past the way sinful humans operate, and see God through the lens of Jesus, we understand love never imposes or coerces; love wins the heart and love leaves free.

- We cannot win God's causes by using earthly methods.
- If God's kingdom were based on imposed law, then his followers would use coercive tactics, tactics of might and power. But God's kingdom is the kingdom of love, and love cannot be achieved by threat, intimidation, coercion, or command.
- God is sovereign, and his laws rule supreme over all creation. The confusion arises when we replace God's design laws with human imposed-law constructs, and instead of God's sovereignty being clearly seen we obstruct it.
- Coercive power does not achieve transformed people who are reliable and trustworthy. Coercive power cannot win people to love and trust.
- The only power that achieves God's goal of healing sinners, the only power that cannot be broken, is the power of love and truth combined.
- God's sovereignty is his constant sustaining of the operation of his universe, maintaining the laws on which all reality is built to function, and using his power to heal and fix all deviations from his design—but only and always in harmony with his nature and character of love.

12

Law or Love in the Real World

> Whenever you did this for one of the least important of these members of my family, you did it for me!
>
> Jesus Christ

On October 7, 1998, twenty-one-year-old Matthew Wayne Shepherd, a gay man and a student at the University of Wyoming, met Aaron McKinney and Russell Henderson in a bar. Later, McKinney's and Henderson's girlfriends would testify that the two men went to the bar looking for a homosexual to beat up. They pretended to befriend Shepherd and offered him a ride home. Instead, they robbed, pistol-whipped, and tied him to a fence post in a desolate area, where he was found eighteen hours later by a cyclist. He was unconscious and had suffered a fractured skull, severe brain stem damage, and multiple lacerations to his head. His injuries were too severe to operate, and he died on October 12, 1998.

McKinney and Henderson were arrested and found with Shepherd's wallet and the bloody gun. Henderson pleaded guilty and agreed to testify against McKinney to avoid the death penalty. McKinney was found guilty, and as the jury began deliberating the death penalty, Shepherd's parents intervened to save McKinney's life and brokered a deal for him to receive two consecutive life sentences.

At Matthew Shepherd's funeral, the Westboro Baptist Church of Kansas picketed with signs that read: "Matt Shepherd rots in hell," "God hates fags," and "AIDS kills fags dead."

What is a healthy Christian understanding of homosexuality? Do you think those so-called Christians who picketed Shepherd's funeral accurately represented Jesus? Is homosexuality a "sin" that needs to be punished?

As we have seen in previous chapters, level four and below methods of determining right and wrong require little to no thinking. Behaviors are judged based on some external authority or rule without thought and without consideration for others. Level five and above thinkers, however, are motivated by love for others, a genuine desire to understand what is actually wrong and why, and a desire to live in harmony with God's design and fulfill his purposes.

Level four and below thinkers have little tolerance for investigation, thinking, or reasoning and prefer a simple explanation with global application and no exceptions. Exceptions require thinking and cause tension; they have not developed the capacity to tolerate such tension. Level five and above thinkers realize cookie-cutter rules don't explain the complexity of human circumstances and seek answers that work for all individuals in harmony with God's nature and design.

Homosexuality and how the Christian church deals with it have caused great conflict in many Christian groups. Could much of this fracturing be a result of persons operating at different levels of moral development? Let's examine the question of homosexuality and the church's response to it.

God designed human beings in Eden as male and female and human marriage as a relationship between one male and one female in a life partnership of genuine trust, love, affection, self-sacrifice, and service. But when humankind sinned, various defects entered the human condition. As Paul states in Romans 8, all nature groans under the weight of sin (vv. 20–22). Because nature is out of harmony with God and his unveiled sustaining presence, many deviations have occurred throughout the natural world. Thorns, thistles, and poisonous plants were not created in Eden but are now present because sin altered God's design. Yet the plants themselves are not committing sin or considered "sinful." Likewise, all congenital malformations are a result of sin, yet children born with cardiac defects, spina bifida, or microcephaly are not condemned because of such conditions. Gene defects that increase the risk of breast cancer, Alzheimer's disease, hypercholesterolemia, and every such problem are a result of sin but in themselves are not acts of sin. Every single human being is born with a biology that is described in Scripture as mortal and corruptible, but the saved will one day be changed to immortal and incorruptible (1 Cor. 15:53–54).

Everything that deviates from God's original design is a result of sin and in some way misrepresents God. However, not everything that deviates from God's original design is sin. For instance, God designed Adam and Eve to be "fruitful and multiply" (Gen. 1:28 NLT). Today, some people are born sterile and are incapable of having children. This is a deviation from God's design, which has resulted because of sin in the world, and fails to represent God as accurately as he intended (God can create life but such individuals cannot procreate life), yet such a deviation in itself is not sin. Those born sterile are not told by their church they cannot be saved unless they get some type of therapy to fix them. We all recognize that such defects are a result of sin but not sin—because sin is not biological, it is characterological.

The disciples asked Jesus, "'Rabbi, who sinned, this man or his parents, that he was born blind?' 'Neither this man nor his parents sinned,' said Jesus, 'but this happened so that the works of God might be displayed in him'" (John 9:2–3). Despite biological defects, God's plan works to transform hearts and heal minds. And God's power to transform hearts is no less today than when Christ walked upon the earth.

Today, because of sin damaging God's creation, there are many individuals born with biological defects not of their choosing. The question is, what is sin and what is merely a result of sin? To explore this difference, we need to understand something about normal human development.

Androgen Insensitivity Syndrome

Maybe you heard the worldwide news coverage a few years ago of Caster Semenya. She is the South African athlete who won gold at the world track competition. After her win, however, it was discovered she has a disorder, unbeknownst to her, called Androgen insensitivity syndrome (AIS). What this means is she is genetically XY (male) yet was born a healthy female and was raised as a female her entire life. How did this happen?

Women have two X chromosomes (XX) and men have an X and a Y (XY). During reproduction, women can only donate an X chromosome because that is all they have. Men donate either an X or a Y chromosome. If a Y chromosome is donated, the embryo will normally develop testes and become a male child. In normal embryological development, all fetuses start out female and require masculinization to become male.

When the Y chromosome is present, the testes develop, and they produce two hormones: antimullerian hormone (AMH), which prevents the vagina and uterus from developing, and testosterone, which normally causes the labia to become the scrotum, the clitoris to become the penis, and the brain to masculinize (change from female to male).

But in order for testosterone to have its masculinizing effect, there must be a receptor that "sees" the testosterone and responds to it. This receptor is coded for on the X chromosome. The problem with AIS is that the gene that codes for the testosterone receptor is defective, so that even though there are testes producing the proper hormones, there are no receptors to see the testosterone, so the XY baby is born a healthy baby "girl," but without a full vagina or uterus. The AIS infant is given a female birth certificate and raised her entire life as a female. Such individuals typically are identified in adolescence when they fail to have menstrual cycles. Physicians will surgically extend the vagina, remove the testicles so they don't become cancerous, and place the girl on estrogen.

All governments of the world recognize the right of these women to marry men. Their brains are female as they are incapable of responding to testosterone. Yet because of AMH, these women do not have a uterus or full vagina and so are sterile. This is clearly a deviation from God's design that results from sin in the world, yet itself is not sin.

There is another condition called Swyer syndrome. In this syndrome, no gonads form at all. Therefore, an XY (male) embryo doesn't have testes to produce either AMH or testosterone, so these babies are born healthy (XY) baby girls with a vagina, uterus, and fallopian tubes but no ovaries. They are genetic males yet are physical females. These individuals are sterile as they have no ovaries or testes, yet because they have a uterus they can become pregnant by implantation of a donated embryo. At least four cases have occurred in which such (XY) women have received donated embryos, become pregnant, and given birth to healthy babies. All governments recognize the legal right of such individuals to marry men.

There are numerous biological conditions such as these that have altered God's original design and are a result of sin in the world but in themselves are not sin, just as being born blind is not sin. These conditions include:

- 5-alpha reductase deficiency
- Aphallia
- Clitoromegaly
- Congenital adrenal hyperplasia
- Gonadal dysgenesis
- Kallmann syndrome
- Klinefelter syndrome
- Micropenis
- Ovo-testes
- Progestin induced virilisation

- Turner syndrome
- Cryptorchidism
- 17-beta-hydroxysteriod dehydrogenase deficiency
- Mosaicism

According to the intersex society of North America, 1–2 percent of live births have some form of sexual ambiguity, and 0.1–0.2 percent of live births have defects severe enough to require medical intervention.[1]

Jane

And if these biological defects are not confusing enough, consider the case of the patient known as Jane. In 1998, Jane, a fifty-two-year-old woman, was upset because tests had just revealed something about two of her three sons that most people would never believe. Genetic testing showed that even though she conceived all her children through natural means with her own husband who is genetically proven to be their father, and gave birth to all three, she was not their mother. What was going on?

Doctors were stumped for months, repeat testing was done, and the findings were put out in medical circles to see if anyone had an explanation. And then a breakthrough came when Jane's siblings were tested. The tests revealed that two of her sons shared markers with Jane's brother, supporting that her sons were related to her. At that point, doctors decided to test tissue from different parts of Jane's body, her thyroid, mouth, and hair. What they discovered is that Jane had cells from two different people! She is what is known as a chimera.

When Jane's mother conceived, two eggs were fertilized, which normally would have resulted in fraternal twin girls. But in early embryonic life, these two fertilized eggs merged into one. As a result, parts of Jane's body have her cells while other parts of her body have cells from her fraternal twin sister.[2]

Human chimeras are thought to be rare, but no definitive data really exists. While most are same-sex chimeras, there have been cases of male/female chimeras, a situation in which fraternal twin brother and sister merged into one person. What if such a person's brain was from the brother but the reproductive organs were from the sister? Who sinned that such a child was born?

Human Sexuality

While I have heard conservative pastors say, "Every person on earth is either male or female," the scientific facts would disagree. The issue of human sexuality isn't as neatly black and white as some individuals would like it to be.

So what determines one's sexuality?

- Chromosomes?
- Hormones?
- Genitalia?
- Mental orientation, identity, individuality?
- Behavior?

What do the science and the various factors impacting sexuality mean for our understanding of homosexuality?

The defects discussed above are a result of sin damaging creation, but that does not mean they are active sin. "People look at the outward appearance, but the LORD looks at the heart"

(1 Sam. 16:7). It is not our place to judge others. We don't know their circumstances (Matt. 7:1–2).

In addition to specific chromosomal and genetic makeup, we now have identified epigenetic factors that contribute to human sexuality. Epigenetics are the chemical markers that sit above the actual genes giving instructions to the genes on how they should be expressed.

In embryological development, the human brain starts out female but will masculinize under the influence of testosterone. Epigenetic markers can be passed from parent to child, which means not only are genes passed along but also instructions on how those genes are to be expressed. Scientists now believe epigenetics are involved in sexualization of the human brain. Epigenetic markers normally protect female brains from the masculinizing effects of testosterone while different markers make male brains more sensitive.

If something goes wrong and the epigenetic markers that protected a mother's brain from testosterone are not properly cleared and she passes those markers on to her son, this could contribute to a male child with a feminized brain. Conversely, if a mother's epigenetic markers that protected her brain from masculinization are cleared and not passed on to her daughter, this could contribute to a female child with a masculinized brain. And because there are billions of brain cells, each with its own DNA and epigenetic markers within, there can be varying degrees of penetrance. This means that in addition to homosexual orientation, we can have effeminate heterosexual males and tomboy heterosexual females.[3]

But this still isn't the entire story, because not only is our sexuality affected by our genetics and epigenetics, it is also affected by our environment.

Tara

Tara was desperate when she first came to see me, unable to sleep and experiencing panic episodes, confusion, and intrusive nightmares. She was in her early thirties, married to her only husband, and had one five-year-old daughter. Yet during her initial presentation, she described herself as bisexual. She told me she thought of herself as lesbian until her early twenties, and then realized she was bisexual.

When I took her history, she disclosed that her father sexually molested her from her earliest memories. But she described the molestation not as coercive, violent, frightening, or abusive but as seductive, loving, and romantic. She described how her father treated her like a little princess and actually romanticized their relationship with gifts, trips, presents, and sexual activity, treating his daughter like a wife in many ways.

This treatment by her father during her childhood caused her mind to develop significant confusion regarding healthy sexuality and intimacy. Where children are to have love and trust in their parents without sexual arousal, Tara had these desires merged.

She described how when she went to a Christian boarding school at the age of fourteen, she had her first lesbian relationship with her roommate. This repeated itself with several more female roommates in high school and college. In her mind, when you love someone you have sex with them. So in her early adolescence she considered herself lesbian.

However, in college she became friends with some men, came to love them, began having sexual relations with them, and changed her view of herself to bisexual, eventually marrying a man and having a family. In our therapy I never directly addressed her sexual orientation. Instead, we focused on her identity as a person: separation, individuation, intimacy, and resolving trauma issues from childhood.

Because of her father's treatment and her merged and confused desire for love, trust, and sexuality, whenever Tara came to love and trust someone, she had sexual arousal and typically sexual relations with that person. After about a year into therapy, she said, "Dr. Jennings, I have never been intimate with someone I didn't have sex with." To which I responded, "What about us?" Therapy, opening one's self, heart, mind, soul, fears, and desires to a therapist, is a very intimate experience, though we always maintain healthy professional boundaries.

Her eyes popped open in surprise, and she sat back in reflection for several minutes after my comment. When she came in the following week, she said, "Dr. Jennings, I'm not lesbian. I'm not bisexual. I'm heterosexual." We never discussed her sexual orientation; we simply focused on healing the wounds inflicted in her early childhood, which allowed her true self to emerge. While I am grateful that people such as Tara can find healing, naive individuals may hear testimony from persons like Tara, describing how they have been "delivered" from the homosexual lifestyle, and falsely conclude that all homosexuals, if they would only get into therapy, could be changed. Such a conclusion is false.

The point of all this evidence is that sexuality is complex. Those on the liberal left want every case of homosexuality to be considered genetically preprogrammed, and those on the religious right want every case to be either a sinful choice or a result of some traumatic experience that can be resolved by therapy. Both extremes fail to present an honest and helpful view of this complex situation.

The Bible and Homosexuality

With these considerations in mind, we can now examine Scripture and come to a mature understanding of this difficult topic. In Romans 1, Paul describes the decadence of the human condition when the truth about God is rejected. There were those who didn't think it worthwhile to retain the knowledge of God. They exchanged the truth of God for a lie and preferred images made with their own hands to the knowledge of God. "Because of this, God gave them over to shameful lusts. Even their women exchanged natural relations for unnatural ones. In the same way the men also abandoned natural relations with women and were inflamed with lust for one another" (Rom. 1:26–27).

Many Christians have used this passage to condemn homosexuals in our society and throughout history. But what Paul actually condemns in Romans 1 is false worship—rejecting the truth of God and preferring a lie, which *results* in a variety of destructive consequences, including *exchanging* natural relations for unnatural ones. But, can a person *exchange* something they don't possess? Can a person *exchange* a pair of white shoes for black ones, if they don't actually possess a pair of white shoes? Can a person *exchange* natural relations if they don't currently *possess* natural desires?

Paul in Romans is not speaking of people with biological aberrations, who make up the vast majority of homosexuals in today's society, but of those individuals with natural heterosexual desires who through destructive worship practices exchange them for homosexual relationships. What other evidence is there to support this conclusion?

Throughout recorded history, what we call homosexuality has been documented to be about 1 to 3 percent of the population, consistent with defective biologic mechanics as described above. However, when one looks at the city of Sodom the Bible states, "*All* the men from every part of the city of Sodom—both young and old—surrounded the house" (Gen. 19:4). One hundred percent of the men turned out demanding to sexually abuse the visitors to Lot's home. This is *not* what we call homosexuality today; this is something entirely different. This is the debasing of normal heterosexual desire from persistent rejection of God and indulgence of self. These men of Sodom *exchanged* their normal heterosexual desires for lust for each other, and became so selfish that they would abuse visitors rather than show hospitality. Thus, Ezekiel documents the real sin of Sodom: "Now this was the sin of your sister Sodom: She and her daughters were arrogant, overfed and unconcerned; they did not help the poor and needy. They were haughty and did detestable things before me" (Ezek. 16:49–50).

Having rejected God, they rejected love. They rejected compassion and became self-indulgent, lust-filled exploiters of others. This is true sodomy. Does anyone really believe that if the angels who came to visit Lot had come in the form of women instead of men, and *all* the men of the city had turned out demanding to rape them, God would have said, "Well done, you heterosexual men"?

I would suggest that the so-called Christians from the Westboro Baptist Church of Kansas who cruelly picketed Matt Shepherd's funeral are the true modern-day Sodomites! This is the religion of imposed law. This is the religion of level four and below thinkers. This is what happens when the truth of God's character of love is exchanged for a lie!

The liberal principles of our modern society, which seek to protect employees from exploitation and abuse from profit-seeking greed, have done exactly what the Bible has done—written warnings to protect. The US Department of Labor has the following rule for employers regarding eye protection for welders:

> The employer shall ensure that each affected employee uses equipment with filter lenses that have a shade number appropriate for the work being performed for protection from injurious light radiation.[4]

We, as a society, prohibit, condemn, and even criminalize actions that willingly and knowingly cause blindness—yet we do not criminalize the blind, especially those who were born blind. And we never tell a person born blind, "We know you did nothing wrong to be born this way, yet we expect you to live like you can see."

Many Christians are confused when dealing with homosexuality because they view it through imposed law rather than design law. They misread the Bible's guidance, which is given to protect and to deter people from activities that will cause harm. They know the Bible condemns something, but they misunderstand what.

What does the Bible condemn? It condemns purposeful actions that damage and corrupt God's design. It would be like a person with good eyesight poking hot irons in their eyes or welding without eye protection. Such acts that lead to blindness are to be condemned. But a child born blind is not to be condemned! The Bible condemns false worship, fertility cults, pornography, and viewing, watching, or engaging in behaviors that would destroy love in a person's character such that a Christian would treat other human beings with cruelty rather than the love of Jesus.

Modern-Day Lepers

Two thousand years ago, persons with a skin disease of any kind—vitiligo, psoriasis, eczema, as well as leprosy—were all castigated as lepers. They not only had the biological sickness with which to contend, they were also shunned by their community and condemned by the religious authorities. This is what we have done to homosexuals today!

As Christians we are called to live like Christ, to love like he loves, and how did he treat lepers? How did he treat a woman who was caught in the very act of undeniable sexual sin? He said, "Neither do I condemn you" (John 8:11).

It is not our responsibility to convict another person of sin; that is the job of the Holy Spirit. Our job is to reveal Christ so clearly and fully that people are drawn to him. He will change what needs to be changed in each person's heart. He will convict of sin that needs to be repented of; he will transform people into his likeness. Christians operating at level four and below, with their focus on rules, concern with behavior, and protection of the institution, have placed untold barriers between struggling people and God.

God is waiting for a mature Bride, people who have grown up to love like he loves.

KEY POINTS FROM CHAPTER 12

- Because nature is out of harmony with God and his sustaining presence, many deviations to his original design have occurred throughout the natural world—thorns, thistles, weeds, sickness, disease, congenital defects, and so on.

- Everything that deviates from God's original design is a *result of* sin and in some way misrepresents God. However, not everything that deviates from God's original design *is* sin.
- The issue of human sexuality isn't as neatly black and white as some individuals would like it to be.
- Despite biological defects, God's plan works to transform hearts and heal minds.

13

God's Action in the Old Testament

Love or Law?

Legalism says God will love us if we change. The gospel says God will change us because He loves us.

Tullian Tchividjian, former pastor

The crowds were overwhelming. The exhibit hall was enormous. We could barely keep up with the demand for our DVDs, books, study guides, pens, and cards. Tens of thousands of people swarmed our ministry booth to get the free materials we were offering. People from over seventy countries around the world were at the event, and multiple times a day our hearts were thrilled as someone came to us in tears and told how our ministry had changed their lives. Frequently, people told us that they had believed in God their entire lives, but now they were no longer afraid of him, now they loved and trusted him! And for the first time they had real peace. Others told us how the contradictions in their belief system were finally gone and the Bible now made sense—what a relief. During the ten-day event, our ministry gave away twenty-five thousand books, thirty thousand DVDs, and fifteen thousand Bible study guides. What a joy it was to give freely what God had given to us.

But one day, in the middle of the event, a person came up to me with a concerned look, pulled me aside, and said, "There is a man going through the convention passing out business cards telling people 'Dr. Jennings teaches heresy. Learn the truth at this website.'" And then the man smiled and said, "So I had to come over right away and see what it is you are teaching." I happily gave him a copy of all our materials. The following day, I ran into the gentleman who was misrepresenting me and asked about his concerns.

He looked me straight in the eye and with great seriousness asked, "Do you believe that when we confess our sins and ask God to forgive us, our sins are removed from the record books in heaven?"

I smiled and replied, "God isn't in the business of erasing history. God wants to remove sin from the hearts, minds, and characters of his children. When we confess and invite God into our hearts, the Holy Spirit comes in and blots sinfulness out of our characters. We get new hearts and right spirits. We become partakers of the divine nature, and the books in heaven register that change. But no history is erased."

His eyes narrowed and he said, "That's what I thought. You deny the Bible."

As I have presented God and his design law of love around the world, the primary obstacle I have encountered is preconceived ideas. Persons who already hold a view of God as dictator-like have formed an entire system of belief—definitions of words, explanations of Bible stories—all filtered through and in harmony with the imposed-law construct. With this system of thinking in place, the view of God as love and his law as design protocols causes many to feel uncomfortable, fearful, and even insecure. They often respond with concerns that such an approach is not being true to Scripture or is denying evidence in Scripture.

What is actually happening is that the picture of God I present is at odds with *their understanding* of Scripture, not with Scripture itself. In other words, they have classified and codified the Bible stories into categories that support the imposed-law dictator view of God and haven't yet seen how these same stories are better understood through design law. Therefore, in this chapter we will examine some of the stories of Scripture that are commonly used to promote the dictator view of God and demonstrate that, in reality, they reveal a God who is love.

One of the first stories cited as proof that God uses divine power to inflict punishment for sin is found in Genesis 3. The punishing-God adherents claim that because of sin God cursed the ground and inflicted the death penalty upon Adam. When you read Genesis 3:17–19, what do you think?

> Cursed is the ground because of you; through painful toil you will eat of it all the days of your life. It will produce thorns and thistles for you, and you will eat the plants of the field. By the sweat of your brow you will eat your food until you return to the ground, since from it you were taken; for dust you are and to dust you will return.

Level one through four thinkers conclude: God has rules. Those rules were broken. Therefore, God had to inflict punishment so that justice was served. Level five through seven thinkers understand a larger reality. They understand that God's laws are design parameters—the protocols on which nature operates. And when Adam sinned, nature became infected with an antagonistic principle along with an enemy that was now afoot infecting God's creation with deviations (mutations) from his design (Matt. 13:28). The mature include in their understanding of Genesis what Paul wrote in Romans, that all nature groans under the weight of sin (8:22). Thus, design-law adherents realize God is not inflicting punishment but accurately diagnosing and announcing reality—what Adam's actions have naturally resulted in—that nature will now bring forth thorns, thistles, and weeds, and it will be harder to produce the desired crop. And that Adam, out of harmony with God's design for life, disconnected from God's full life-giving presence, will slowly deteriorate and die.

What about Genesis 3:16; how do you understand it? "Your desire will be for your husband, and he will rule over you." The immature think God is inflicting this upon women and wrongly conclude it is God's desire or will for wives to be subjugated to the authoritarian rule of their husbands. But the mature realize what naturally happens when love is replaced by selfishness in the heart—the strong dominate the weak and the weak long to be protected by the strong! Again, God is *not* using power to inflict an outcome but *is* accurately diagnosing the condition of humanity and announcing what will now transpire as a result of their sin-infected hearts.

Throughout the entire history of humankind as recorded in Scripture, God, who is love, has been working through his methods of love, truth, and freedom to heal and restore, while the evil one has been working to infect our minds with false interpretations of God's actions, primarily the idea that God is punishing people for sin.

Some might argue that this presents only part of the picture, that I am leaving out other examples when imposed rules were broken and punishments were inflicted, such as when Moses struck the rock and was denied entry into the promised land.

But Moses didn't simply break a rule; Moses, for a brief moment, lost trust in God and became angry, allowing selfishness to take control. This is a violation of design law, of how God constructed the human mind to operate. This act not only misrepresented God to the people but was also damaging to the heart, mind, and character of Moses. God, in love, intervened therapeutically and put Moses in a position where he had to *choose*—trust God or resist God and do what self wants. We know this was a struggle for Moses, but it was in this struggle with his own selfish desires that Moses finally experienced complete victory over selfishness and was fitted for heaven! And he was then taken to the true promised land by Jesus himself!

King David

Consider the lessons from the life of King David. Early in his life, he experienced incredible victories over a lion and in single combat with the giant Goliath. Yet later, he suffered crushing defeat with Bathsheba and Uriah. How could David have such singular victories with the lion and Goliath only to fail so horribly with Bathsheba?

Was the defect in David's character that was revealed in his actions with Bathsheba not present within him when he faced the lion and Goliath? Or was that defect there, in his heart, at those earlier times in his life but simply not yet fully exposed and therefore not yet removed? What was the most significant difference about the situations David faced with the lion and Goliath when compared to Bathsheba?

Would objective reality with the lion and Goliath provide David with confidence in his own human ability to defeat them, or were both those situations beyond David's innate ability to handle? Were they the types of situations that would almost automatically cause David to look outside of himself for help, to seek another power to overcome, to not trust in himself and thus turn to God? In those situations David did indeed trust in God and not in his own strength.

Throughout much of David's life, he found himself in situations when his own human strength was not sufficient for the task—not only with Goliath and the lion but also a bear, years of running from Saul, and in combat with enemies. Each of these situations instinctively caused him to reach out to God for help. As the old saying goes, "There are no atheists in foxholes."

But when David saw Bathsheba bathing below his balcony, he was in a different place. David was now king. He was in a position of authority, power, apparent control, safety, security, and wealth. He was a beloved and popular ruler. Perhaps David thought he could handle it. He didn't need God for this. This situation was in his ability to manage. (This is likely the reason God instructed him not to take a census, because David would be tempted to believe his strength was in his spearmen, infantry, bowmen, and cavalry and forget his true strength had always been in God.) But this is when David's hold on God collapsed. This is when selfishness took control of David's heart.

Did the selfishness manifested in David when he took Bathsheba suddenly originate at this point in his life for the first time? Or was this selfishness always within David, but it wasn't until this time, when trials, challenges, and tribulations seemed in the past, that David was most vulnerable to its corrupting influence breaking out into the open?

What was necessary for David to be saved? To be reborn, to die to self, to have a new heart and right spirit re-created within—to be healed in the inner man! When do you think this ultimate conversion experience happened for David? Wasn't it after his failure with Bathsheba, after Nathan confronted him?

It was then that David finally understood that he had a terminal condition of the heart with which he was born and that he could not change. He needed God to heal and transform him from within. His action with Bathsheba wasn't the problem, it was the manifestation, the outward symptom of a problem deep within that, if not removed, would ultimately destroy him. When David realizes his true condition, he doesn't seek a legal solution. He doesn't perform rituals. He finally understands reality and writes Psalm 51. Reading this psalm through the lens of design law, David's amazing wisdom comes into stunning clarity.

> [1]Have mercy on me, O God, according to your unfailing love;
> according to your great compassion blot out my transgressions.

From where do you think David wants his sin blotted out—recorded history or his heart, mind, and character?

> [2]Wash away all my iniquity and cleanse me from my sin.

He realizes something is wrong within his heart that needs purifying.

³For I know my transgressions, and my sin is always before me.

⁴Against you, you only, have I sinned and done what is evil in your sight; so you are right in your verdict and justified when you judge.

He acknowledges his condition is terminal and that he cannot run from it; no matter where he goes he carries his sinful self there. God's diagnosis of his terminal condition is perfectly accurate.

⁵Surely I was sinful at birth, sinful from the time my mother conceived me.

He realizes this problem has been within him his entire life. He was born this way, infected with fear and selfishness.

⁶Yet you desired faithfulness even in the womb; you taught me wisdom in that secret place.

He understands that what God wants is to heal what is broken in his heart and mind.

⁷Cleanse me with hyssop, and I will be clean; wash me, and I will be whiter than snow.

He acknowledges that only God has the healing solution. Only the Creator can re-create him back to God's original intent.

⁸Let me hear joy and gladness; let the bones you have crushed rejoice.

⁹Hide your face from my sins and blot out all my iniquity.

He is asking to be renewed, to have the crushing guilt and shame taken out of his heart, to be glad again, and to have fear and selfishness blotted out of his character so that he can one day see God face-to-face.

> [10]Create in me a pure heart, O God, and renew a steadfast spirit within me.

He again acknowledges his need and desire for God to heal his heart, change his motives, and renew his mind so that they operate upon other-centered love.

> [11]Do not cast me from your presence or take your Holy Spirit from me.

He acknowledges God's presence is where he wants to be, and only the Holy Spirit can fix what is broken inside and enable him to stand in God's presence.

> [12]Restore to me the joy of your salvation and grant me a willing spirit, to sustain me.

He asks for the joy of healing and strength to stay compliant with God's treatment plan.

> [13]Then I will teach transgressors your ways, so that sinners will turn back to you.

He acknowledges the responsibility and privilege to share God's remedy with others dying of the same condition.

> [14]Deliver me from the guilt of bloodshed, O God, you who are God my Savior, and my tongue will sing of your righteousness.

He specifically requests to have his heart healed from murder, from willingness to kill another child of God, and knows such freedom results in rejoicing and praise.

¹⁵Open my lips, Lord, and my mouth will declare your praise.

He acknowledges that his natural heart cannot even praise God, but all praise is the outflow of God's healing love transforming him.

¹⁶You do not delight in sacrifice, or I would bring it; you do not take pleasure in burnt offerings.

He recognizes that rituals are meaningless, and God doesn't want them.

¹⁷My sacrifice, O God, is a broken spirit; a broken and contrite heart you, God, will not despise.

He realizes God wants the healing and restoration of his children back into harmony with him—his design of love—his protocols of life.

¹⁸May it please you to prosper Zion, to build up the walls of Jerusalem.

He asks God to make his helpers effective in revealing the truth and distributing the remedy to the world.

¹⁹Then you will delight in the sacrifices of the righteous, in burnt offerings offered whole; then bulls will be offered on your altar.

He understands that if Israel rightly represents God, then the rituals will be effective teaching tools to help people open their hearts and minds to experience the genuine remedy—the Lamb of God who takes away the sin of the world.

All through Scripture the message is the same. Humankind is infected with fear and selfishness (sin), which is deviant from

God's design for life and is a terminal condition (dead in trespasses and sin). God is working through Christ to heal each person, restoring in them God's heart of love! This is what God is seeking to achieve in each of us—complete transformation of heart.

The Question Legal Theologies Cannot Answer

Design law, love in the heart, heals and removes confusion and misunderstanding, but imposed law injures and obscures. If you have friends stuck in imposed-law constructs, ask them this question: When did sexual relations between David and Bathsheba no longer constitute sin for David? This question has no right answer for those operating at level four and below. Every answer they provide is flawed. The following are typical level four answers:

- When he repented. But isn't repentance turning away from one's sinful behavior? Did David turn away from Bathsheba or to her?
- When God legally forgave and pardoned. Does that mean if a person today has a sin problem, for example, adultery or pornography, that once they ask God for forgiveness they can continue with ongoing adultery or pornography and it is no longer sin?
- When David married her. Is God's law superseded by human culture and tradition? Is polygamy not a violation of God's law even when local customs accept it? If today a Christian moved to a country where polygamy is legal, would it be acceptable to have more than one wife? Or would it still violate God's law to do so?

Sinful humanity (and level four thinking) looks on the outward appearance, but God looks on the heart (1 Sam. 16:7). The issue is not primarily the behavior but the motivation of the heart. The relationship between David and Bathsheba was sinful when it was motivated by selfishness in the heart. It was selfishness that caused David to commit adultery. It was selfishness that caused David to murder Uriah—and all of this was sinful.

However, after David was confronted by Nathan, he had a true change of heart motive. He died to self, love replaced selfishness in his heart, and he wrote Psalm 51. With a heart that genuinely loved others more than self, David's motivation was no longer to exploit Bathsheba for his own pleasure but instead to heal and restore to her what his selfishness had taken from her. And what had he taken from her? By his adultery and the murder of her husband, David had taken her name, reputation, station, livelihood, property, and home, and she likely would have ended up homeless and perhaps a prostitute. David had also taken away the one who loved and cherished her, the one who adored her and poured love into her life. The only way, in that society, that David could restore to her what he had taken was to marry her and genuinely love her.

This is real repentance, not merely turning away from a behavior but turning away from the selfishness in the heart and living a life of love. The penal theologies, based on level four thinking and focused on the bad deed, would have added injury to injury by demanding that David turn his back on Bathsheba and abandon her to a devastated life. But love heals, love restores.

Those at level four also misunderstand the death of the child from David and Bathsheba's first pregnancy. The imposed-law view alleges this story is another example of God punishing sin—God killing the infant to punish David. Not so! We must remember Israel at that time was functioning in the role of God's actors to display God's plan to heal and restore from sin (1 Cor. 4:9; see chap. 10 above). David, as king, was on center stage. The eyes of the world have been reviewing his life for millennia. The child that failed to survive (who was born with some condition that was not consistent with life, some congenital defect that caused death) was the product of selfishness. This is an exact object lesson: selfishness does not bring life; selfishness violates God's design for life and results in death. However, when love rules in the heart, then life, health, and wisdom occur. After David's heart was transformed, he and Bathsheba had a child born of love—Solomon—blessed with the wisdom of God!

The Face-Off

In Scripture, whenever imposed law–keeping faced off with design law, God went with design law: Jesus said, "Have you never read what David did when he and his companions were hungry and in need? In the days of Abiathar the high priest, he entered the house of God and ate the consecrated bread, which is lawful only for priests to eat. And he also gave some to his companions" (Mark 2:25–26). Jesus points out that the laws of health and the law of love (David caring for the welfare of his men) were what mattered, not keeping imposed rules that were merely theater to teach the true reality of design law.

Jesus heals a man on the Sabbath and instructs him to carry his bed home. The Jews immediately accuse Jesus of being a lawbreaker (John 5:8–10). The Jews wanted to inflict punishment for breaking rules; Jesus focused on design law, healing the physical and spiritual brokenness in the paralyzed man.

When a woman was caught in adultery and dragged before Christ, the religious leaders focused on broken rules and wanted to inflict punishment. Jesus focused on design law, on reaching this daughter of God with his healing love! When he said, "Neither do I condemn you. . . . Go now and leave your life of sin" (John 8:11), he was saying, "I know where you just were. And had you not been caught and brought before me, you would have snuck home with your head hung low, burdened with guilt and shame because you were choosing to act outside of my design for relationships, and such behavior is damaging to you. I don't need to condemn you because your actions are inherently destructive to you. Go now and live in harmony with my design for life!"

This is the same all through Scripture. Ever since Adam chose to deviate from God's design and change his own nature, human beings have been born in sin, born with a terminal condition, from which God has been working to save and to heal. All the while, Satan has been working to blind us to this fact and get us to accept the lie that the problem is not in our condition but is instead a legal problem based on a false law construct.

A Corrupt Gospel

What is the power of God that enables us to stand firm? "I am not ashamed of the gospel, because it is the *power* of God that brings salvation to everyone who believes" (Rom. 1:16).

What is the gospel (good news) and its power that heals and saves? The answer often given was presented in a sermon in a church near my home recently, and it goes like this:

Jesus died on Calvary. Here's a question: "What did it do for God?" It is called, in theological terms, the "objective" side of the atonement. What did it do for God? God was involved. The Bible says, "God was in Christ reconciling the world unto himself." So, what did it do for God? There was a legal issue. Man had broken the law, the punishment was death. How is it God can preserve his law, preserve his righteousness, preserve his integrity, and take care of man at the same time? The cross has an objective side—what God did, what God accomplished—it's called by theologians the "forensic" side, forensic meaning legal. There was a legal issue and God solved it with the cross. . . . What did the cross do for God? Well, it settled the legal problem. It gave mankind the opportunity to be right with Him.[1]

Good news? Really? This is level four thinking: God is angry his law was broken, and he needs a legal payment to keep him from using infinite power to torture and kill us. I want to suggest that, expressed in this way, it is not good news at all but a corruption based on a false law construct. In reality, it is quite bad news because it would mean that God is coercive, not loving, a being from whom we must be protected.

Would it be good news to spend eternity with God if God is the type of being Satan alleges him to be? Would you be happy to spend eternity with an all-powerful deity who is the *source* of eternal pain, suffering, and death, and who burns with anger and rage, except for his Son who stands beside him to pay him off with his blood?

This false gospel leads directly to the distortion of many beautiful godly illustrations. Rather than seeing God as our eternal Friend who uses all the resources of heaven to heal and save, we instead deform Christian theology into a system of mental constructs that function to separate us from God rather than reconcile us to him. Consider how the following doctrines are often taught throughout Christianity and ask functionally what they are doing. How many are operating to, in some way, protect or hide us from God?

- *Covered by the robe of righteousness*: Is this metaphor taught as the removal of sinfulness from the heart of the sinner and re-creation of Christlikeness within so that we actually "become the righteousness of God" (2 Cor. 5:21) (design law), or is it a covering that obscures the Father's ability to see our sin and thus functions to protect us from the Father (imposed law)?

- *Jesus as our advocate with the Father*: Is this metaphor taught as Jesus, *along with* the Father, working to oppose evil and sin for our healing and restoration (Rom. 8:28–34) (design law), or is Jesus legally representing us as a lawyer *to* the heavenly magistrate arguing his merits/sacrifice to protect us from the inflicted punishment the heavenly judge would otherwise mete out (imposed law)?

- *Jesus our intercessor*: Is this illustration taught as Jesus being the Father's envoy, representative, ambassador *to* us to lead us back into unity with the Father—Jesus pleading with us to convince us the Father is just like he has revealed (design law), or is it taught as Jesus pleading *to* the Father to protect us from the Father's anger and wrath and convince the Father to be merciful (imposed law)?

- *Having our sins erased*: Is this metaphor taught to mean that God erases sin (sinfulness) from the hearts, minds, and characters of his children, re-creating them into the likeness of his Son (design law), or that our sins (history of bad deeds) are erased from historical records kept in the heavenly court so the Father won't know what awful things we have done (imposed law)?

- *Washed in the blood* or *cleansed by the blood*: Is this metaphor taught as the heart, mind, and character of the believer being cleansed from lies, selfishness, and sin, writing the law of love on the heart and having the mind of Christ, by the regenerating power of the Holy Spirit taking Christ's life and producing his righteousness within the individual (design law), or is the blood being applied to record books in heaven and erasing the record of deeds or paying the legal debt because if God found a record of bad deeds God would have to punish (imposed law)?

When we make theologies to protect ourselves from God, we obstruct his healing love. Such ideas create a fear-based religion not a loved-based religion, and people falsely believe that no one could love them if their sins and defects were known.

These ideas undermine trust and worsen people's actual spiritual condition. Why? Because of the design law of worship—by beholding we become changed—we actually become like the God we worship. Therefore, holding such beliefs will not only incite fear but also harden hearts inside inflexible, legal mental constructs (modern-day Pharisees) that cut us off from the transforming power of God.

Satan knows that the truth about God's character of love is so overwhelmingly beautiful, consistent, reliable, trustworthy, altogether lovely, and compelling that anyone who really comes to know God will trust him. Therefore, Satan misrepresents God to be like himself—a coercive dictator and inflictor of pain and death—all to prevent us from genuinely knowing and thereby trusting God.

The Ultimate Good News

The ultimate good news is not about us; the ultimate good news is about God—that God is *not* the kind of being Satan alleges. The good news is that *God* "so loved the world he gave his Son" that whoever trusts him will not perish but will be restored to unity with him and live eternally! Yes, we have the incredible good news of the promise of eternal life through Jesus Christ our Lord—through his victory over death—but this is only good news because of who God is! The truth about God is the ultimate good news!

When we consider the power of God, the power that wins our trust, that transforms hearts and heals minds, that results in trustworthy friends of God who will not be shaken though the heavens fall—that power is the good news about God's character of love. Truth and love are the prevailing power, the power that prevails over all evil, sin, and death.

The Crosswalk

Imagine crossing the street and as you step into the crosswalk a truck comes barreling right toward you. What emotion do you experience? Fear!

Now imagine you are out with your three-year-old firstborn child. You get distracted and look up and see your child in the street with a truck barreling toward him. There is just enough time if you act right now to shove your child out of the way, but if you do, you will get hit. What do you do? You shove your child out of the way. And as you see your child hit the grass on the other side and know he or she is safe, what emotion do you experience? Relief and joy—wait a minute, you are getting hit by a truck! Notice, in both circumstances you are getting hit by a truck. In the first there is only fear. In the second, *your love has cast out your fear*!

This isn't just imaginary—it happened. An April 2, 2016, news report reads, "Hero Nanny Pushes Baby out of SUV's Path, Gets Hit Herself." Loretta Penn, a sixty-two-year-old Long Island nanny pushed a nine-month-old boy in his stroller out of the way of an oncoming vehicle, but she was hit in the process. According to CBS news:

> "Witnesses said that she was crossing the crosswalk, the operator of the vehicle never saw her, and as she saw the car was going to strike her, she pushed the stroller out of harm's way," Rockville Centre Police Commissioner Charles Gennario told 1010 WINS. "She knew she was going to get struck by the vehicle and had the wherewithal to protect the baby." . . .
>
> The baby whom Penn pushed free suffered barely a scratch. His grateful parents were overcome, according to investigators.
>
> "She's practically family to us," Twah Dougherty, Penn's employer, told CBS2's Brian Conybeare. "I'm not surprised that, you know, she did what she did."
>
> Witnesses and police officials alike called Penn's actions heroic.
>
> "That is the kind of people we need around in the community—people who care for other people," said witness Alex Padrone.[2]

"That is the kind of people we need around in the community—people who care for other people." Yes, that is exactly the kind of people we need—people with God-shaped hearts, people who love others more than self! People who have been restored to God's design for life!

Love, originating in God, manifested fully in Christ, and infused into our hearts by the indwelling Spirit is the only power to free us from fear and selfishness! But it all starts with the truth about who God is. The breach in love began with lies about God, and the entire healing cascade hinges on embracing the truth about God! While lies believed break the circle of love and trust,

- Truth believed destroys lies and wins trust.
- Restored trust opens the heart and God pours his love into our hearts (Rom. 5:5).
- Love and trust overcome fear and result in acts of righteousness, acts of service, acts of giving, and acts of love.
- Acts of righteousness result in growing in godliness and witnessing God's kingdom—a healing progression.

But it all starts with coming back to the truth about God! This is the only method, the only power that is able to free us, transform our hearts, and prepare us to meet Jesus!

Truth prevails over lies, and love prevails over fear and selfishness. If we want to prevail in this war, we must come back to an accurate understanding of God's character and government—that is, his methods and design for reality. The truth of who he is and how he works is power, experiencing God's love is power, and partaking of the divine nature is power—the power to live in harmony with God!

"This is eternal life: that they know you, the only true God, and Jesus Christ, whom you have sent" (John 17:3). I invite you to embrace the God who is love!

KEY POINTS FROM CHAPTER 13

- One of the primary obstacles to embracing the truth about God and his character of love is a preconceived system of beliefs based on imposed human law.

- Throughout human history, God, who is love, has been working through his methods of love, truth, and freedom to heal and restore, while the evil one has been working to infect our minds with false interpretations of God's actions, primarily the idea that God is punishing people for sin.

- All through Scripture the message is the same. Humankind is infected with fear and selfishness (sin), which is deviant from God's design for life and is a terminal condition (dead in trespasses and sin). God is working through Christ to heal each person, restoring in them God's heart of love.

- Real repentance is not merely turning away from a behavior but also turning away from selfishness in the heart and living a life of love.

- In Scripture, whenever imposed law–keeping faced off with design law, God went with design law.

- When we make theologies to protect ourselves from God, we obstruct his healing love.

- Love, originating in God, manifested fully in Christ, and infused into our hearts by the indwelling Spirit is the only power to free us from fear and selfishness.
- Truth prevails over lies, and love prevails over fear and selfishness. If we want to prevail in this war we must come back to an accurate understanding of God's character and government—that is, his methods and design for reality.

14

Love and Eternal Judgment

> Darkness cannot drive out darkness: only light can do that. Hate cannot drive out hate: only love can do that.
>
> Martin Luther King Jr., *Strength to Love*

Richard was reluctant to come to my office. His head was hung low, shoulders drooping. He looked crushed; his eyes were hollow with an empty stare almost oblivious to his surroundings. When he finally spoke, his voice was devoid of life, no melody, just flat and empty. He sounded hopeless and defeated when he asked, "Why?"

I wondered, *why what?* What would be his concern? What was overwhelming him? I have heard this question many times before, but it was always associated with some tragedy, loss of a job, breakup in relationship, or death of a loved one. I didn't expect what Richard said next.

"Why hasn't the Lord returned? Why doesn't the Lord put an end to all the wickedness, pain, and suffering? Why does God allow all the evil in the world to continue?"

It was a question I had heard many times at church and have asked myself on more than one occasion, but one I had rarely heard in my office and never before as an initial complaint. Richard was beginning to wonder if the Bible was true, if the Lord would ever return.

Have you asked this question or heard it asked? What answers were you given or heard? I typed the question "Why hasn't Jesus returned?" into an internet search engine and was saddened by the responses I read.

Some were mocking:

- Because he never left.
- Because science has advanced to the point his "tricks" wouldn't impress anyone.

Others took a more fatalistic and helpless approach:

- Because he is too busy with some other petri dish in the cosmos.
- He's not ready.
- His preset time hasn't arrived.
- The signs of the Bible haven't occurred.

Still others saw compassionate reasons:

- He is waiting for people to repent.
- He is waiting for the gospel to go to the world.
- He is waiting for people to get ready.

As I read, I realized that the reasons given by the various respondents revealed insight into the view of God they held. Those who rejected the idea of God answered with such ideas as he never left. Those who believed in God but saw him through level four and below lenses described him as a being of arbitrary power experimenting on his lab animals, or too busy to care, or having a preset time that hasn't arrived.

But the mature—those who viewed God as love and understood more clearly how reality is built to operate—realized God is concerned for us, desires our welfare and eternal healing, and knows that what he wants he cannot get by the exercise of might and power. God is love and what he wants is our love and trust and our eternal restoration to how he designed life to operate. But love and trust cannot be obtained by force, threat, control, or coercion. Love and trust can only be gained by truth and love presented in an atmosphere of freedom. This is why the Bible says, "'Not by might nor by power, but by my Spirit,' says the LORD" (Zech. 4:6). And the Spirit is the Spirit of truth and love!

The reason God waits to return is because there are still billions of people who could be won to love and trust, if only they heard the truth about God and understood his character and methods. "The Lord is not slow in keeping his promise, as some understand slowness. Instead he is patient with you, not wanting anyone to perish, but everyone to come to repentance" (2 Pet. 3:9).

Jesus said, "This gospel of the kingdom will be preached in the whole world as a testimony to all nations, and then the end will come" (Matt. 24:14). What kingdom? Would it not be the kingdom of love—the kingdom of the God of love, presenting the truth about his law of love, his design protocols on which life is based? Has this gospel gone to the world, or instead has an imperial Roman dictator god, a deity who imposes rules and inflicts punishment for disobedience, gone to the world?

Eternal Judgment

In chapter 4 we identified the "elementary teachings" described in Hebrews 6 that we must move beyond in order to mature, to become acquainted with righteousness. We have examined the problem of misunderstanding law and getting stuck on rituals. Now, we turn to another basic teaching that is important for the newborn, those just converted to Christ who come to God self-focused, like a child caught with their hand in the cookie jar and fearful of getting punished. But also like children consumed with self, they want to be sure everything is "fair" and those who haven't repented get what is due them. So God gives them the assurance that there will be a final judgment: *You can stop worrying, stop keeping score, stop holding resentments, forgive your enemies, and trust me with how it all turns out. I will ensure everyone receives exactly what they are due.* God spoke his assurance of equity in many places:

> As I judged your ancestors in the wilderness of the land of Egypt, so I will judge you, declares the Sovereign LORD. (Ezek. 20:36)

> You, then, why do you judge your brother or sister? Or why do you treat them with contempt? For we will all stand before God's judgment seat. (Rom. 14:10)

> For we must all appear before the judgment seat of Christ, so that each of us may receive what is due us for the things done while in the body, whether good or bad. (2 Cor. 5:10)

Since you call on a Father who judges each person's work impartially, live out your time as foreigners here in reverent fear. (1 Pet. 1:17)

And I saw the dead, great and small, standing before the throne, and books were opened. Another book was opened, which is the book of life. The dead were judged according to what they had done as recorded in the books. (Rev. 20:12)

How do you hear such passages? It really depends on which law lens (stage of moral development) you are looking through.

People who view judgment through level one through four (imposed-law) lenses envision a judicial proceeding in which record books are opened that describe in vivid detail every sin, shortcoming, evil, and wrong deed ever committed in order for God to *determine* one's eternal destiny and mete out appropriate punishment. But not to worry, if the sinner has claimed the legal payment of Jesus, then Jesus stands next to them acting as their defense attorney, their heavenly court-appointed advocate, to plead their case to the heavenly Judge. And what, in this model, does Jesus do? He begs his Father, holding up his pierced hands, "My blood, my blood, Father! I have paid the price. You can't punish them. I have taken their punishment. Remember you vented all your anger and rage on me. You don't have the legal right to hurt them. So just wipe their misdeeds from the record books. . . . Oh, and also from your memory and the memory of all the angels and all the other saved, so when you (and everyone else) look at them you will be enabled to see them with the love you have for me . . . please, do it for me, Father!"

Such gross distortions, which are commonly taught in Christianity, are all based on believing the lie that God's law functions like laws made by sinful human beings—imposed rules that require judicial proceedings. Such concepts, rather than removing fear, instilling trust, and healing hearts actually instill fear, break down trust, and harden hearts.

When we mature past level four and realize God is love and his laws are the protocols on which reality is constructed, we understand that judgment is simply the accurate diagnosis of the condition of each person's heart. Has each person accepted the truth about God, opened their heart, and received the indwelling Spirit, who reproduces Christ within? Do they have God-shaped hearts or not? This is the question. One example of God's judgment is found in Hosea 4:17: "Ephraim is joined to idols; leave him alone!"

What is God's judgment in this case? Ephraim cannot be separated from his idols, so leave him the way he is. It is a diagnosis of his actual condition of heart.

It is all about reality, the actual condition of each person. We've either been restored to God's design for life, so that we can live in his presence, or not. This is what Jesus meant when he said: "Judge not, that you be not judged. For with what judgment you judge, you will be judged; and with the measure you use, it will be measured back to you" (Matt. 7:1–2 NKJV).

Those viewing the world through imposed-law lenses read this to mean that God keeps track of how you treat others and will use that same standard against you. But those who understand God's design law realize that what a person says and does reveals the actual condition of *their* heart.

When you see a white supremacist burning a cross (yes, a cross, as these villains claim to be Christians) in the yard of an African American, shouting vile epitaphs, whose character is being revealed? Do you realize what is transpiring in the heart, mind, and character of the white supremacist? Every act of sin reacts upon the sinner, makes a change in their inner being, searing their conscience, hardening their heart, deadening their moral sensibilities, and warping their character further and further out of harmony with God and his design of love.

Thus Jesus said,

> Make a tree good and its fruit will be good, or make a tree bad and its fruit will be bad, for a tree is recognized by its fruit. You brood of vipers, how can you who are evil say anything good? For the mouth speaks what the heart is full of. A good man brings good things out of the good stored up in him, and an evil man brings evil things out of the evil stored up in him. But I tell you that everyone will have to give account on the day of judgment for every empty word they have spoken. For by your words you will be acquitted, and by your words you will be condemned. (Matt. 12:33–37)

Infants hear Jesus's words and say, "See, Jesus is keeping track of every bad thing you do or say and one day he will make you pay." The mature, however, have grown up to realize that sin damages the sinner, and those who refuse the infusion of Christ via the Holy Spirit will be diagnosed as terminal and let go to reap what they have sown. By their *own* words they will be condemned. From their *own* terminal condition they will reap destruction: "Whoever sows to please their flesh, *from the flesh will reap destruction*" (Gal. 6:8). This is design law. It is exactly like saying, the one who ties a plastic bag over their head will, from their own actions, reap destruction. Or, the anthrax-infected patient who refuses the antibiotic infusion (remedy) will, from their own infection, reap destruction. According to Scripture, God's judgment is when he says, "Let the one who does wrong continue to do wrong; let the vile person continue to be vile;

let the one who does right continue to do right; and let the holy person continue to be holy" (Rev. 22:11).

What determines our eternal destiny is not God's judgment upon us but our judgment of God. We either judge him to be a being we can trust, and thereby open our hearts to, or not. This choice in turn makes us either fit or unfit for living in God's system of other-centered love. If we judge God trustworthy, then we open our hearts and his Spirit heals us from sin. If, instead, we accept Satan's lies and judge God untrustworthy, then we cling to legal theologies and pile up doctrines to protect and hide us from God—which keeps our hearts closed and eventually moves us beyond his healing reach—while all too frequently maintaining strict religious observance.

Why is this the case? Because of design law, it is how God constructed reality to actually work. While God can create life, sinless perfect life, God cannot create loyalty, trust, or love by the exercise of power. God can create robots, programmed to operate reliably, but robots are not loyal; they don't make choices of devotion, they don't trust, and they can't love. God cannot create, by use of divine power, mature character in the inner being of a free sentient intelligence. Mature character must be formed/developed by the choices of the individual. After Adam sinned, no human being could accomplish such a feat—so Jesus came to do what we could not. As a human, Jesus chose to love perfectly; he chose to restore God's design into the human species.

God's endgame—God's goal—is unity, a universe united in never-ending love and trust. This can be accomplished only through God's methods of truth, love, and freedom. Each intelligent being must be fully persuaded (about God) in their own mind (Rom. 14:5). We must individually choose whom we will trust. It is the only way to heal our characters and transform our hearts, while preserving our individuality.

Martin Luther King Jr. described this reality when he said, "Darkness cannot drive out darkness: only light can do that. Hate cannot drive out hate: only love can do that."[1] Selfishness cannot drive out selfishness—only love can do that. God cannot drive fear and selfishness out of the hearts of sinners by the exercise of might, power, and threats—only selfless love and unwavering trustworthiness can do that. Jesus provides the remedy we need: the truth to free us from lies and a new character to heal us from within. Jesus is the evidence of God's true nature and character. Though God possesses all power, he is not corrupted by absolute power. Jesus demonstrated, for the entire universe to see, that he would rather die, he would rather allow his creatures to kill him, than use his power to take their freedom, control them, or coerce them.

At the cross, God's character of selfless love proved to be absolutely trustworthy. God will never abuse his power. This is the only way to bring the universe back to unity—to at-one-ment. This is the only way to transform hearts—by "speaking the truth in love, we will grow to become in every respect the mature body of him who is the head, that is, Christ" (Eph. 4:15). Truth spoken in love, in freedom, without coercion, without threat, is the only means to transform hearts, the only method that can restore unity in God's universe. But people at different levels of moral development have varying understanding of the incredible accomplishments of Christ. As the writer of Hebrews said, the immature, those stuck on milk, are not acquainted with the teaching about righteousness. They have different explanations for why Christ had to die—what atonement means. Let's look at why Jesus had to die through the seven levels of moral development:

1. *Reward and punishment*: People disobeyed and did what God said not to do. This dishonored God. God was offended and in his justice responded with angry vengeance to execute the disobedient and satisfy his outrage. But Jesus stepped in and became humanity's substitute. God killed him in our place and is satisfied that his honor and justice have been preserved. This is the Satisfaction theory of atonement.

2. *Marketplace exchange*: Because earth and humanity were now the legal property of Satan, the devil claimed legal rights to this earth and the lives of the sons and daughters of Adam and Eve. Therefore, God struck a bargain with the devil to exchange the life of Christ for the lives of the rest of humanity. This is the Ransom theory of atonement.

3. *Social conformity*: Somebody had to pay so that God could be seen as fair in how he deals with sin and sinners; Jesus is the one who paid that price. This is the Governmental theory of atonement.

4. *Law and order*: In this view, Jesus died to pay the legal penalty the law demanded and the heavenly judge imposed. The law must be kept. Humans broke the law and justice requires the imposition of the proper punishment. Someone had to be executed to pay the legal penalty. Jesus became our substitute and was executed in our place (by the Father as the righteous judge) to pay that penalty. The integrity of the law is maintained and sinners can be pardoned if they claim the legal payment made by Jesus. This is the Penal Substitution theory of atonement.

5. *Love for others*: Sin separated us from God and corrupted our hearts so that we no longer trusted God. But God loved us too much to let us go, and Christ's death was the

means to reach us with his love and restore us to trust in him. This is the Moral Influence theory of atonement.

6. *Principle-based living*: In this view, Christ's life, death, and resurrection are understood to be the only means to fix what sin had done to God's creation. When humankind sinned, the condition of humankind was changed and was now out of harmony with God and his design for life. Humankind was now held in bondage by their own condition of sinfulness (carnal nature), their terminal state (death), and the lies about God told by Satan. Christ came to break these powers and fix what sin did to creation. Thus, "God made him who had no sin to be sin for us, so that in him we might become the righteousness of God" (2 Cor. 5:21). These are the Recapitulation and Christus Victor theories of atonement.

7. *Understanding friend of God*: At this level, the plan of salvation is understood to have a deeper and broader intent than just the redemption of the human species.

Level seven includes level five understanding that humanity is held captive by lies about God that undermine our ability to trust him. God loves us too much to let us go, so he sent Jesus who, as part of his mission, revealed truth so as to destroy Satan's lies and win (morally influence) us back to trust (John 8:32; Heb. 2:14).

Level seven also includes all the elements of level six understanding. Humankind is not only held in bondage by the lies of Satan but also by our own carnal (selfish) natures. But God through Christ not only destroyed the lies of Satan, thereby destroying the devil's power (Heb. 2:14), and the carnal nature, thereby destroying death, he also perfectly restored God's law of love—God's character—back into the human species, thereby perfecting the species and bringing life and immortality to light (2 Tim. 1:9–10; 1 John 3:8; Heb. 5:8–9). As the early church fathers would have said, Jesus picked up humankind broken off in Adam and carried it to completion.

But level seven also understands that God has a larger purpose than just saving humanity. God is also working to secure the unfallen beings in their confidence, trust, and loyalty to him—to protect them from disaffection and keep them eternally safe. All things *in heaven* and in earth *are reconciled to Christ at the cross* (Col. 1:20).

Atonement at level seven is understood in its true biblical meaning of at-one-ment—complete unity with God—a universe without any deviation from God and his design of love. As Jesus himself prayed just before his crucifixion: "I pray also for those who will believe in me through their message, *that all of them may be one, Father, just as you are in me and I am in you*" (John 17:20–21).

This unity is the mystery of God. It is his secret plan to heal all who trust him, while eliminating all deviations from his design (sin and unrepentant sinners), so that all the saved along with the unfallen beings will be solidified in the unshakable unity of love and trust. This is possible only through the accomplishments of Jesus Christ:

And he made known to us the *mystery* of his will according to his good pleasure, which he purposed in Christ, to be put into effect when the times reach their fulfillment—*to bring unity to all things in heaven and on earth under Christ.* (Eph. 1:9–10)

This is God's healing plan of atonement. Imposed law divides, as evidenced by theories one through four above. But true unity, genuine at-one-ment, is achieved when we return to design law. Through a level seven lens, the metaphors in the various atonement theories radiate the same beautiful healing message:

1. Satisfaction is understood in the light of a creation out of harmony with the protocols of life, dead in trespasses and sin. In such a state, God, like a parent whose child is dying, would only be satisfied with the healing and restoration of his creation. In this light we understand why God was pleased that Christ was bruised. It was only through his death that the remedy to save his children could be achieved (Isa. 53:10). Anything short of perfect healing of his children would not satisfy, but "he will see the fruit of his suffering and will be satisfied" (Isa. 53:11, margin note).

2. Ransom is the price necessary to free someone from bondage. Level seven understands that sinners are held in the bondage of lies about God and their own carnal natures. Christ, through his perfect life, selfless death, and resurrection, has revealed the truth about God that destroys the lies of Satan and frees us to trust God (Heb. 2:14). In trust we open our hearts, and the Holy Spirit takes the perfect character developed by Christ and reproduces it in us (John 16:14–15; 1 Cor. 2:16; Heb. 5:9). We become new beings, freed from the slavery of our carnal natures (2 Cor. 5:17). We become partakers of the divine nature (2 Pet. 1:4)!

3. Governmental theory, understood in its proper sense, is that God is fair in how he governs, which is by design law. To repair the deviation from his design, God himself took

the responsibility of providing the remedy to heal and restore. God wins the loyalty, love, devotion, and trust of his intelligent creatures only through his methods of truth, love, and freedom. The universe stands secure for all eternity not because angels with flaming swords stand on every street corner to police the populace but because it is inhabited by only those who, having been convinced beyond a doubt of God's method of governing, are like Jesus in character.

4. In terms of law and order, God is Creator and his design protocols are his law. But God in his mercy added a written codification of his law specifically designed to protect, diagnose, and bring sinful humans back to him for healing. God's law is immutable and unchangeable because it originates in the heart and character of God, who is love. And God, who is love, constructed all reality to operate in harmony with his own nature of love. Human imposed-law concepts are eliminated, and God is seen in his true light as Creator and sustainer of all.

5. Moral influence is accepted as a reality that is part of the healing plan. Humans living in the darkness and despair of sin, fearful and survival-driven, need love and truth to penetrate their clouded minds to influence them, draw them, woo them back to God again. But it is also understood that moral influence alone is not enough to fix the damage sin has done, that a true remedy is also needed to restore in the sinner a God-shaped heart!

6. Christus Victor and recapitulation are understood to be Christ's victory over all opposition to his methods: truth overcoming lies; love overcoming selfishness; Christ, in

his humanity and exercising his human will, overcoming fears and selfishness to develop a perfect human character in harmony with God's design for life—God's law of love. Jesus took up humanity, damaged and broken by sin, and perfected it. In Jesus the human race is restored to its right place in God's kingdom of love.

7. All things in heaven and earth unite under one head, Jesus Christ. This is true at-one-ment. All metaphors, rightly understood, teach the same reality!

The Judgment of God

One day, every intelligent being will stand in God's presence and their true condition will be revealed—this is God's judgment, his accurate diagnosis of each person. It is our very condition that determines our eternal destiny. We cannot make ourselves good. We can only be made good by the power of God working in us. And what determines whether God's healing power is experienced within our hearts and minds is whether we trust God and open our heart to him.

John the Revelator, looking through the corridors of time, describes the very events that precede the second coming of Christ. He pens an incredible message for the people at this time in earth's history:

> Then I saw another angel flying in midair, and he had the eternal gospel to proclaim to those who live on the earth—to every nation, tribe, language and people. He said in a loud voice, "Fear God and give him glory, because the hour of his judgment has come. Worship him who made the heavens, the earth, the sea and the springs of water." (Rev. 14:6–7)

At the end of time, a worldwide message is to go forth centering on the eternal gospel—the *eternal* good news—the good news that has been true even in eternity past, even before sin entered the world. And what is the good news that existed even before the need of a Savior to die for sinners? It is the truth about God's amazing character of love! God is not an arbitrary dictator who makes up rules and inflicts punishment. God is not an enemy we must fear but our eternal friend who, when needed, died for our healing and salvation.

As we have discovered throughout this book, there are two law lenses through which people can view Scripture and the world around them: the imposed-law lens of rules coercively enforced or the design-law lens of the protocols of love built into the fabric of reality. Those who continue to interpret life through the imposed-law lens read Revelation 14:7 in this way:

> Tremble and be afraid of God and be sure to sing praises to him because God is powerful, and it is time for him to sit in judgment of those who have broken his rules. You better worship him in the right way, keep the right rituals, and observe the right forms of worship indicating your acknowledgment of him as Creator so that you can pass his test of loyalty.

But those who have grown past level four of moral development stand with the apostle Paul who wrote: "Let God be found true, though every man be found a liar, as it is written, 'That You may be justified in Your words, *And prevail when You are judged*'" (Rom. 3:4 NASB). The mature realize it is God who has been lied about, and a time must come when the truth about him is presented with such overwhelming clarity that people are able to make a right judgment about him. They read Revelation 14:7 differently:

Be overwhelmed with awe of God and his amazing character and methods of love. Reveal his character of love by practicing his methods in your lives (glorify him), for the time has come in earth's history for people to make a right judgment about him. He has been lied about. He has been misrepresented. The minds of billions are darkened by the dictator views of God stemming from the false imposed-law construct. Worship "him who made the heavens, the earth and the seas." Worship the Creator—the designer—and reject the dictator views of God. Embrace God's design law of love and reject the imposed-law construct.

It is time for God's true worshipers to stand up and reveal the God who is like Jesus in character, the only true God—the builder of space, time, matter, energy, life, and all reality—the Creator whose universe runs on the design law of love, so that the rest of the world may judge him trustworthy, reject the lies they have been told their entire lives, and turn to him for eternal healing and restoration. "By this everyone will know that you are my disciples, if you have love for one another" (John 13:35 NRSV).

Becoming a Spokesperson for God

What, then, is God waiting for? Why hasn't he yet returned? Because billions of his healable children have still not heard of his true remedy. They remain trapped in a legal religion that has a form of godliness but without the transforming power of love! The gospel of the kingdom of love has not yet gone to the world. Instead a false gospel based on imposed law promoting a dictator god who is the source of inflicted punishment and from whom we need protecting has gone to the world.

God is holding back the final events in earth's history waiting for something incredible to happen. At the end of earth's history, as order on earth seems to be breaking down, God sends an angel from heaven with an urgent message to the four angels holding back the winds of strife. He tells them to hold, to not let go, until something specific occurs—until God's "servants" receive a "seal on their foreheads" (Rev. 7:1–3).

In Bible language, God's "servants" are his prophets. "Surely the Sovereign LORD does nothing without revealing his plan to *his servants the prophets*" (Amos 3:7). The primary role of a prophet was not prognostication, not predicting future events. The primary role was being a spokesperson for God, to speak the truth the people needed to hear, to take God's message for that time to the people.

Likewise, at the end of time, God is holding back the final unraveling of events on earth until his spokespersons—the people who will speak the truth about him—are sealed on their foreheads. This seal is not a physical mark but a spiritual seal—the solidification of our characters into Christlikeness. Our prefrontal and anterior cingulate cortices, the parts of the brain right behind our foreheads, are where we reason, understand truth, worship, experience other-centered love, and choose whom we will serve. The imagery of Revelation beautifully illustrates that something needs to happen in our minds and hearts—that our minds and hearts need to be sealed to God.

When we recall that we are in a war for our minds, centering on the knowledge of God, this makes perfect sense (2 Cor. 10:3–5). And what does a seal do? It "locks" something as is, complete, finished. When you seal a letter, it is done. When you seal a document, it is finalized. When God's spokespersons are sealed, they are so settled into the truth about God that nothing can shake them from it. They are solidified in their loyalty, devotion, understanding of reality, and their practice of his methods—they have died to self and have God's perfect character of love restored within. These are the ones who do "not love their lives so much as to shrink from death" (Rev. 12:11). Fear and selfishness have been replaced with God's character of self-sacrificing love. Understandably, then, this incredible group is described as having the name (character) of the Lamb and the Father written on their foreheads—they are sealed of God (Rev. 14:1)! They have God-shaped hearts (characters)!

God is holding back the final events on planet Earth, waiting for his friends to prepare themselves to be his spokespersons—to tell the truth about him, to take the true good news of his kingdom of love to the world—then he will let the four winds blow. And when the four winds are loosened, terrible calamities will happen all over the earth in such intensity and rapidity as the world has never seen. Why? Level four and below thinkers will claim God is punishing the world for wickedness and sin. But the mature will realize something altogether different is occurring.

The mature understand that billions of people are so caught up in the routines of life—just trying to survive, pay the bills, find a meal, work, or get lost in mind-numbing entertainment—that they are unaware of the truth about God and their own terminal condition. The unraveling of nature will cause these people to awaken from their spiritual slumber and ask what is happening. At that time, God's spokespersons, who are already on the scene and settled into the truth, will present the truth about God to them, and a "great multitude that no one could count, from every nation, tribe, people and language" (Rev. 7:9) will respond and be saved.

Could one factor in our Lord's long delay be that the church, God's people all over the world, has never grown up, has never become the mature bride he longs to receive? If so, what is obstructing that growth, that sealing, that settling into the truth about God so that nothing can move her? Is it not the distorted ideas about God himself that undermine our trust in him, primarily the lie that God's law is imposed?

According to Revelation 14:6–7, what God is working to achieve is the preparation of his spokespersons to tell the truth about him. Then the latter rain will fall upon them, the earth will be lightened with the knowledge of God, and Christ will return!

We stand at the threshold of eternity; all heaven is eager to bring an end to this long conflict with sin. But God's message to his angels at the four corners of the earth is still—hold. God's message to you and me is this:

Make a choice. Make a judgment. I have been lied about. I have been presented as the one you must fear, the one you need protecting from, and the time has come in universal history for you to decide. Will you believe the lies of the enemy or the testimony of my Son? Will you believe that my Son and I are one, that everything you have seen in Jesus is true of me (John 10:38; 14:9)? Will you believe my Son when he said that he will not pray to me in your behalf, because there is no need—I love you myself (John 16:26)? In fact, I love you so much I sent you my Son (John 3:16)! Will you believe that I was in my Son working to restore you back into unity with me (2 Cor. 5:19)? Will you believe that I am, and always have been, for you (Rom. 8:31)? Don't you hear me knocking at the door to your heart? Won't you open the door, open your heart, and trust me? Won't you let me in? Please! Let me heal you. Let me pour my love into your heart (Rom. 5:5) and remove your guilt, eradicate your shame, cleanse your thoughts, purify your desires, and write

*my design for life (law of love) into your inmost being (Heb. 8:10)!
Please remember my promise, "A new heart also will I give you"
(Ezek. 36:26 KJV). It is you whom I love! Won't you let me reshape
you—transform you, re-create you, and regenerate you? Won't you
let me restore in you a God-shaped heart?*

KEY POINTS FROM CHAPTER 14

- Love and trust cannot be obtained by force, threat, control, or coercion. Love and trust can only be obtained by truth and love presented in an atmosphere of freedom.

- What determines our eternal destiny is not God's judgment upon us but our judgment of God—do we judge him to be a being we can trust and thereby open our hearts to, or not—which in turn makes us either fit or unfit for living in God's system of other-centered love.

- Character must be formed/developed by the choices of the individual. After Adam sinned, no human being could accomplish such a feat—so Jesus came to do what we could not. As a human, Jesus chose to love perfectly; he chose to restore God's design into the human species.

- God cannot drive fear and selfishness out of the hearts of sinners by the exercise of might, power, and threats; only selfless love and unwavering trustworthiness can do that. And that is what Jesus does. He provides our remedy: the truth to free us from lies and a new character to heal us from within.

- Truth spoken in love, in freedom, without coercion, and without threat is the only means that can transform hearts, the only method that can restore unity in God's universe.

- Atonement at level seven is understood in its true biblical meaning of at-one-ment—complete unity with God—a universe without any deviation from God and his design of love.

- It is time for God's true worshipers to stand up and reveal the God who is like Jesus in character, the only true God—the builder of space, time, matter, energy, life, and all reality—the Creator whose universe runs on the design law of love, so that the rest of the world may judge him trustworthy, reject the lies they have been told their entire lives, and turn to him for eternal healing and restoration.

Appendix A

Summary of God's Design Laws

Throughout this book we have made a clear distinction between God's laws (the laws reality is built on) and imposed laws (the laws we humans enact and enforce with inflicted punishments).

Below is a brief summary of some of God's design laws. This is not an exhaustive list but a simple, quick reference guide.

Law of love: the principle of giving. This law is the law of life for the universe. All living beings and systems operate on this law. If it lives, it gives. Violation of this law damages health and, if not resolved, will result in death.

Examples:
- Respiration (give away CO_2, plants give O_2)
- Water cycles (oceans give to clouds, which give to lakes, rivers, and streams, which give back to oceans)
- Pollination (insects pollinate, plants give pollen)

When giving stops, death ensues—this is the law of sin and death.

Law of liberty: the principle of freedom. Love only exists in an atmosphere of freedom. Violate liberty in a relationship, and three predictable consequences always occur:

1. Love is damaged and eventually destroyed.
2. Rebellion (to reclaim freedom) is instilled.
3. When one chooses to stay in such a relationship, individuality is slowly eroded and autonomy is lost.

Example: A young man asks a woman to marry him; when she hesitates, he puts a knife to her throat and threatens to kill her if she doesn't. What happens? Any love that she might have had for him is damaged. A desire to rebel and get away is instilled. If she chooses to stay in a relationship with him, over time she will lose the ability to think and reason for herself and instead think through the lens of what she believes he would have her do.

Law of worship: by beholding we are changed; also known as modeling. It is the principle that we become like whatever we spend time admiring, valuing, thinking about, worshiping, or esteeming.

Examples:

- Theatrical entertainment activates emotion circuits, diminishes activity in reasoning circuits, and increases inattention and propensity for violence, regardless of whether the programming is R- or G-rated.
- Meditating on a God of love activates the brain's love circuits and calms the brain's fear circuits. Positive brain changes are observed in as little as thirty days.

- The mind (software) chooses what we focus on, believe, value, and the behaviors in which we engage. Such choices determine which neural circuits are activated, and this results in actual change to our brain structure and genetic expression.

Law of exertion: strength comes by exercise. If you want something to get stronger, you must exercise it. If you don't use it, you will lose it.

Examples:
- Physical strength—stronger muscles require exercise
- Skill—greater ability in golf requires practice
- Intelligence—improved mathematical ability requires working problems

Law of sowing and reaping: you reap what you sow.

Examples:
- Farming—plant wheat, reap wheat
- Character—sow a pattern of lying, deceiving, and cheating and reap an untrustworthy character
- Health—eat an unhealthy diet, stay indoors, and never exercise and reap worsening health; eat a healthy diet, get outdoors, and exercise regularly and reap improved health

Laws of physics: the fixed laws on which the material universe operates.

Examples:
- Laws of motion
- Laws of thermodynamics

- Laws of friction
- Law of gravity

Laws of health: the fixed parameters on which biological systems are designed to operate.

Examples:
- Hydration
- Nutrition
- Respiration (fresh air)
- Avoid toxins
- Sunshine
- Rest

Law of heredity: we procreate beings in our image, with our features, strengths, and weaknesses, through passing along our genetic information, with specific gene sequences and the epigenetic instructions directing how those gene sequences are to be expressed.

Examples:
- Physical attributes such as hair color, eye color, blood type, height, and so on
- Risk for various diseases (breast cancer, Alzheimer's, etc.)
- Risk for addictions
- Epigenetic modification that alters longevity, taste, smell, and brain development

Laws of mathematics: the fixed protocols on which mathematics operates.

Examples:

- Commutative law of addition: it doesn't matter in what order numbers are added together; the sum total of those same numbers is always the same
- Commutative law of multiplication: it doesn't matter in what order numbers are multiplied together; the answer is always the same

Appendix B

Another Resource—
The Remedy

As you have discovered in this book, the idea of imposed law has infected Christianity and altered the view of God held by many good-hearted Christian people.

Many people struggle when they read the Bible because they find numerous expressions that seem to support the imposed-law idea. This is due to the fact that by the time the Bible was translated into our modern language, the imposed-law construct was deeply ingrained orthodoxy that was accepted as fact by most translators. All Bible translations have been produced since Constantine converted and the idea of imposed law became assumed orthodoxy. This means that Bible translators, though honest and with good intent, have artificially introduced into the translations much of the legal language with its fear-inducing ideas about God. Such words as *justice*, *justification*, *expiation*, and *propitiation* all connote legal processes that were often not intended by the original authors.

My understanding of inspiration is that God inspired his human agents with wisdom and insight, and those human beings chose which words to use when writing Scripture. God is not presented as an author in Scripture. Thus, the specific words of Scripture are not inspired, but the concepts, ideas, and truths contained within Scripture are. This is why any translation of the Bible is legitimate, because the original Hebrew, Greek, and Aramaic words don't have special value or inspiration and can be replaced with words from a new language—as long as those new words present the same truths, ideas, and concepts as clearly and accurately as possible. Sadly, many of the modern translations introduce legal (level four) thinking not in the original languages.

For this reason, I spent twelve years systematically paraphrasing the New Testament through the lens of design law—the law of love. *The Remedy* is a New Testament expanded paraphrase that offers an alternative to the imposed-law bias found in so many translations. My view is that God is the Creator, designer, and builder of reality, and when he constructed his universe, he built it to operate in harmony with his own nature of love. Thus, God's law is not a set of imposed rules but the design parameters on which he built life to exist. *The Remedy* is intentional in its focus to reorient the Christian mind toward God's character of love and his mission to heal and restore humankind back into unity with himself, as taught by the early church.

For those who might question the legitimacy of a physician, who does not hold a degree in theology, paraphrasing the New Testament, I would remind them that 27 percent of the New Testament was written by Luke—a physician with no seminary training. Paul, the theologian, wrote 23 percent of the New Testament but only after spending three years in the desert being reeducated by the Holy Spirit (Gal. 1:15–18). And John—a fisherman also with no seminary training—wrote 20 percent.[1] God has always used people who are open to being led by his Spirit, not people approved by human academia. I claim no special revelation or insight beyond that of any honest-hearted Christian who humbly seeks the guidance of the Holy Spirit in order to communicate as effectively as possible God's healing truth (Acts 4:13).

I hope you will find *The Remedy* an aid in developing your trust relationship with God, culminating in becoming a partaker of God's eternal Remedy—Jesus Christ!

NOTES

Chapter 1 Heart Disease in Christianity

1. R. D. Drumm et al., "Intimate Partner Violence in a Conservative Christian Denomination: Prevalence and Types," *Social Work & Christianity* 33, no. 3 (2006): 233–51; P. Tjaden and N. Thonnes, *Full Report of the Prevalence, Incidence, and Consequences of Violence against Women Research Report: Findings from the National Violence against Women Survey* (Washington, DC: U.S. Department of Justice/Centers for Disease Control and Prevention, November 2000); A. L. Coker et al., "Frequency and Correlates of Intimate Partner Violence by Type: Physical, Sexual, and Psychological Battering," *American Journal of Public Health* 90, no. 4 (2000): 553–59; J. Schaefer, R. Caetano, and C. L. Clark, "Rates of Intimate Partner Violence in the United States," *American Journal of Public Health* 88, no. 11 (1998): 1702–4.

2. Nate Cohn, "Big Drop in Share of Americans Calling Themselves Christian," *New York Times*, May 12, 2015, http://www.nytimes.com/2015/05/12/upshot/big-drop-in-share-of-americans-calling-themselves-christian.html?_r=0; Baylor University Religion Survey, September 2006, available at http://www.baylor.edu/mediacommunications/news.php?action=story&story=41678; Frank Newport, "In U.S., 77% Identify as Christian," December 24, 2012, http://www.gallup.com/poll/159548/identify-christian.aspx.

3. Centers for Disease Control and Prevention, "Youth Risk Behavior Surveillance—United States, 2007," *Surveillance Summaries* 58, no. SS-4 (June 6, 2008).

4. *Drug and Alcohol Dependence* 74, no. 3 (June 11, 2004), 223–34.

5. "Christian Views on Alcohol," Barna, December 22, 2013, https://www.barna.com/research/christian-views-on-alcohol/.

6. S. Dein, "Religion and Mental Health: A Critical Appraisal of the Literature," *World Cultural Psychiatry Research Review* (June 2014): 42-46, https://www.wcprr.org/wp-content/uploads/2014/06/2014.02.42-46.pdf; J. Park et al., "The Relationship between Religion and Mental Disorders in a Korean Population,"

Psychiatry Investigation 9, no. 1 (2012): 29–35, https://www.ncbi.nlm.nih.gov/pmc/articles/PMC3285738/.

7. "New Research Explores the Changing Shape of Temptation," Barna, January 25, 2013, https://www.barna.com/research/new-research-explores-the-changing-shape-of-temptation/.

8. Pornography Addiction Survey (conducted by Barna Group), Proven Men, 2014, available at www.provenmen.org/2014pornsurvey/pornography-use-and-addiction.

9. Boz Tchividjian, "Startling Statistics: Child Sexual Abuse and What the Church Can Begin Doing about It," Religion News Service, January 9, 2014, http://boz.religionnews.com/2014/01/09/startling-statistics/.

10. David B. Barrett, George T. Kurian, and Todd M. Johnson, *World Christian Encyclopedia*, 2nd ed. (New York: Oxford University Press, 2001), 1:16–18, http://www.philvaz.com/apologetics/a106.htm.

Chapter 2 The Infection

1. J. H. Hay, "A British Medical Association Lecture on the Significance of a Raised Blood Pressure," *British Medical Journal* 2, no. 3679 (July 11, 1931): 43–47, doi:10.1136/bmj.2.3679.43 PMC2314188, PMID 20776269.

2. Paul D. White, *Heart Disease*, 2nd ed. (New York: MacMillan, 1937), 326.

3. A. J. Crum et al., "Mind over Milkshakes: Mindsets, Not Just Nutrients, Determine Ghrelin Response," *Health Psychology* 30, no. 4 (July 2011): 429, http://psycnet.apa.org/index.cfm?fa=buy.optionToBuy&id=2011-13978-002.

4. C. Gaser and G. Schlaug, "Brain Structures Differ between Musicians and Non-Musicians," *Journal of Neuroscience* 23, no. 27 (October 8, 2003): 9240–45.

5. A. Ai et al., "Prayers, Spiritual Support, and Positive Attitudes in Coping with the September 11 National Crisis," *Journal of Personality* 73, no. 3 (June 2005): 763–92; A. Ai et al., "Wartime Faith-Based Reactions among Traumatized Kosovar and Bosnian Refugees in the United States," *Mental Health, Religion & Culture* 8, no. 4 (2005): 291–308.

6. S. van der Oord et al., "The Effectiveness of Mindfulness Training for Children with ADHD and Mindful Parenting for their Parents," *Journal of Child and Family Studies* 21, no. 1 (February 2012): 139–47.

7. R. Teper and M. Inzlicht, "Meditation, Mindfulness and Executive Control: The Importance of Emotional Acceptance and Brain-Based Performance Monitoring," *Social Cognitive and Affective Neuroscience* 8, no. 1 (January 2013): 85–92, doi:10.1093/scan/nss045.

8. "Reported Prank Call Leads to Business Damage at Morro Bay Burger King," KSBY6, updated January 31, 2016, http://www.ksby.com/story/31102605/reported-prank-call-leads-to-business-damage-at-morro-bay-burger-king.

9. S. L. Greenslade, *Church and State from Constantine to Theodosius* (London: SCM Press, 1954), 10, emphasis mine.

10. Thomas Lindsay, *A History of the Reformation*, International Theological Library (Edinburgh: T&T Clark, 1906), 168, emphasis mine.

Chapter 3 Growing Past the Rules

1. "Time Magazine Cover of Breastfeeding Mom Sparks Intense Debate on 'Attachment Parenting,'" *CBS News*, May 11, 2012, http://www.cbsnews.com /news/time-magazine-cover-of-breastfeeding-mom-sparks-intense-debate-on -attachment-parenting/.

2. M. Mercer, "Officer Put on Leave after Chase Arrest," *Chattanooga Times Free Press*, June 22, 2010, http://www.timesfreepress.com/news/news/story/20 10/jun/22/officer-put-leave/21018/.

3. Anne Colby and Lawrence Kohlberg, *The Measurement of Moral Judgment*, vol. 1 (New York: Cambridge University Press, 1987), 20–31. For comparison, following are Kohlberg's six stages:

Level 1: Heteronomous morality
Level 2: Individualism, instrumental purpose, and exchange
Level 3: Mutual interpersonal expectations, relationships, and interpersonal conformity
Level 4: Social system and conscience
Level 5: Social contract or utility and individual rights
Level 6: Morality of universalizable, reversible, and prescriptive general ethical principles

4. "Pakistani Family Stones Daughter to Death for Marrying Man She Loved," *Daily News*, March 27, 2014, http://www.nydailynews.com/news/world/pakistani -woman-stoned-death-family-article-1.1806700.

5. "Daily Quote from Pope Paul VI," Integrated Catholic Life, October 17, 2010, http://www.integratedcatholiclife.org/2010/10/daily-quote-from-pope -paul-vi-4/.

6. Stephen King, Facebook post, December 23, 2013, https://www.facebook .com/OfficialStephenKing/posts/345033688969553, from an interview in London's *The Independent on Sunday*, March 10, 1996.

Chapter 4 Spiritual Failure to Thrive

1. T. Jennings, *The Remedy: A New Testament Expanded Paraphrase in Everyday English* (Chattanooga: Lennox Publishing, 2015).

2. Ibid., Romans 3:19–20.

Chapter 5 Law, Love, and Healing

1. "Debate about the Mass and Transubstantiation," Amazing Discoveries, October 24, 2012, http://amazingdiscoveries.org/12.10.24-debate-about-the -mass-and-transubstantiation (transcribed by T. Jennings).

2. "Police: Parents Beat Son to Death in Church 'Counseling Session,'" *CBS News*, October 14, 2015, http://www.cbsnews.com/news/police-parents-beat -son-to-death-in-church-counseling-session/.

3. John Kekis, "Teen Brutally Beaten to Death by Parents, Sister and Church Members in Bid to Expose Sins, Police Say," *National Post*, October 14, 2015,

http://news.nationalpost.com/news/world/teen-brutally-beaten-to-death-by
-parents-sister-and-church-members-in-bid-to-expose-sins-police-say.

4. Baylor University Religion Survey.

5. Timothy Longman, *Christianity and Genocide in Rwanda* (Cambridge: Cambridge University Press, 2010), 6–7.

6. *Wikipedia*, s.v. "Four Chaplains," https://en.wikipedia.org/wiki/Four _Chaplains.

7. "Felix Manz: Anabaptist Radical Reformer and Martyr," Christian History for Everyman, http://www.christian-history.org/felix-manz-martyrdom.html.

Chapter 6 The Evidence

1. Robert Sungenis, *Not By Faith Alone* (Santa Barbara, CA: Queenship, 1997), 107–8, emphasis mine. *Sungenis is the founder and president of Catholic Apologetics International Publishing.*

2. D. Neff, "A Call to Evangelical Unity," *Christianity Today*, June 14, 1999, emphasis mine.

3. Guy P. Duffield and Nathaniel M. Van Cleave, *Foundations of Pentecostal Theology* (Los Angeles: LIFE Bible College, 1983), 188, emphasis mine.

4. Albert Mohler, "The Wrath of God Was Satisfied," August 12, 2013, emphasis mine, http://www.albertmohler.com/2013/08/12/the-wrath-of-god-was -satisfied-substitutionary-atonement-and-the-conservative-resurgence-in-the -southern-baptist-convention/.

5. David King, "God Isn't Looking at Us with an Angry Face," *Chattanooga Times Free Press*, December 5, 2015, E-1, emphasis mine.

6. Ministerial Association General Conference of Seventh-Day Adventists, *Seventh-day Adventists Believe: A Biblical Exposition of 27 Fundamental Doctrines* (Hagerstown, MD: Review and Herald Publishing Association, 1988), 111, emphasis mine.

7. Woodrow W. Whidden, "Sinners in the Hands of God," *Ministry Magazine*, February 2007, emphasis mine, http://www.ministrymagazine.org/archive/2007 /February/sinners-in-the-hands-of-god.html.

8. A. Rodriguez, "The Revelation of Salvation," *Adventist World Review*, December 2007, 26, emphasis mine.

9. Joseph Fielding Smith, *Doctrines of Salvation*, vol. 1 (Salt Lake City: Bookcraft, 1954–56), 84, emphasis mine.

10. Brigham Young, *Journal of Discourses*, vol. 4 (Liverpool: S. W. Richards, 1857), 53–54, emphasis mine, http://scriptures.byu.edu/jod/jodhtml.php?vol =04&disc=10.

11. I am not teaching universalism. I am not advocating for cheap grace. I am not promoting there is no punishment for sin. I am not suggesting there is no consuming fire and eternal burning. I am stating that all of these ideas have been misconstrued through the warp of imposed law and have resulted in our misunderstanding of reality and the truth about God's character of love. Instead, far too many people view God as being no different in character than a sinful human magistrate.

12. Max Lucado, *When Christ Comes* (Nashville: Thomas Nelson, 1999), 117.

13. Chris Fabry Live, interview with Elizabeth Smith, Moody Bible Institute, March 5, 2015, trans. T. Jennings.

14. Ben Carson, *America the Beautiful* (Grand Rapids: Zondervan, 2012), 29.

15. Derek Flood, *Healing the Gospel: A Radical Vision for Grace, Justice, and the Cross* (Eugene, OR: Wipf and Stock, 2012), 8, emphasis mine.

16. "J. B. Phillips," World of Quotes, http://www.worldofquotes.com/author /J.+B.+Phillips/1/index.html.

17. "Bart Whitaker Talks about Killing Family, Death Row Complaints," Click2Houston, August 2, 2012, http://www.click2houston.com/news/bart -whitaker-talks-about-killing-family-death-row-complaints_201511241607 36126.

18. Keith Johnson has a Master's degree in Correctional and Alternative Education and has worked for thirty-four years in federal, state, county, and private prisons and juvenile detention centers. Used with his permission.

19. Augustine, *On the Trinity*, 13.4.15, emphasis mine.

Chapter 7 Love and Worship

1. Tjaden and Thonnes, *Full Report of the Prevalence, Incidence, and Consequences of Violence against Women*; Coker et al., "Frequency and Correlates of Intimate Partner Violence by Type"; Schaefer, Caetano, and Clark, "Rates of Intimate Partner Violence in the United States."

2. Jurgen Moltmann, *Sun of Righteousness, Arise: God's Future for Humanity and the Earth* (Minneapolis: Fortress, 2010), 86.

3. Philip Yancey, *The God I Never Knew* (Grand Rapids: Zondervan, 1967), 267.

4. Moltmann, *Sun of Righteousness, Arise*, 89.

5. J. Decety et al., "The Negative Association between Religiousness and Children's Altruism across the World," *Current Biology* 25, no. 22 (November 16, 2015): 2951–55.

6. *Wikipedia*, s.v. "Murder of David Gunn," modified December 11, 2016, https://en.wikipedia.org/wiki/Murder_of_David_Gunn.

7. Jared Malsin, "Christians Mourn Their Relatives Beheaded by ISIS," *TIME*, February 23, 2015, http://time.com/3718470/isis-copts-egypt/.

8. *New Bible Dictionary*, 3rd ed., s.v. "baal (deity)."

9. Ibid.

10. Some may attempt to argue that what made Baal worship false was its gross and hedonistic practices. We assert that all such degradation is the outgrowth of worshiping a god who must be appeased, assuaged, or propitiated. In the Dark Ages these ugly practices of worshiping such a god were evidenced in the inquisition and burning people at the stake. The gross forms of their worship were the fruit of the real problem, which was accepting a god who had to be paid by sacrifice to grant blessings, a god who would inflict punishment if sacrifices were not brought. And Revelation tells us that those who hold to this view of God will again torture and kill in the name of their god.

11. W. A. Elwell and P. W. Comfort, ed., *Tyndale Bible Dictionary* (Wheaton: Tyndale, 2001), Logos Bible Software ebook, s.v. "baal (Deity)."

12. P. J. Achtemeier, ed., *Harper's Bible Dictionary* (San Francisco: Harper & Row, 1985), Logos Bible Software ebook, s.v. "baal (Deity)."

13. Do not conclude that because I assert that Jesus's death was not needed to appease/assuage/propitiate the Father that I am saying humankind could be saved without the death of Christ, or that Christ's death was unnecessary for our salvation. Absolutely not! We could not be saved without the incarnation, life, death, and resurrection of Christ. His death was a nonnegotiable requirement for the salvation of humankind. It just wasn't needed to do anything to the Father or God's law, for nothing was wrong with the Father or the law. His death was required for other reasons, all of which are consistent with God's character of love.

Chapter 8 Love and the Institution

1. Oswald Chambers, "The Spiritually Self-Seeking Church," My Utmost for His Highest, http://utmost.org/the-spiritually-self-seeking-church/, emphasis mine.

2. Erica Ritz, "Tenn. Church under Fire after Allegedly Forcing Mother of Lesbian to Choose between the Church and Her Daughter," the blaze, August 23, 2013, http://www.theblaze.com/stories/2013/08/23/tenn-church-under-fire-after-allegedly-forcing-mother-of-lesbian-to-choose-between-the-church-and-her-daughter/.

3. "John Wesley's Dream," CRYOUT!, http://www.cryoutreach.com/john-wesleyss-dream.html.

4. John Wesley, "The Character of a Methodist," Global Ministries, http://www.umcmission.org/Find-Resources/John-Wesley-Sermons/The-Wesleys-and-Their-Times/The-Character-of-a-Methodist.

5. Barrett, Kurian, and Johnson, *World Christian Encyclopedia*, 1:16–18, http://www.philvaz.com/apologetics/a106htm.

Chapter 9 Rituals, Metaphors, and Symbols

1. William Bennett, *Tried By Fire: The Story of Christianity's First Thousand Years* (Nashville: Thomas Nelson, 2016), 339.

2. Online Etymology Dictionary, s.v. "hocus-pocus," http://www.etymonline.com/index.php?term=hocus-pocus.

3. P. Pugliatti, *English Renaissance Scenes from Canon to Margins* (Oxford: Peter Lang, 2008), 340.

4. Tom J. Nettles et al., *Understanding Four Views on Baptism* (Grand Rapids: Zondervan, 2007).

5. C. S. Lewis, *The Last Battle* (New York: HarperCollins, 2005), 164–65.

6. Nancy Pearcey, *Finding Truth* (Colorado Springs: David C. Cook, 2015), 30.

7. Christopher Mcdougall, "The Hidden Cost of Heroism," nbcnews.com, updated November 26, 2007, http://www.nbcnews.com/id/21902983/ns/health

-behavior/t/hidden-cost-heroism/#.UPAaY2eP9uY. For other inspiring stories, see http://listverse.com/2013/01/15/the-top-10-most-inspiring-self-sacrifices/.

8. *Wikipedia*, s.v. "Liviu Librescu," https://en.wikipedia.org/wiki/Liviu_Librescu.

9. Judith Crosson, Kerry Wills, and Bill Hutchinson, "'Dark Knight Rises' Shooting: Three Heroes Died in Aurora Taking Bullets for Their Girlfriends," *New York Daily News*, updated July 23, 2012, http://www.nydailynews.com/news/national/aurora-shooting-died-bullets-sweeties-article-1.1119395#ixzz21TPAUdXi.

Chapter 10 The Little Theater

1. Chris Fabry Live, interview with Michael Vanlaningham and Michael Rydelnik, Moody Radio, hour 2 at 12:25, March 23, 2016, trans. T. Jennings, http://www.moodyradio.org/Chris-Fabry-Live/2016/03-2016/2016-03-23---The-Centurion---Bible-Q---A/, emphasis mine.

Chapter 11 The Power of Love and Truth

1. Stephanie Pappas, "God's Hand?," LiveScience, March 25, 2011, http://www.livescience.com/13422-americans-natural-disasters-god.html.

2. State of the Union address to joint session of Congress, The Guardian, September 21, 2001, https://www.theguardian.com/world/2001/sep/21/september11.usa13.

3. Christian de Chergé, "Last Testament," Eternal Word Television Network, http://www.ewtn.com/library/MARY/LASTTEST.HTM.

4. *Wikipedia*, s.v. "Andrea Yates," https://en.wikipedia.org/wiki/Andrea_Yates.

Chapter 12 Law or Love in the Real World

1. "How Common Is Intersex?," Intersex Society of North America, http://www.isna.org/faq/frequency.

2. Claire Ainsworth, "The Stranger Within," *New Scientist* 180, no. 2421 (2003): 34, https://www.newscientist.com/article/mg18024215-100-the-stranger-within/.

3. W. R. Rice, U. Friberg, and S. Gavrilets, "Homosexuality as a Consequence of Epigenetically Canalized Sexual Development," *The Quarterly Review of Biology* 87, no. 4 (2012), http://www.jstor.org/stable/10.1086/668167?seq=1#page_scan_tab_contents; W. R. Rice, U. Friberg, and S. Gavrilets, "Homosexuality Via Canalized Sexual Development: A Testing Protocol for a New Epigenetic Model," *BioEssays* 35, no. 9 (2013), https://www.ncbi.nlm.nih.gov/pubmed/23868698.

4. "Personal Protective Equipment," 1910.133(a)(5), Occupational Safety and Health Administration, https://www.osha.gov/pls/oshaweb/owadisp.show_document?p_table=STANDARDS&p_id=9778.

Chapter 13 God's Action in the Old Testament

1. http://s3-us-west-2.amazonaws.com/audio.collegedalecommunity.com/2016/EN-2016-01-30-Faith-and-Works.mp3.

2. "Hero Nanny Pushes Baby Out of SUV's Path, Gets Hit Herself," CBS News, April 2, 2016, http://www.cbsnews.com/news/hero-nanny-loretta-penn-pushes -baby-out-of-suvs-path-gets-hit-herself/.

Chapter 14 Love and Eternal Judgment

1. Martin Luther King Jr., *Where Do We Go from Here: Chaos or Community?* (Boston: Beacon Press, 1968), 67.

Appendix B Another Resource—*The Remedy*

1. "Who Wrote Most of the New Testament?," ApoLogika, May 3, 2014, http:// apologika.blogspot.com/2014/05/who-wrote-most-of-new-testament.html.

Timothy R. Jennings, MD, is a board-certified Christian psychiatrist, certified master psychopharmacologist, Distinguished Fellow of the American Psychiatric Association, Life Fellow of the Southern Psychiatric Association, and past president of both the Tennessee and Southern Psychiatric Associations. Dr. Jennings served in the US Army as the division psychiatrist for the 3rd Infantry Division and the chief of psychiatry at Winn Army Hospital. He has spent more than two decades researching the interface between biblical principles and modern brain science and is the founder and president of the not-for-profit Christian ministry Come and Reason Ministries. He is a highly sought after lecturer and international speaker and is the author of *The God-Shaped Brain: How Changing Your View of God Transforms Your life, Could It Be This Simple? A Biblical Model for Healing the Mind, The Journal of the Watcher,* and *The Remedy: A New Testament Expanded Paraphrase.* Many of Dr. Jennings's materials can be found at www.comeandreason.com.

Come and Reason Ministries was founded by Christian psychiatrist Dr. Tim Jennings. Our mission is to help you hone your mental faculties by providing free materials that integrate Scripture, science, and experience to reveal the beauty of God's character of love so you can grow in your relationship with God.

Join Dr. Tim Jennings in Come and Reason Ministries' weekly interactive Bible study as he answers tough biblical questions by applying God's design law.

Visit **comeandreason.com** to find out how to stream live or watch directly from the app. Search Come and Reason from your device's app store.

CONNECT WITH THE AUTHOR AT

Interested in having Dr. Jennings speak to your group?
Email us at Requests@comeandreason.com

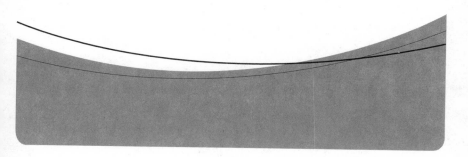